Whitewater Rafting
in North America

Whitewater Rafting in North America

The 200 Best Rafting Adventures in the
United States, Canada, Mexico, and Costa Rica

by Lloyd Armstead

An East Woods Book

The Globe Pequot Press

Old Saybrook, Connecticut

Library of Congress Cataloging-in-Publication Data
Armstead, Lloyd Dean.
  Whitewater rafting in North America : the 200 best rafting adventures in the United States, Canada, Mexico, and Costa Rica / by Lloyd Armstead. — 1st ed.
      p.   cm.
  An East Woods book.
  Includes index.
  ISBN 1-56440-362-9
  1. Rafting (Sports)—North America—Guidebooks. 2. North America—Guidebooks.
  I. Title.
GV776.05.A76 1994
797.1'22—dc20   93-39424
                                                                      CIP

Manufactured in the United States of America
First Edition/Second Printing

*Dedicated to the late Georgie de Ross-White (1910–1992),
a dearly loved river runner and professional rafting outfitter
whose spirit of adventure and determination
opened the depths of the Grand Canyon of the Colorado
for countless generations to enjoy.*

Contents

PART II

PART III

PART IV

LIST OF MAPS

North America

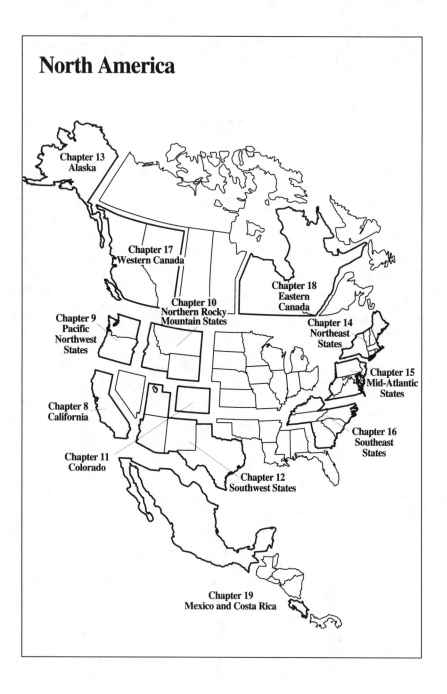

Chapter 13
Alaska

Chapter 17
Western Canada

Chapter 18
Eastern Canada

Chapter 10
Northern Rocky
Mountain States

Chapter 9
Pacific
Northwest
States

Chapter 14
Northeast
States

Chapter 15
Mid-Atlantic
States

Chapter 8
California

Chapter 16
Southeast
States

Chapter 11
Colorado

Chapter 12
Southwest States

Chapter 19
Mexico and Costa Rica

Foreword

Discover the thrill and adventure of whitewater amid some of the continent's most spectacular scenery. Shoot rapids through the mist of deep mountain gorges with your most adventuresome friends. Or take the family on a fun float trip down a tree-lined river punctuated by a few small rapids. There's a river for every person and every season. Professional outfitters provide the equipment and know-how to help you discover some of North America's most special places—our precious heritage of free-flowing rivers.

Whitewater rafting is not just for thrill-seekers, as it is commonly perceived. There are many river trips during which participants can relax, swim, hike, bird-watch, and experience the same sort of adventure Huck Finn found nearly a century ago. Many rivers still offer the pristine wilderness and sense of discovery that inspired the continent's original pioneers.

Today's whitewater rivers are very precious resources. Dams, reservoirs, and diversions have claimed all but a few whitewater runs. That's not to say that all dams are bad. Some actually help sustain recreation flows throughout the summer while producing electric power or improving water quality. We cannot, however, afford to sacrifice the heritage and recreational opportunities offered by our remaining streams.

America Outdoors is a national trade association of professional outfitters established to preserve opportunities for outdoor recreation. Most outfitters care deeply about the beauty and recreational value of the river resources listed in this book. Their business is to provide you with a service and the opportunity to join with us in a lifelong enjoyment of free-flowing streams.

DAVID L. BROWN
Executive Director
America Outdoors

Preface

Whitewater Rafting in North America is a nontechnical guide for both first-time and frequent rafters. The book details the enjoyable, exciting, and sometimes even daring sport of whitewater rafting. It also describes several relaxing float trips suitable for families, seniors, or for that matter, anyone who enjoys the outdoors. It is the most complete and authoritative source of information on whitewater and float trips in North America.

As with my earlier regional whitewater editions, *Whitewater Rafting in Western North America* (The Globe Pequot Press, 1990) and *Whitewater Rafting in Eastern North America* (The Globe Pequot Press, 1989), I wrote this book with the desire to introduce people not only to the sport of rafting and the excitement of whitewater, but also to the total river experience—the grandeur and solitude of isolated mountain and desert canyons, the imprints of past civilizations, and an incredible oneness with nature. I also wrote this book to share and protect the solitude and isolated beauty of the remaining wilderness areas of North America that I have come to know and love. To be able to appreciate and enjoy the river wilderness, while knowing that I have left no trace of my presence for those who follow, is a cherished memory.

Fellow writers and readers will recognize that the compilation of this book required enormous and detailed research. It is almost inconceivable for me to imagine attempting this task without a modern computer and fax machine. While the preparation of this book obviously required countless hours of personal time that I would otherwise have spent paddling on local rivers, or with family and friends, it has not been without its memorable and rewarding moments. Were it not for the preparation of this book, there are undoubtedly many miles of rivers and unforgettable canyon beauty that I would not have seen.

Not all commercially rafted rivers in North America are included in this book. Likewise, the names and addresses of all professional rafting outfitters are not listed. Editorial limitations required that I be selective in both cases. I have purposely omitted a number of infrequently rafted rivers whose seasons are ordinarily fairly short or whose water flows are often unpredictable. For the most part, I have used two principal criteria in the selection of outfitters. First, I have sought to list those outfitters who most frequently run these rivers and who have been in business for at least three years. Second, I have favored those outfitters who are members of America Outdoors, North America's only national organization or trade association for professional rafting outfitters.

With the assistance of countless professional rafting outfitters, *Whitewater Rafting in North America* became a reality. Their information, photos, and suggestions were most helpful in compiling and writing this book. Those deserving special credit include George Wendt, O.A.R.S.; Bill McGinnis, Whitewater Voyagers; Marty McDonnell, Sierra Mac River Trips; Bill Carlson, All Rivers Adventures–Wenatchee Whitewater; Casey Garland, Downstream River Runners; James Moore, Orion Expeditions; David King, Olympic Raft and Guide Service; Robert Rafalovich, Rogue Wilderness; David Mills, Rocky Mountain River Tours; Betsy

Barrymore Stoll, The River Company; Jerry Hughes, Hughes River Expeditions; Jerry Myers, Silver Cloud Expeditions; Peter Grubb, River Odysseys West (ROW); Julia Page, Yellowstone Raft Company; Ron Blanchard, Wyoming River Trips; Dick Barker, Barker-Ewing Float Trips; Frank Ewing, Barker-Ewing River Trips; Bill Dvorak, Bill Dvorak's Kayak/Rafting Expeditions; Sheri Griffith, Sheri Griffith River Expeditions; Patrick Blumm, Rio Grande Rapid Transit; Steve Harris, Far Flung Adventures; Beth Garcia, Big Bend River Tours; Sandy Neily, Eastern River Expeditions; Patrick Cunningham, Hudson River Rafting Company; Phil Coleman, Precision Rafting Expeditions; David Arnold, Class VI River Runners; Debbie Dean and Tom Blue, Nantahala Outdoor Center; Jeff Stanley, Wahoo's Adventures; Brian Leighton, Whistler River Adventures; Bernie Fandrich, Kumsheen Rafting Adentures; Joan Mitrovic, Mirage Adventure Tours; Claudia and Dirk Van Wijk, Owl Rafting and Madawaska Kanu Centre; and Chris Phelan, New World River Expeditions.

I owe an extra special thanks to the several regional river authors who reviewed portions of the manuscript and added much-needed suggestions: Doug North, *Washington Whitewater I* and *Washington Whitewater II;* Jim Cassady, *California Whitewater* and *Western Whitewater;* Karen Jettmar, *The Alaska River Guide;* and Rafael E. Gallo and Michael W. Mayfield, *The Rivers of Costa Rica.*

Lastly, I thank my wife, Connie, for her patience and support during this year-long effort, and the publisher for making it possible for me to share the white-water rivers of North America with you.

Introduction

The canyon explorations of John Wesley Powell and his brave companions are among the first recorded river-running expeditions in western North America. Written accounts of their whitewater journeys through the spectacular canyons of the Southwest's Green and Colorado rivers in 1869 have fascinated armchair travelers for more than a century. Only in the past twenty-five years, however, has it been possible for tens of thousands of rafters a year to experience these and a host of other whitewater canyons throughout North America.

After Powell, nearly a half-century passed before other adventure-seeking boaters regularly navigated these forbidding canyon waters. While many entrepreneurial boatmen, including Bus Hatch and Norman Nevills, successfully operated commercial whitewater trips in wooden boats in Utah, Idaho, and Oregon during the 1930s and 1940s, their unusual river exploits received little attention outside their local area.

The birth of modern commercial rafting in the mid-1950s is largely attributable to the determination and innovativeness of a Chicago-born woman, the late Georgie de Ross-White. Georgie, unwilling to accept that river running was for men only, successfully lashed together surplus Army bridge pontoons from World War II, creating the first oar-guided rubber raft. News of her successful adventures down the Grand Canyon of the Colorado spread rapidly, attracting customers as well as competing river outfitters. In just a decade, at least two dozen professional outfitters were offering whitewater trips in rubber rafts on numerous western rivers. Another three decades later, hundreds of professional outfitters offer whitewater raft and float trips in North America.

The growth of the whitewater rafting industry has led to many equipment innovations. The variety of rafts and other river equipment available to outfitters makes it possible for almost anyone to participate safely in some level of whitewater rafting. Outfitters, using state-of-the-art self-bailing rafts, offer energetic rafters an opportunity to run rivers that just a few years ago were considered unrunnable. Oar-guided rafts with lightweight aluminum rowing frames make it possible for senior citizens and families with young children to enjoy both single-day and multiday Class I, II, and III whitewater trips. Motor-equipped rafts enable those with less time to experience otherwise inaccessible canyons like those of the Colorado's Grand and Cataract canyons and of British Columbia's Thompson and Fraser rivers. In addition, there are dories and inflatable kayaks for those wanting a personal river experience.

Many outfitters have made a remarkable effort to make whitewater rafting both possible and affordable for disabled individuals. On several of the popular river trips of easy and moderate difficulty—such as California's South Fork American, Utah's Green and Colorado, Colorado's Arkansas, New York's Sacandaga, and North Carolina's Nantahala—it is not at all uncommon to see a person who is paraplegic or quadriplegic, a deaf person, or even a blind person experiencing the unique thrill of whitewater.

The lure of whitewater and the access to spectacular canyons provided by rafting have also created an international market. Outfitters attract increasingly large numbers of customers from England, France, Germany, Japan, Australia, and elsewhere. Many outfitters employ bilingual guides to serve their foreign clientele. While the multiday Grand Canyon of the Colorado rafting adventure has been the traditional favorite of foreign visitors, each year more and more of them are discovering the equally fascinating wilderness canyon adventures of Idaho, Colorado, and Utah as well as the wild rivers of Alaska and British Columbia.

Competition among outfitters has spurred creative approaches to maintain or increase their market share and to enhance the river experience for customers. This is particularly shown by the growing number of specialty rafting trips including gourmet dinners and wine tastings, storytellers, concerts in the canyon, and personal and professional development seminars and workshops. Multiday trips are offered on many rivers and are becoming increasingly popular as rafters realize that such trips offer the best—often the only—way to experience isolated river canyons. Many rafters find the quiet solitude of the wilderness canyons as memorable a part of the river experience as the whitewater.

HOW TO USE THIS BOOK

If you are about to become a first-time rafter or if you are an infrequent rafter, read Part I first. Here you will find most of the essential information needed to plan and prepare for a river trip, including the clothing and personal items you should bring. In addition, there is a description of the river equipment provided by outfitters and a brief introduction to the fundamentals of whitewater rafting.

Once you have decided to take a whitewater raft or float trip, you are ready to select a river that best suits your group's skill or interest level. Parts II, III, IV, and V describe more than 200 rafting options in thirteen geographic or political regions of North America—nine in the United States, two in Canada, and Mexico and Costa Rica.

The River Comparison table at the beginning of each chapter provides a handy reference that will enable you to become familiar with a region's raft trips during normal-season water level. Small paddle symbols (one, two, or three), showing relative **Difficulty**, are used to help beginning rafters choose an appropriate river and should not be confused with the international Class I–VI rapids classification system. A single paddle denotes the easiest rivers, two paddles the intermediate rivers, and three paddles the hardest rivers; there are times, though, when high or low water levels will change the rating categories of a river.

Minimum Age provided for each river follows general guidelines recommended by outfitters. Minimum ages also depend upon seasonal water levels or temperatures, the adult-to-child ratio, and the experience or confidence level of the guide or outfitter. Most minimum ages shown in the table apply to the normal family rafting season. Consult individual guides about minimum age requirements.

The **Time** shown for each river trip includes the shuttle ride, orientation talk, lunch if included, and the actual rafting trip. For comparison, half-day trips are those lasting approximately four hours or less. Trips lasting more than four hours are listed as one day. The time and distance of a trip may vary considerably, however, depending on water levels.

Rafting **Season** refers to the months during which commercial rafting trips are normally offered on any given river. A number of factors, including unsatisfactory water levels (either too high or too low) and unseasonal weather, not only affect the beginning and end of any rafting season, they may also cause cancellation of river trips in mid-season.

Finally, **Raft Type** indicates the various raft options that are normally available on a river trip—paddle raft, oar raft, motorized raft, inflatable kayak, or dory. Two cautionary notes must be remembered. First, all raft types may not be available with every outfitter. Second, water levels may preclude the use of some raft types such as the inflatable kayak.

Once you have narrowed your river choices, write or call several of the professional outfitters requesting their brochures. When reviewing these colorful brochures, you may wish to re-read the section of chapter 5 entitled, "How to Choose a Professional Outfitter."

If your raft trip requires an overnight stay, use the accommodations directory at the back of the book for a range of options including both lodging and campgrounds. While most of these accommodations are located well within an hour's driving time of the river trip, the specific location of an outfitter or the meeting place for your trip may not be. Unless you are sure of your meeting place, it is best to consult with your outfitter prior to your choice of accommodations. In addition to these accommodations, many outfitters offer their own private lodging or campgrounds.

That's it! Happy reading! Happy rafting! May this book open a whole new world of whitewater or flatwater rafting for you, your family, and your friends!

WORDS OF CAUTION

Whitewater rafting is one of the safest and most enjoyable recreational activities in North America. In any such outdoor activity, however, there are certain elements of risk. Accidents and injuries occasionally occur in whitewater rafting, but by using professional outfitters and heeding the advice of their guides, you can reduce the chances of injury to a minimum. While the author and publisher cannot assume liability for accidents to any reader engaged in whitewater rafting, they caution you to respect the dangers of swift-flowing rivers and whitewater rafting and thereby increase your enjoyment of this sport many times over.

PART I

■ ■ ■

The Basics of Whitewater Rafting

CHAPTER I

■ ■ ■

Early Preparations

WHO SHOULD GO?

Every year more people of all ages and occupations are finding whitewater rafting to be one of the most challenging and exciting forms of recreation they have ever enjoyed. Many people are finding that rafting offers a perfect escape from the pressures and tensions of their daily routines. No matter who you are or what your career, if you feel comfortable around water, chances are you will enjoy whitewater rafting and will want to go again and again. Almost anyone can enjoy some level of whitewater rafting.

Rafting is fun to do alone, but it is even more enjoyable when you go with friends or family. It is an ideal recreational activity for people from your plant or office, church or school group, or civic or social organization. Families and seniors find that whitewater raft and float trips add a new and long-remembered dimension to their summer vacation.

For safety and insurance reasons, outfitters often have minimum-age requirements on each river they travel. These age limits, usually between ten and eighteen on trips rated Class III and above, have been set after careful consideration of river conditions by experienced outfitters. In recent years an increasing number of relatively easy whitewater trips allow children as young as five or six to enjoy rafting. Often a child's size—whether or not the smallest life jacket will fit—determines whether an outfitter will allow a child to participate.

The maximum age for rafting can only be determined by a person's health and enthusiasm. A person with a heart condition, shortness of breath, or a serious physical disability should consult a physician as well as the river outfitter before attempting a raft trip. Many people over ninety years old enjoy moderate-level whitewater each year.

Should a nonswimmer go whitewater rafting? Many nonswimmers go rafting each year. On less demanding rivers, outfitters often leave the decision to the individual after pointing out that life jackets provide adequate flotation and that standard swimming techniques are not used in the rapids. Whatever is decided, it is important not to coax or dare someone to go whitewater rafting against that person's wishes. Fear of water may lead to moments of panic should a nonswimmer fall overboard in fast-moving rapids. The ability to swim is recommended for all whitewater rivers rated Class IV and above.

BEST TIMES TO GO

Rain or shine, you can go whitewater rafting; you probably will get wet regardless of the weather.

Most outfitters welcome disabled paddlers on Class I–III rivers.

Rafting seasons vary depending upon region, snowfall and precipitation, and controlled water releases from dams and reservoirs. In the United States and Canada, most rafting is done from April through October. Outfitters who wear wet suits, however, begin rafting the snow runoff in the early spring and, if fall water levels permit, run raft trips well into November. It's difficult to say what time is best for whitewater rafting. If you are interested in big whitewater action, the early spring runoff should provide it. Days following periods of extended rain during the summer and fall offer the same thrills, but the water is usually hard to catch at sustained levels.

If scenery is a prime consideration, remember that two of the most beautiful times of year are when the rhododendron, mountain laurel, desert cacti, and other flowers bloom (usually May and early June) and during the appearance of fall colors. Rafting during the summer months usually provides a welcome relief from heat as well as an enjoyable opportunity to swim and relax.

There are three advantages to weekday rather than weekend rafting trips: most outfitters offer reduced rates on weekdays; popular rivers usually have fewer rafters on weekdays; and weekday trips are usually available on much shorter notice (many outfitters fill up their weekend reservations far in advance).

Rafters frequently find it enjoyable to raft the same river during different seasons and water levels. The complexity and characteristics of the rapids vary dramatically with water levels, offering very different challenges.

High water after periods of heavy rain, or low water after extended dry periods in the late summer and fall, can temporarily halt river rafting. This is particularly true of uncontrolled or free-flowing rivers. When making reservations, ask the outfitter about cancellation and rescheduling policies in the event of high or low water. Often this information is stated in the outfitters' brochures. If you have questions about water levels or conditions, it is also advisable to check with your outfitter a day or two before your trip.

CHOOSING THE RIGHT RIVER

Choosing the right river is an important consideration when planning a rafting trip. Whether there are few or many rivers to choose from, the basic decision hinges upon the level of whitewater adventure you want, and what you can afford.

In general, the first priority for choosing a river is selecting one that does not exceed the ability of any member of your family or group, including the oldest, youngest, weakest, and least-experienced.

Seniors, families with children, and tentative first-time rafters should pay special attention to the length of their proposed rafting trip. Unless warm weather is expected, it is best to select a rafting trip lasting a half-day or less. The attention span of smaller children may also be a reason for family rafters to select a shorter trip.

Finally, rivers take on very different personalities during different water levels and seasons. While some rivers become less difficult during low water levels, others become significantly more technical and difficult. If a river is located nearby, enjoy rafting it during different seasons and water levels. Families and seniors, however, are commonly advised by outfitters to plan rafting trips during the warm summer months.

Once you have selected a river and reserved the dates of your trip, carefully review the clothing and planning suggestions in the following chapters. If you still have unanswered questions or concerns, call your professional outfitter.

Planning Your Rafting Trip

MAKING RESERVATIONS

Reservations are recommended for all rafting trips. They enable outfitters to plan for each trip and ensure an adequate number of guides. Even on popular rivers, there are many days when "walk-ons" can join a rafting trip, but it is advisable to check in advance.

While many of the more popular multiday trips are booked weeks, even months, in advance, late cancellations occasionally make it possible for a person to join a trip, such as one on the Grand Canyon or Salmon River, on fairly short notice. Outfitters often keep standby lists of those wishing to join already booked multiday trips. Although whitewater outfitters have widely differing reservations/requirements, some general observations can be made.

The sooner you make reservations, the greater your chance of obtaining the rafting dates of your choice. Most outfitters will accept an initial reservation by telephone but will send a final confirmation only after receiving your deposit or, in many cases, full payment. Outfitters normally require a deposit shortly after your reservation and full payment from fourteen to thirty days prior to the trip. To avoid any possible confusion, always ask the outfitter to confirm your reservation in writing. Outfitters' brochures detail the terms for reservations.

In the event that a trip is cancelled by the outfitter due to high water or a lack of water, a refund or rescheduling can almost always be arranged to the mutual satisfaction of the rafter and the outfitter. Many outfitters reserve the right to run alternative rivers or sections of rivers when unfavorable water conditions prevail on the scheduled river.

Notable exceptions to the general rule that reservations are needed are the family- and tourist-oriented rafting trips near national parks and other popular tourist centers. Outfitters are normally able to accommodate visitors on numerous daily rafting excursions lasting from one or two hours to a half day with fairly short notice. Such river trips include:

· Animas River (Lower), Colorado
· Arkansas River, Colorado
· Bow River, Alberta
· Colorado River (Glenwood Canyon), Colorado
· Colorado River (Professor Valley), Utah
· Elwha River, Washington
· Flathead River (Middle Fork), Montana
· Green River, British Columbia

- Hoh River, Washington
- Lowe River, Alaska
- Nantahala River, North Carolina
- Nenana River, Alaska
- Rio Grande (Pilar), New Mexico
- Rogue River (Recreation), Oregon
- Sacandaga River, New York
- Shoshone River, Wyoming
- Snake River (Grand Teton), Wyoming
- Snake River (Upper), Wyoming
- Watauga River (Section V), Tennessee
- Yellowstone River, Montana

HOW MUCH WILL IT COST?

Few generalizations can be made about the cost of whitewater rafting. Rafting trips normally cost from $10 to $30 for a one- or two-hour trip, $15 to $40 for a half-day trip, $50 to $100 or more for a full-day trip, and $75 to $150 per day for multiday trips. The cost of multiday expedition-type trips may be considerably higher. A trip's price depends on the day of week, time of year, difficulty of the river, number of guides needed, length of shuttle transportation required, and prices charged by competing outfitters.

Wet-suit rentals, if not included in the raft trip price, normally cost an additional $5 to $15 a day. A security deposit may be required at the time of the wet-suit rental.

The cost of all rafting trips and terms of payment—including group, weekday, and special season discounts—are detailed in each company's brochure. Although it is a good idea to compare the prices of companies competing on the same rivers, cost should not be the only criterion used to select an outfitter. Chapter 5 lists several criteria for selecting an outfitter.

In addition to payment by cash, traveler's checks, or personal checks, most outfitters accept major credit cards.

ORGANIZING GROUP TRIPS

Whitewater rafting is more enjoyable in the company of friends. Office and professional groups, church and school groups, social and civic clubs, and other organizations have found rafting to be an ideal recreational activity.

Outfitters prefer one person to serve as trip leader or organizer. The trip leader should make the group's reservation, deposit, and payment as required and should handle all arrangements with the outfitter. The selection of the right person as trip leader or coordinator greatly influences the success of the trip. A well-organized individual who pays careful attention to detail should find trip planning a relatively easy task. For others, organizing a group rafting trip may be a frustrating and unpleasant experience.

To someone organizing a group rafting trip for the first time, the following suggestions should be beneficial.

- Begin your planning months in advance. Start with an initial interest survey to determine approximately how many reservations you will need. The size of your group may well influence your choice of outfitter and river.
- Learn as much about your group as you can before you select a river trip. Carefully consider the likely participants, their ages, experience, and physical limitations. Don't plan a trip beyond their abilities. Unless the group has been rafting before, it may be best to plan a late-spring or summer trip.
- Select an outfitter, river, date, and time, and begin promoting the trip. Several larger outfitters have films, photos, posters, and other materials to assist in the organization and promotion of group trips. Request an adequate supply of outfitter brochures or reproduce the pertinent information for everyone. Early planning may enable you to take advantage of your organization newsletter and bulletin boards.
- Obtain either a check or cash from interested participants when they sign up. Only those who have paid should be considered definite participants. If you have a specific number of guaranteed reservations, persons should be informed in advance that after a certain date their money can be refunded only if someone is found to replace them.
- As the date of the trip nears, make sure all drivers and participants have necessary trip information, including a detailed map with the location, name, and telephone numbers of the outfitter. Advise anyone who has unexpected car trouble or illness on the day of the trip to call the outfitter.

Outfitters offer varying price reductions or incentives for group rafting; trip leaders should decide how these savings can be passed on to participants. Some outfitters offer percentage discounts above a specified number of rafters. Others offer a free space for every rafter over a certain number. No one should object to a leader accepting a free trip in exchange for the time and effort put into organizating the outing. It may be necessary for a trip leader to include a per-rafter charge to cover out-of-pocket expenses such as telephone calls, promotional materials, or postage.

CHAPTER 3

■ ■ ■

Clothing and Personal Items

Wearing the proper clothing is essential to the enjoyment of each river outing. Consider the season, location, water temperature, and both forecasted and unforecasted weather when selecting clothing for rafting trips. Afternoon thunderstorms, common in mountainous areas, can bring sudden drops in temperatures along with heavy downpours.

Other than tennis shoes or sneakers, which are required for all rafting trips, plan your dress according to three general types of water and weather conditions: warm, cool, and cold.

The following suggestions are for half- and one-day trips.

WARM-WEATHER CLOTHING

· Swimming suit and/or shorts or cutoffs
· T-shirt and windbreaker
· Sneakers

Three factors should be considered in addition to the expected daytime temperatures. First, in the late spring, early summer, or early fall, water temperatures can be considerably colder than air temperatures. Second, if water is released from a dam or reservoir, it will likely be many degrees colder than expected. Third, many rivers pass through narrow, steep-walled gorges or canyons that remain shaded and cool during much of the day. Even on warm days (especially on northern rivers) and during the cool morning hours or along the shaded portions of a river, you may feel more comfortable with a water-repellent jacket, pants, or windbreaker. Most outfitters have dry bags to carry extra clothing.

COOL- AND RAINY-WEATHER CLOTHING

· Long wool underwear and pants
· Wool, polyester, or acrylic sweater
· Heavy windbreaker, poncho, or rain jacket
· Wet suit
· Sneakers
· Wool socks
· Wool hat
· Gloves

Short of a wet suit, wool or synthetic long underwear such as polypropylene or capilene provide the best protection against the cold since they absorb less water and retain body heat better than cotton.

COLD-WEATHER CLOTHING

- Wet suit
- Wet-suit booties or sneakers
- One or two pairs of wool socks
- Wool hat
- Gloves

Wet suits are necessary apparel on most northern rivers. They enable rafters to take advantage of exciting whitewater during spring runoff in comfort. Rafters also use them during chillier fall temperatures. If wet suits are needed, most outfitters either include them in the trip price or rent them. It is advisable to wear a pair of shorts or cutoffs over the wet suit to minimize contact of the rubber suit with the raft, which causes unnecessary wear to both the suit and the raft.

The importance of being properly dressed for both cool- and cold-weather rafting cannot be overemphasized. Many rafters have had otherwise enjoyable trips ruined because they were cold and wet.

If there is any question about weather and water temperatures, be sure to take along extra clothing. Check with your outfitter prior to the trip about the best river attire. Being improperly prepared for cold waters and air temperatures can also lead to hypothermia—a dangerous lowering of body-core temperature. A little extra thought about your river wear should guarantee an enjoyable time in almost any rafting season or weather.

MULTIDAY RAFTING CHECKLIST

Check with your outfitter for a recommended list of personal items for a multiday rafting adventure. The following items are fairly standard.

- Sleeping bag
- Air mattress or foam pad
- Towel and personal toiletry items
- Biodegradable soap
- Insect repellent
- Sunscreen
- Sunglasses and sun hat
- Bathing suit and shorts
- Underwear
- T-shirts (two or more)
- Long-sleeved shirts
- Long pants
- Warm jacket and sweater
- Shoes for hiking
- Shoes for rafting
- Wool or polypropylene socks
- Rain gear
- Camera and film
- Flashlight and batteries

CAMERAS

Almost anytime you take a camera, you are taking a risk. Remember, most cameras are not waterproof. All too often, expensive cameras are damaged or lost by

Grand Canyon campsite

well-intentioned photographers because of careless or improper handling or packing. No rafting outfitter can be held responsible for a lost or damaged camera. Many outfitters employ river photographers who offer color photo prints of your raft trip. These photos are usually of fairly high quality. If you take a camera, follow these guidelines:

- Cushion your camera in a waterproof bag. Although many outfitters provide these bags, none will guarantee the bag is waterproof. Make sure the container is watertight before you begin the trip. Most outfitters do not allow ammunition boxes for cameras because they might puncture a raft or rafters.
- Secure your camera container to the raft with a small rope or strap.
- Use extreme caution when photographing from a raft. Survey your downriver situation carefully before taking out your camera. Sit in a stable position on the raft. Make sure nearby rafters are aware you are using your camera. Sudden water fights or horseplay may catch you by surprise. It is best to photograph from the riverbank.
- If your camera becomes thoroughly wet or submerged, get it to an authorized dealer as soon as possible.

OTHER CONSIDERATIONS

For half- and one-day rafting trips, the less you take, the better. Other than what you are wearing, try to get by with as few extra items as possible. Include a safety strap or string to keep glasses or sunglasses securely fastened. You may find the streaked and fogged lenses that result from splashing water make glasses only an annoyance.

Waterproof sunscreens should be in a small plastic or metal container that will fit into a pocket.

Try to leave your car keys with the outfitter. If you must take keys, put them in a zippered pocket or bag. It is a good idea to hide an extra key with the car.

Nearly all outfitters furnish lunch on one-day trips, high-energy snacks on half-day trips, and all meals for two-day or longer trips. Information on meals is either described in individual outfitter brochures or can be obtained from the outfitter.

CHAPTER 4

■ ■ ■

Rafting Equipment

One of the primary reasons for the popularity of whitewater rafting is the simplicity of the sport. With professionally guided trips, you don't have to buy any special equipment, carry a heavy pack, bring lunch, or worry about extra supplies. There are few easier ways to enjoy the wilderness. The outfitter will provide the basic items of equipment: the raft, the life jacket, and the paddle. Helmets are also furnished on many rivers. In rafts that are not self-bailing, buckets or bailers will be provided for bailing excess water.

RAFT

Depending upon water volumes, river levels, and the difficulty of the whitewater, the raft provided by your outfitter may be a four- to six-person craft or a larger eight- to twelve-person size. Larger rafts are more commonly used on high-volume rivers in the southwestern United States and western Canada. The main types of rafts used on North America's whitewaters are described below.

· **Paddle rafts:** Teamwork and fun are the key elements of paddle rafting! Generally, each paddle rafting particiapant is expected to assist the guide with the propulsion and navigation of the raft. Paddle raft commands are ususally very basic, for example, "all paddle forward," "all back," "right-side back," "left-side back," and "stop paddling." Paddle rafts are normally 12 to 18 feet long and carry four to ten passengers and a guide. Whitewater rafting in the eastern United States and Canada is predominantly a participation sport.

· **Oar rafts:** A variety of oar rafts, mostly used in the western United States and western Canada, enable families, seniors, and other guests to experience easy and moderate whitewater and enjoy the surrounding environment without having to paddle. Custom-made aluminum frames with wooden oars allow skilled guides to navigate the raft single-handedly. Food, tents, sleeping bags, and personal items for multiday river trips are normally carried on oar rafts.

· **Paddle/oar rafts:** On paddle-oar rafts, passengers are expected to use paddles to assist their oarsman throughout the river trip. Generally, a skilled oarsman is positioned at the rear of the paddle raft to provide extra manueverability during technical Class IV–V whitewater.

· **Inflatable kayaks:** One- and two-person inflatable kayaks, or duckies, allow guest to enjoy whitewater paddling during moderate and low water levels in the summer. Paddlers with no prior experience can enjoy a thrill similar to that of real river kayaking.

Most rafts are made of neoprene, nylon, polyester, or Hypalon (a DuPont product). Although the rafts are flexible and can bend and bounce off rocks, use care to avoid permanently damaging the rafts.

Rafters often are asked to help carry rafts for short distances to or from trucks either at put-in or take-out points. Everyone doing his or her part can save guides considerable time and effort.

LIFE JACKET

The most important item of equipment on any river is the life jacket. The guides will provide you with one at the beginning of your trip; make sure it fits properly and fastens securely. Ask a friend or guide to help you with necessary adjustments. Should you fall into swift-moving water, a loosely fitted life jacket can slip up around your face, causing disorientation and confusion.

Wear the life jacket at all times on the river. Also wear it when climbing on rocks near the water's edge as it may cushion a fall. Don't risk being without it even for a few minutes, no matter how well you are able to swim. Remind your rafting companions to wear theirs, and likewise don't be offended if someone reminds you to "put on or secure your life jacket."

PADDLE

The single-bladed paddle (not an oar) is an important item in making your whitewater outing a success. During the orientation and safety talk, the guide will demonstrate its use. Pay careful attention to the guide's instructions for propelling and maneuvering the raft with the paddle. Your quick mastery of the correct paddle techniques will add greatly to your enjoyment and enhance your value as a team member. The use of the paddle is not optional. You are expected to do your share of the paddling.

HELMET

Safety helmets are often worn while rafting to prevent head injuries from rocks or flailing paddles. The use of helmets is the decision of the individual outfitter. If helmets are provided, rafters will be required to wear them and to keep them fastened during whitewater stretches.

Surprisingly, even on some fairly difficult rivers, some outfitters feel helmets are unnecessary and do not provide them. If you desire the added safety that a helmet provides, you can make this a priority when selecting an outfitter or you can bring one of your own.

BAILER

When rafts are not self-bailing, they are usually supplied with one or more bucket-like containers for removing excess water from the floor.

Water weighs one kilogram per liter, more than eight pounds per gallon. Unless water is removed, the added weight will slow the raft and reduce your ability to maneuver it.

If you engage in water fights with other rafters, use the bailer and not the paddle to throw water. Paddle blades are generally sharp, and injuries may result from their improper use.

CHAPTER 5

■ ■ ■

Outfitters and Guides

OUTFITTERS

The importance of using the services of competent professional outfitters on swift-flowing whitewater rivers cannot be overemphasized.

Although this book lists more than three hundred professional whitewater rafting outfitters in North America, it is not a complete list. The inclusion or omission of any outfitter should not be considered an endorsement or rejection.

Professional outfitters are experienced in whitewater rafting and familiar with the rivers they run. Naturally, some outfitters and guides are better prepared than others and extend a greater effort to provide enjoyable and safe rafting experiences. The safety record for commercial outfitters on whitewater rivers is excellent, and serious injuries or deaths are rare.

Outfitters are usually required to be licensed by states or provinces, and by various authorities (such as the United States Forest Service) if there is passage through lands that they administer. Most of these licensing agencies require liability insurance by outfitters. Many outfitters also belong to various river safety and conservation organizations.

Most of the outfitters listed in this book are members of America Outdoors, a national organization created for the advancement of safety on rivers, for improving the quality of the river trip experience, and for the promotion, preservation, and conservation of the wilderness and wildlife areas. Today, much of the effort of America Outdoors is focused on preserving the opportunities for whitewater rafting throughout North America.

Outfitters are responsible for accurately advertising, promoting, and scheduling river trips. Outfitters must also ensure adequate guide preparation and safety training. They must maintain all equipment, including rafts, life jackets, paddles, helmets, and any company vehicles needed to transport rafters to or from the put-in or take-out. Furthermore, it is the outfitters who decide when river water levels are either too high or too low to be run safely and who decide which persons should not be permitted on a rafting trip because of age or physical limitations.

HOW TO CHOOSE AN OUTFITTER

On the more popular rivers, rafters have the opportunity to choose from several professional outfitters. Write or call several of them for information. Study their brochures carefully. How quickly did they respond? How long have they been in business? What river safety and conservation organizations or associations do they belong to? Are they licensed? Are they insured? What aspects of river running do they emphasize? Finally, you may wish to rely on the recommendations of people who have rafted the river. Ask the outfitter for the name of one of their customers in your area to whom you can talk.

As you run a river, you may want to watch for a few points in helping you evaluate the outfitter's performance. Was the orientation briefing informative and complete? Did the outfitter have an adequate number of responsible guides who are concerned about safety? Were the guides concerned about your personal comfort and enjoyment? Was the number of people per raft kept low enough to avoid overcrowding? Were swimming and horseplay sensibly discouraged near rapids or unsafe areas? Was the transportation to or from the river carefully planned and executed to avoid unnecessary delays?

Outfitters appreciate receiving feedback from rafting customers. If the guides have done a good job in providing a quality river trip, take time to write the outfitter a note of appreciation. Likewise, if an essential part of a river trip was lacking or inadequate, politely bring this to the attention of the outfitter. Your comments, criticisms, and suggestions will help outfitters provide better river trips.

GUIDES

Experienced and good-natured guides are essential to the safety and enjoyment of whitewater rafting trips. Outfitters provide one or more guides on each trip, de-

Guide demonstrates proper floating position through rapids should one fall out of raft.

pending on the size of your group. On most rivers, there is usually one guide per raft. On a few rivers requiring less skill, guides sometimes ride only in selected rafts or in kayaks near the rafts.

Guides will review key safety points during the orientation briefing and position people in the raft for optimum balance and maneuverability. He or she will also demonstrate a system of commands for controlling the raft and give you an opportunity to practice your responses. If your raft is unguided, your group should select a leader with previous rafting experience and should practice responding to a set of commands for manuevering the raft.

In addition to being experienced in paddling techniques, raft control, and the skills of river reading, most guides have had training in first aid, cardiopulmonary resuscitation (CPR), and rescue methods. Prior to running difficult rapids, guides will often scout the best routes for existing water conditions and may even set up rescue procedures and safety rope lines. Once these decisions have been made, the guides will assemble the group of rafts and explain the best procedures through the rapids.

Guides are usually selected not only for their whitewater skills, but also for their amiability and willingness to help make each river trip a safe and memorable experience. Although guides have widely varying interests, most are knowledgeable about the unique features of the particular river area, its geography, history, and folklore. You will find few professions in which people enjoy their work more than river guides.

RIVER ORIENTATION AND SAFETY

Prior to all river trips, professional river guides give rafters an orientation and safety briefing. It is important to pay close attention as guides discuss the river, the proper use of the equipment, and safety procedures.

The orientation and safety briefing should cover the following key points.

· A general description of the river and the rapids you will run.
· An explanation of basic equipment: raft, life jacket, and paddle.
· A demonstration of basic techniques for paddling and controlling the raft.
· A discussion of potential hazards.
· A demonstration of what to do if you fall in.
· An introduction to the flora and fauna of the river.
· Information about the care and conservation of the river.
· An opportunity for any questions.

Don't be alarmed if during the orientation and safety briefing the guides exaggerate tales and joke about the upcoming trip. It is often an effective psychological method to "break the ice" with a new group, and it sometimes helps tense rafters to relax.

The outfitters and guides conducting your trip will take the necessary precautions to ensure a safe and enjoyable trip for all rafters. Your chances of sustaining an injury requiring medical attention are slight if you follow a few basic rules. Listen for additional ones given by your guides.

- Always wear your life jacket on and near the river. Make sure it is tight enough and securely fastened.
- Do not drink alcoholic beverages before or during the the river trip.
- Always wear sneakers.
- Avoid wearing or carrying sharp objects.
- Be careful with your paddle when going through rapids. Hold on to it with both hands. If you must release the paddle with one hand, keep it outside the raft; many rafters' injuries result from flailing paddles.
- Should you fall from your raft, or if it should capsize, get out from under it. Once in the water, lean back, point your feet downstream, and let the water carry you. Don't try to stand up in swift water or your feet may become lodged between rocks. Try to propel yourself toward a raft, calm water, or shore. Keep your feet up!

LIABILITY WAIVER

Although whitewater outfitters and guides make every effort to provide safe trips, river rafting does include some danger. Due to the potential hazards, the terms are that you participate at your own risk. You can, however, minimize the risks by using good personal judgment and by following the instructions of your guides.

You will be given an "Assumption of Personal Liability" form prior to your trip; you must read and sign it, and responsible adults must sign for children. Among other things, it states that you are expected to follow the outlined rules on the river. You also agree that you will not hold the rafting outfitter liable for any personal injuries, loss of property, or damages resulting from your river trip. If you have any handicaps or medical problems that might hinder your ability to watch out for your own safety, you should inform the guides before the trip. Finally, the personal liability form may ask your permission to use photographs taken of you on the river for publicity or other purposes.

CHAPTER 6

■ ■ ■

Whitewater Fundamentals

RAPIDS CLASSIFICATIONS

Whitewater rapids are rated, based on relative difficulty, on a scale of one to six, usually written in Roman numerals. Class I is the smallest of rapids and waves, and Class VI the extremely difficult rapids.

The classification or rating of a river varies considerably with fluctuating water levels. Although higher water levels normally increase the difficulties of rapids, high water occasionally covers rocks sufficiently to wash out rapids. Conversely, some rapids become more difficult at lower water levels because more rocks are exposed.

Outfitters and guides are familiar with rapids classification and are always glad to explain the rating system in more detail.

Class I: Very small rapids with low waves, slow current, no obstructions.

Class II: Fairly frequent rapids of medium difficulty, few or no obstructions.

Class III: Difficult, large, irregular waves up to four feet, numerous rapids. The course requires some maneuvering of the raft.

Class IV: Very difficult, long, extended rapids that require careful maneuvering of the raft. Powerful irregular waves and dangerous rocks are common. The course is hard to determine and scouting is necessary.

Class V: Long and violent rapids. Large waves that are unavoidable and irregular. Extremely difficult and complex course. Scouting is essential.

Class VI: Maximum difficulty. Nearly impossible and extremely dangerous. Class V carried to the limit of navigability. Involves risk of life.

WHITEWATER GLOSSARY

Bailer: An open-ended container or bucket used to remove water from a raft.

Chute: A narrow channel through which the flow of water is swifter and deeper than the normal flow.

Duckie (or ducky): An inflatable kayak.

Eddy: A current of reverse water flow sometimes creating a small whirlpool.

Gradient: Drop in elevation during the downstream flow of a river. Rate of gradient is usually expressed in number of feet decreased per mile.

Hole: A depression in the river caused by reverse water flow. Also may be called a hydraulic.

Hydraulic: A very large hole with reverse water flow.

Hypothermia: A dangerous lowering of body-core temperature, caused by losing heat faster than it is produced by the body. Hypothermia is a threat when water temperatures are below 60° Fahrenheit or air temperatures are below 50° Fahrenheit.

Pool: An area of flatwater between rapids.

Pool drop: A whitewater rapid, usually of short duration, that begins and ends with fairly calm water rather than continuous water flow.

Portage: To carry a raft around unraftable or unsafe rapids or falls.

Put-in: The starting point of a rafting trip, where rafts are put into the river.

Rapids: A series of waves and turbulences.

Riffle: A very small rapid or wave caused by a shallow sand bar or rocks extending across a stream bed.

Scout: To visually survey a rapid from the riverbank to select the best route.

Standing waves: A series of stationary waves caused by water converging at the end of a tongue or a submerged object.

Take-out: The point where the rafting trip ends and the rafts are removed from the river.

Throw bag: A small bag containing a coiled rope that is used to rescue rafters in a river.

Tongue: A narrow depression between waves.

Whitewater: Moving water whose surface becomes turbulent or frothy by passing either over rocks, through a narrow river channel, or down a steep gradient.

CHAPTER 7

Savoring the River Experience

RIVER MEMORIES

Long after the final splash of the last rapid, you will remember the excitement and fun of your raft trip. With your rafting companions you will relive the river, your passage through the whitewater, what you did right, what you did wrong, and how you will run it the next time. During each retelling of the story, the rapids become more savage, your raft maneuvering more exacting, and the lure of the river stronger.

The challenge of whitewater rafting seems to draw you back. You want to run the river again, improve your technique, or have a second shot at the big one. The wilderness solitude and beauty strengthen the magnetic force. You remember stretches of quiet water dotted with sunlight, wildflowers adorning the shoreline, or the woods vibrant with fall colors. You savor the thrill of fast water—the incredible feeling of the natural river high. You want to remember it all.

Perhaps it is the intensity of these feelings that makes a river runner try to capture a bit of the river, to hold onto those memories.

Color photography is the most lasting visual reminder. Because of the difficulty of getting good pictures while on the water, many outfitters offer the services of a photographer positioned at key points along the river. In such cases color prints of your raft can be ordered from the outfitter following the trip.

Probably the most popular river souvenirs are the colorful and artistic T-shirts sporting river slogans or river maps. Several outfitters use a portion of the proceeds from T-shirt sales for river conservation and preservation projects. Other memorabilia available at outfitters and nearby shops are posters, postcards, Frisbees, insignia patches, key chains, and photographs.

The excitement and pleasure of rafting are addictive. Once you've run a river, you'll likely be hooked. At the conclusion of your river trip, chances are that as you shed your life jacket and say goodbye to your friends, you will add, "Until next time."

RIVER PRESERVATION

Rivers all over the continent face threats to their free-flowing existence. A significant number of popular rivers have been lost to dams, channelization, and other encroachments. Rivers can be exploited and wasted; they cannot be replaced.

Despite our legacy of poor stewardship, it appears to no longer be true that more river miles are being destroyed each year than are being saved. Dams and other threats have been fought off by people who recognize the value of endangered rivers. Many of these river miles are protected through the National Wild and Scenic Rivers program of the United States, which limits development on free-flowing rivers or river segments that possess outstanding scenic, recreational, geological, fish-and-wildlife, historic, or archaeological values. Dozens of dams have been stopped. More than 10,500 miles on 152 rivers have received legal protection from dams and water development, and their adjacent lands are managed for their natural values.

In just one recent year, twenty-seven rivers were added to the National Wild and Scenic Rivers system, totaling more than one thousand miles in Michigan, Arkansas, California, Pennsylvania, and New Jersey. Another 700 river miles were given temporary protection while they are studied for wild-and-scenic status, and 124 rivers and streams in Alaska's Tongass National Forest were found eligible for designation. Other recent river victories include a new flow regime for Glen Canyon Dam that will stop water releases from eroding important beaches in the Grand Canyon, defeat of the Auburn Dam on the American River in California, and protection of the Tatshenshini and Alsek rivers in British Columbia.

Conservationists are seeking wild-and-scenic status for hundreds of other threatened rivers. The most effective forces in river preservation are those closest to the source. No river—no matter how beautiful, appreciated, used, or endangered—will be protected without action by the people who raft, kayak, or canoe it, fish in it, or hike or live along it. Although many rafters admire and enjoy the resource they use, few are aware of the constant threats to the rivers or of the work required by national, state, and local organizations to preserve them.

American Rivers, the only national organization in the United States dedicated exclusively to protecting outstanding natural rivers, has been amazingly successful in its fight to preserve what remains of America's heritage of free-flowing streams. Founded in 1973 to help expand the five-year-old but sluggishly growing National Wild and Scenic Rivers system, American Rivers helps shape national and state rivers policy by focusing on six areas: nationally significant rivers, hydropower policy reform, urban rivers, clean water protection, endangered aquatic and riparian species protection, and water allocation issues of the western United States. It has a growing national membership and relies largely on the support of its members to make certain that the defenders of free-flowing rivers have a voice in Washington. Membership in American Rivers is one of the more basic ways to become involved in river conservation. To join, contact American Rivers, 801 Pennsylvania Avenue SE, Suite 400, Washington, DC 20003; (202) 547–6900.

PART II
■ ■ ■
Western United States

The South Fork of the American River, which flows through nineteenth-century gold rush country, is the site of California's most popular rafting trip.

CHAPTER 8

■ ■ ■

California

California, most populous of the United States, has some of the country's best recreational whitewater opportunities. Professional outfitters offer guided raft trips on rivers ranging from very easy to extremely difficult. Such offerings include half-day, one-day, and multiday trips, as well as trips especially for families, senior citizens, and the disabled.

California's most popular rafting trips are located in the western Sierra foothills near the agriculture-rich Central Valley. Here, free-flowing snowmelt from the High Sierra and controlled water releases from irrigation reservoirs and power dams are the source of much of the state's finest whitewater. These trips include the following rivers:

- The South Fork of the American River, in historic gold-rush country, the state's most popular whitewater run, offers exciting daily trips suitable for first-timers and families.
- The North and Middle forks of the American River, more difficult than the South Fork, feature both one-day and multiday trips through wilderness-like canyons. North Fork's Giant Gap run, with Class V whitewater, is reserved for physically fit adventure paddlers.
- Cache Creek, north of San Francisco, is an easy yet fun river for families in small rafts and inflatable kayaks.
- The Yuba River's North Fork, near the historic gold-rush town of Downieville, has Class III–IV and Class V sections.
- The North Fork of the Stanislaus, which passes through the breathtaking gorges of Calaveras Big Trees State Park west of Yosemite National Park, and the lower Stanislaus, which cuts through Goodwin Canyon near Knights Ferry, both provide challenging Class III–IV whitewater.
- The Tuolumne, designated a National Wild and Scenic River, is a whitewater classic through scenic wilderness canyons. The Tuolumne has a dynamic Class V+ Cherry Creek tributary.
- The Merced River offers continuous and lively Class III–IV whitewater just west of Yosemite National Park.

Southern California's Kings and Kern rivers, which originate in Kings Canyon and Sequoia national parks, provide several rafting options. While both have challenging Class III–IV+ whitewater sections in the springtime, they have family rafting trips during moderate summertime flows.

Northern California's coastal mountain ranges and rain-fed forests provide action-packed spring-season whitewater excitement as well as reliable summer

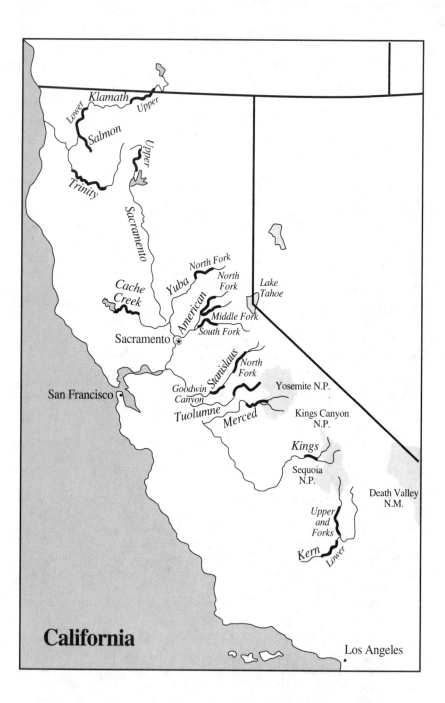

California
River Comparison

	Difficulty	Min Age	H	D	M	Season	P	O	K
Central California									
American (South Fork)									
Chili Bar	/ /	7	✗	✗		Apr–Oct	✗	✗	✗
Gorge	/ /	7	✗	✗		Apr–Oct	✗	✗	✗
American (Middle Fork)	/ /	14	✗	✗		May–Sep	✗	✗	
American (North Fork)									
Chamberlain Falls	/ /	14	✗	✗		Apr–Jun	✗	✗	
Giant Gap	/ / /	16	✗	✗		Apr–May	✗		
Cache Creek	/	6	✗	✗		May–Sep	✗		✗
Yuba (North Fork)									
Upper	/ / /	16	✗			Apr–Jun	✗	✗	
Lower	/ /	12	✗	✗		Apr–Jun	✗	✗	
Stanislaus (North Fork)	/ /	14	✗			Apr–Jun	✗		
Stanislaus (Goodwin Canyon)	/ /	16	✗			May–Sep	✗	✗	
Tuolumne									
Main	/ /	14	✗	✗		Apr–Oct	✗	✗	
Cherry Creek	/ / /	18	✗			Apr–Aug	✗	✗	
Merced	/ /	12	✗	✗		Apr–Jun	✗	✗	
South-Central California									
Kings	/ /	8	✗	✗		Apr–Aug	✗	✗	✗
Kern									
Forks	/ / /	14		✗		Apr–Jul	✗	✗	
Upper	/ / /	14	✗	✗		May–Jul	✗	✗	
Lower	/ /	12	✗	✗		May–Oct	✗	✗	
Northern California									
Sacramento (Upper)	/ /	12	✗	✗		Apr–Jun	✗	✗	
Salmon	/ / /	16	✗	✗		Apr–Jul	✗	✗	
Trinity									
Upper	/	6	✗	✗	✗	Apr–Oct	✗	✗	
Lower	/	6	✗	✗		Apr–Oct	✗	✗	
Trinity (Burnt Ranch Gorge)	/ / /	16		✗		May–Aug	✗	✗	
Klamath (Upper)	/ /	12	✗	✗		May–Sep	✗	✗	
Klamath (Lower)	/	4	✗	✗	✗	Apr–Oct	✗	✗	✗

/   Beginner—Easy whitewater. Fun for everyone.

/ /   Intermediate—Moderate whitewater.
No previous rafting experience is necessary.

/ / /   Advanced—Difficult whitewater.
Previous Class IV paddle rafting experience is recommended or required.

H—Half-Day Trip, D—Day Trip, M—Multiday Trip
P—Paddle Raft, O—Oar Raft, K—Inflatable Kayak

rafting excitement for adventurous and first-time rafters. Three of California's most challenging Class IV–V+ whitewater trips—the upper Klamath, the Salmon, and Trinity's Burnt Ranch Gorge—are within 75 miles (120 km) of the California-Oregon border. More moderate Class I–III whitewater sections on the Trinity River and the lower Klamath Creek can be enjoyed by families all summer.

Some California outfitters promote charter-bus trips to the more popular rivers for customers from San Francisco, Los Angeles, and other population centers. Interested rafters will find information about these trips described in outfitters' brochures.

AMERICAN RIVER (SOUTH FORK), CALIFORNIA

Sections:	Chili Bar and Gorge
Location:	El Dorado County, central California, between Auburn and Placerville
Driving Time:	Sacramento—1.5 hours
Difficulty:	Class II–III
Trip Length:	Chili Bar—9 miles (14 km); Gorge—12 miles (19 km). Trip lengths may vary between outfitters.
Trip Options:	Paddle raft, oar raft, inflatable kayak; one day on either section or two-day overnight including both sections
Season:	April–October
Cost:	$70–$115 on each section

The South Fork of the American River, between Chili Bar and Folsom Lake, is California's most frequently rafted whitewater stretch. The South Fork American maintains its popularity because of its exciting whitewater, beautiful scenery, historical setting, and proximity to population centers. The river's put-ins are just one and one-half hours from Sacramento by car and less than three hours from the San Francisco area. Many outfitters arrange charter-bus transportation from as far away as Los Angeles and San Diego.

The South Fork American offers a favorable blend of exciting whitewater and slow-moving flatwater and pools in the heart of California's gold country. More than fifty Class II–III rapids—such as Meat Grinder, Racehorse Bend, African Queen, Triple Threat, Ambush Island, Swimmers, Troublemaker, Satan's Cesspool, Lower Haystack, Bouncing Rock, and Hospital Bar—test the skills of both beginning and intermediate rafters. In addition to providing raft trips for groups, children, families, and first-timers, many outfitters are accommodating to the disabled and disadvantaged.

Rafters may choose between one-day trips on the upper Chili Bar Run or the lower Gorge Run, and two-day camping trips that cover the entire 21-mile stretch from Chili Bar to Folsom Lake. On two-day trips, outfitters offer such treats as gourmet meals, saunas, and volleyball games.

The South Fork American flows past the historic town of Coloma, where John Marshall discovered gold and started the famed California Gold Rush of 1849.

Outfitters listed on pages 32–33.

AMERICAN RIVER (MIDDLE FORK), CALIFORNIA

Section:	Oxbow to Mammoth Bar
Location:	Placer County, Auburn State Recreation Area, between Auburn and Foresthill, central California
Driving Time:	Sacramento—2 hours
Difficulty:	Class II–IV
Trip Length:	26 miles (42 km) or less
Trip Options:	Paddle raft, oar raft; one and two days
Season:	May–September
Cost:	$90–$130; $200–$250 two days

The Middle Fork of the American River, in the mid-Sierra foothills, provides rafters a unique opportunity to experience a wilderness river in California's gold-rush country. Beaches, side creeks, and waterfalls alternating with exciting white-water provide a variety of adventures in the picturesque canyons of the Auburn State Recreation Area. Along the calmer areas of the river, the chances of seeing deer, black bears, otters, and bald and golden eagles are excellent.

One of the first rapids encountered on the Middle Fork is Tunnel Chute, a fast, steep, narrow chute leading into a 30-yard granite tunnel that was blasted through the mountainside by early miners. Because of a potential for injury at some water levels, outfitters may not always run Tunnel Chute. Downstream, most Class II–III rapids such as Karma, Gumby, and Bus Wreck are more civilized. The exceptions are Ruck-A-Chucky and Murderer's Bar rapids, which are usually portaged.

Outfitters listed on pages 32–33.

AMERICAN RIVER (NORTH FORK), CALIFORNIA

Sections:	Chamberlain Falls and Giant Gap
Location:	Placer County, central California, near Iowa Hill
Driving Time:	Sacramento—2 hours
Difficulty:	Class III–IV+ (Chamberlain Falls); IV–V+ (Giant Gap); Class IV paddle raft experience required for Giant Gap
Trip Length:	Chamberlain Falls—9 miles (14 km); Giant Gap—14 miles (22 km)
Trip Options:	Paddle raft, oar raft; paddle only on the Giant Gap run; one and two days
Season:	April–June (Chamberlain Falls); April–May (Giant Gap)
Cost:	$85–$130 (Chamberlain Falls); $100–$225 (Giant Gap)

The North Fork of the American River, Chamberlain Falls run, offers a spectacular whitewater run through a wilderness canyon that is protected under the California Wild and Scenic Rivers Act. During the first half of the 9-mile (14-km) trip, the river drops through narrow boulder-filled Class III–IV+ rapids such as Chamberlain and Bogus Thunder falls, Staircase, Nose Stand, and Entrance Exam. On the more mellow lower half of the trip, the river has numerous less-technical Class II–III rapids.

Rafting on the free-flowing North Fork American depends upon snowmelt from the Desolation Wilderness region of the High Sierra, west of Lake Tahoe. Considered a step up from the Class II–III South Fork American, outfitters prefer rafters to have had previous Class III whitewater experience.

The Giant Gap section of the North Fork American is yet another step up in difficulty from the Middle Fork. It is one of California's finest and most technical whitewater stretches. For nearly 14 miles from Euchre Bar to the Iowa Hill Bridge take-out, rafters challenge one Class V rapid after another in a 2,000-foot canyon. Now included in the National Wild and Scenic Rivers system, the Giant Gap run has just recently been opened to a limited number of raft trips. Prospective rafters must be physically fit and have previous Class IV rafting experience. In addition to the difficult rapids, rafters must hike 2 miles into a steep ravine to reach the Euchre Bar put-in. Only two outfitters are licensed to run this section: Sierra Mac River Trips and Whitewater Voyages (see following list for addresses and phone numbers).

American River Outfitters

ABLE Adventure Tours
P.O. Box 18
Coloma, CA 95613
(916) 626–6208

Adventure Connection
P.O. Box 475
Coloma, CA 95613
(800) 556–6060
(916) 626–7385

All-Outdoors Adventure Trips
2151 San Miguel Dr.
Walnut Creek, CA 94596
(800) 247–2387
(510) 932–8993

American River Recreation
P.O. Box 465
Lotus, CA 95651
(800) 333–7238
(916) 622–6802

American Whitewater Expeditions
P.O. Box 4280
Sunland, CA 91041–4280
(800) 576–3205
(818) 352–3205

ARTA River Trips
Star Route 73
Groveland, CA 95321
(800) 323–2782 (California only)
(209) 962–7873

Beyond Limits Adventures
P.O. Box 215
Riverbank, CA 95367
(800) 234–7238 (California only)
(209) 529–7655

Chili Bar Outdoor Center
P.O. Box 554
Coloma, CA 95613
(800) 356–2262
(916) 621–1236

Earthtrek Expeditions
7310 Hwy. 49
Lotus, CA 95651
(800) 229–8735
(916) 626–8175

ECHO: The Wilderness Company
6529 Telegraph Ave.
Oakland, CA 94609–1113
(800) 652–3246
(510) 652–1600

Environmental Traveling Companions
Fort Mason Center
Bldg. C, Room 360
San Francisco, CA 94123
(415) 474–7662

Gold Rush River Runners
P.O. Box 390
Garden Valley, CA 95633
(916) 626–7631

Mariah Wilderness Expeditions
P.O. Box 248
Point Richmond, CA 94807
(800) 462–7424
(510) 233–2303

Mother Lode River Trips
P.O. Box 456
Coloma, CA 95613
(916) 626–4187

O.A.R.S.
P.O. Box 67
Angels Camp, CA 95222
(800) 346–6277
(209) 736–4677

Sierra Mac River Trips
P.O. Box 366
Sonora, CA 95370
(800) 457–2580

(209) 532–1327
Tributary Whitewater Tours
20480 Woodbury Dr.
Grass Valley, CA 95949
(916) 346–6812

Whitewater Connection
P.O. Box 270
Coloma, CA 95613–0270
(800) 336–7238
(916) 622–6446

Whitewater Excitement
P.O. Box 5992
Auburn, CA 95604
(916) 888–6515

Whitewater Voyages
P.O. Box 20400
El Sobrante, CA 94820–0400
(800) 488–7238
(510) 222–5994

Whitewater Expeditions & Tours
P.O. Box 160024
Sacramento, CA 95816
(916) 451–3241

CACHE CREEK, CALIFORNIA

Section:	Cache Creek Canyon
Location:	Lake County near Rumsey, north-central California
Driving Time:	San Francisco—2 hours
Difficulty:	Class II–III
Trip Length:	6–12 miles (10–19 km)
Trip Options:	Paddle raft, inflatable kayak; one and two days
Season:	May–September
Cost:	$60–$65; $125–$150 two days

Cache Creek, a two-hour drive north of San Francisco, offers an excellent introduction to whitewater rafting. Its relatively easy Class II-III whitewater and scenic canyons may be enjoyed by the most inexperienced paddler. Guests above the age of twelve may paddle their own rafts or two-person inflatable kayaks. Families with younger children will enjoy small guided paddle rafts.

Popular one-day trips begin at Cache Creek Canyon Regional Park. Two-day trips put in at Buck Island, some 13 miles (21 km) upriver. Two-day trips include overnight camping on the riverbank.

Daily water releases from Clear Lake and Indian Valley Reservoir normally permit sufficient water for rafting from May through August.

Cache Creek Outfitters

Whitewater Adventures
P.O. Box 2472
Napa, CA 94558
(707) 255–0761

Whitewater Voyages
P.O. Box 20400
El Sobrante, CA 94820–0400
(800) 488–7238
(510) 222–5994

YUBA RIVER (NORTH FORK), CALIFORNIA

Sections:	Union Flat (upper) and Goodyear's Bar (lower)
Location:	Sierra County near Downieville, north-central California
Driving Time:	Sacramento—2.5 hours
Difficulty:	Class IV–V (upper); III–IV (lower)
Trip Length:	Upper—10 miles (16 km); Lower—18 miles (29 km)
Trip Options:	Paddle raft, oar raft; one day (upper), one and two days (lower)
Season:	April–June
Cost:	$120–$140 (upper); $90–$120 (lower); $200–$275 two day

The North Fork of the Yuba River features nearly 30 miles (48 km) of exciting free-flowing whitewater near the historic gold-rush town of Downieville. Its steep Class IV-V upper (Union Flat) section, which cascades for 10 miles (16 km) through numerous boulder gardens containing narrow chutes, concludes with the Class V Rosasso Ravine just above Goodyear's Bar, where the gradient exceeds 100 feet a mile.

North Yuba's 18-mile (29-km) lower (Goodyear's Bar) run offers rafters the choice between a one-day, 9-mile (14-km) run to Fiddle Creek or a two-day trip that ends in the placid waters of New Bullards Bar Reservoir. The highlight of the Goodyear's Bar run is the spectacular Class V Maytag Rapid, just upstream from Fiddle Creek. Rafting guests may choose to walk around Maytag.

Tahoe National Forest's issuance of commercial rafting permits to only three outfitters on the Yuba River assures an uncrowded experience for those who raft this beautiful Sierra river. California Route 49, which parallels much of the river, provides several vantage points from which to photograph the exciting rapids. Rafters should allow time to visit the charming and picturesque town of Downieville.

Yuba River (North Fork) Outfitters

Beyond Limits Adventures
P.O. Box 215
Riverbank, CA 95367
(800) 234–7238 (California only)
(209) 529–7655

Tributary Whitewater Tours
20480 Woodbury Dr.
Grass Valley, CA 95949
(916) 346–6812

Whitewater Voyages
P.O. Box 20400
El Sobrante, CA 94820–0400
(800) 488–7238
(510) 222–5994

STANISLAUS RIVER (NORTH FORK), CALIFORNIA

Section:	Sourgrass to Calaveras Big Trees State Park
Location:	Calaveras County near Dorrington, central California
Driving Time:	San Francisco—3.5 hours
Difficulty:	Class IV+; rafting experience highly recommended
Trip Length:	5 miles (8 km)
Trip Options:	Paddle raft only; one day
Season:	April–June
Cost:	$100–$130

The North Fork Stanislaus River is nestled within the breathtaking granite gorges of Stanislaus National Forest and Calaveras Big Trees State Park in the heart of the mother lode. Along the banks of the whitewater run, giant sequoias tower above azaleas, dogwoods, and side-canyon waterfalls.

The North Fork Stanislaus is not a river for first-time rafters. Highly technical Class III-IV+ pool-drop rapids—Beginner's Luck, Sierra Gate, the Claw, Convulsion, Wallet Slot, and Emerald Falls—require the best from each paddler and leave little time to enjoy some of the river's most spectacular scenery.

Rafters on the North Stanislaus should allow enough time to wander through the North Grove of Calaveras Big Trees State Park and to visit nearby Mercer Caverns and the historic gold-rush towns of Columbia and Murphys.

Stanislaus River (North Fork) Outfitters

ABLE Adventure Tours
P.O. Box 18
Coloma, CA 95613
(916) 626–6208

Beyond Limits Adventures
P.O. Box 215
Riverbank, CA 95367
(800) 234–7238 (California only)
(209) 529–7655

All–Outdoors Adventure Trips
2151 San Miguel Dr.
Walnut Creek, CA 94596
(800) 247–2387
(510) 932–8993

Whitewater Voyages
P.O. Box 20400
El Sobrante, CA 94820–0400
(800) 488–7238
(510) 222–5994

STANISLAUS RIVER (GOODWIN CANYON), CALIFORNIA

Section:	Goodwin Canyon
Location:	Stanislaus County near Knight's Ferry, central California
Driving Time:	Sacramento—2 hours; San Francisco—2.5 hours
Difficulty:	Class III–IV+
Trip Length:	5 miles (8 km)

Trip Options:	Paddle raft, oar raft; one day
Season:	May–September
Cost:	$80–$85

The lower Stanislaus River, between Goodwin Canyon Dam and Knight's Ferry, is a very challenging Class III–IV+ whitewater stretch. Goodwin Canyon's varied terrain and geological formations include Table Mountain, deep granite canyons, and rolling foothills. Technical Class IV+ rapids in the canyons include Mr. Toad's Wild Ride, Pinballs, and Haunted House. Other canyon attractions are its wildlife and the site of a gold-rush town destroyed by floods.

Stanislaus River (Goodwin Canyon) Outfitters

Beyond Limits Adventures
P.O. Box 215
Riverbank, CA 95367
(800) 234–7238 (California only)
(209) 529–7655

Sunshine Raft-Balloon Adventures
P.O. Box 1445
Oakdale, CA 95361
(800) 829–7238
(209) 848–4800

TUOLUMNE RIVER, CALIFORNIA

Section:	Lumsden Launch to Ward's Ferry Bridge (main)
Location:	Tuolumne County, northwest of Yosemite National Park near Groveland, central California
Driving Time:	San Francisco—3.5 hours
Difficulty:	Class III–IV+; IV–V in high water
Trip Length:	18 miles (29 km)
Trip Options:	Paddle raft, oar raft, paddle/oar raft; one, two, and three days
Season:	April–October
Cost:	$125–$160

The Tuolumne, a National Wild and Scenic River since 1984, has all the features that any river adventurer could want: remoteness, wildlife, and swift-flowing and demanding whitewater. In addition, its banks and side canyons are awash with the folklore of the Miwok Indians and early California gold seekers.

For more than two decades, the classic 18-mile (29-km) main Tuolumne has been one of California's premier whitewater trips. Following a breathtaking shuttle ride down the steep canyon to Meral's Pool near Lumsden put-in, the river trip drops to 760 feet at Ward's Ferry Bridge. This steep gradient, varying between 30 and 70 feet per mile, creates fifteen major Class IV–IV+ rapids. Tuolumne's noted rapids include Sunderland's Chute, Hackamack's Hole, Ram's Head, The Squeeze, Clavey Falls, Grey's Grindstone, and Hell's Kitchen. The most exciting rapid is the renowned Clavey Falls, a breathtaking Class IV+ plunge, one of the major drops on western rivers.

Section:	Cherry Creek (upper)
Location:	Tuolumne County, northwest of Yosemite National Park near Groveland, central California
Driving Time:	San Francisco—3.5 hours

Difficulty:	Class V+; Class IV rafting experience is highly recommended
Trip Length:	9 miles (14 km)
Trip Options:	Paddle raft, paddle/oar raft; one day
Season:	April–August
Cost:	$225

Rafters wanting an even greater challenge than the main Tuolumne should ask outfitters about the river's upper run from Cherry Creek to Meral's Pool. Known as the Cherry Creek trip, unbelievable Class V+ rapids cascade and drop almost continuously (at times up to 150 feet per mile) for nearly 9 miles (14 km) to the start of the main Tuolumne trip. Class IV–V+ rapids, such as Mushroom, Miracle Mile, Lewis's Leap, Flat Rock, and Horseshoe Falls, will excite the most experienced rafter.

Self-bailing rafts and more experienced professional outfitters make it possible to descend the steep upper Tuolumne, previously thought unrunnable. Persons interested in the one-day Cherry Creek or upper Tuolumne raft trip should contact any of the outfitters who offer the main Tuolumne trip.

Tuolumne River Outfitters

Ahwahnee Whitewater Expeditions
P.O. Box 1161
Columbia, CA 95310
(800) 359–9790
(209) 533–1401

All-Outdoors Adventure Trips
2151 San Miguel Dr.
Walnut Creek, CA 94596
(800) 247–2387
(510) 932–8993

ARTA River Trips
Star Route 73
Groveland, CA 95321
(800) 323–2782
(209) 962–7873

ECHO: The Wilderness Company
6529 Telegraph Ave.
Oakland, CA 94609–1113
(800) 652–3246
(510) 652–1600

O.A.R.S.
P.O. Box 67
Angels Camp, CA 95222
(800) 346–6277
(209) 736–4677

Outdoor Adventures
P.O. Box 1149
Pt. Reyes Station, CA 94956–9900
(800) 323–4234
(415) 663–8300

Sierra Mac River Trips
P.O. Box 366
Sonora, CA 95370
(800) 457–2580
(209) 532–1327

Whitewater Voyages
P.O. Box 20400
El Sobrante, CA 94820–0400
(800) 488–7238
(510) 222–5994

Zephyr River Expeditions
P.O. Box 510
Columbia, CA 95310
(800) 431–3636 (California only)
(209) 532–6249

MERCED RIVER, CALIFORNIA

Sections: Cranberry Gulch to McCabe Flat (upper); McCabe Flat to Bagby (lower)
Location: Mariposa County near El Portal, central California
Driving Time: San Francisco—4 hours
Difficulty: Class III–IV; rafting experience recommended during spring high water
Trip Length: Upper—15 miles (24 km); Lower—9 miles (14 km)
Trip Options: Paddle raft, oar raft; one and two days
Season: April–June
Cost: $85–$130; $165–$250

Just west of Yosemite National Park's Arch Rock entrance, the Merced River begins a spectacular Class III-IV whitewater journey through a nonglaciated V-shaped canyon alongside California's Route 140. This is in sharp contrast to the tranquil section of the Merced River seen by the millions of people who visit the park's valley floor each year. Merced Canyon was added to the National Wild and Scenic Rivers system in 1987. For part of its course, the river follows the old Yosemite railroad bed, passing abandoned gold mines and water flumes.

The Merced is one of the Sierra's more popular springtime whitewater rivers for experienced rafters. During the high water typical of May and early June, the Merced has exceptional Class III-IV rapids created by a river gradient of up to 70 feet per mile. Although less intense during late June and July, the Merced is still an exciting trip for both experienced and first-time rafters.

Merced River Outfitters

Ahwahnee Whitewater Expeditions
P.O. Box 1161
Columbia, CA 95310
(800) 359–9790
(209) 533–1401

All-Outdoors Adventure Trips
2151 San Miguel Dr.
Walnut Creek, CA 94596
(800) 247–2387
(510) 932–8993

American River Recreation
P.O. Box 465
Lotus, CA 95651
(800) 333–7238
(916) 622–6802

ARTA River Trips
Star Route 73
Groveland, CA 95321
(800) 323–2782
(209) 962–7873

Beyond Limits Adventures
P.O. Box 215
Riverbank, CA 95367
(800) 234–7238 (California only)
(209) 529–7655

Mariah Wilderness Expeditions
P.O. Box 248
Point Richmond, CA 94807
(800) 462–7424
(510) 233–2303

O.A.R.S.
P.O. Box 67
Angels Camp, CA 95222
(800) 346–6277
(209) 736–4677

Whitewater Excitement
P.O. Box 5992
Auburn, CA 95604
(916) 888–6515

Whitewater Voyages
P.O. Box 20400
El Sobrante, CA 94820–0400
(800) 488–7238
(510) 222–5994

Zephyr River Expeditions
P.O. Box 510
Columbia, CA 95310
(800) 431–3636 (California only)
(209) 532–6249

KINGS RIVER, CALIFORNIA

Section:	Garnet Dyke to Kirch Flat
Location:	Fresno County, east of Fresno, south-central California
Driving Time:	Fresno—1 hour; Los Angeles—4.5 hours
Difficulty:	Class II–IV
Trip Length:	10 miles (16 km)
Trip Options:	Paddle raft, oar raft, inflatable kayak; one and two days
Season:	April–August
Cost:	$95–$120; $185–$265 two days

The Kings River is the largest of the Sierra's many fine whitewater rivers. It is free-flowing during its westward descent through Kings Canyon National Park and Sequoia National Forest until it enters Pine Flat Lake, nearly due east of Fresno.

Rafters generally find the best whitewater from early May through June. During peak springtime runoff, more than twenty-five rapids, many in the Class III–IV range, provide a thrilling intermediate–advanced run with numerous large waves and fast currents.

Although considerably less intense during July and August, the Kings still offers fine whitewater and beautiful mountain canyon scenery. From late June until season end (depending on the amount of spring runoff), the Kings calms to a lively Class II–III river. Families with children as young as eight years may enjoy the summertime whitewaters of the Kings.

Kings River Outfitters

Kings River Expeditions
211 N. Van Ness
Fresno, CA 93701
(209) 223–4881

Zephyr River Expeditions
P.O. Box 510
Columbia, CA 95310
(800) 431–3636 (California only)
(209) 532–6249

Spirit Kings River Whitewater
P.O. Box 51040
Pacific Grove, CA 93950–6040
(408) 373–3275

KERN RIVER, CALIFORNIA

Section:	Forks of the Kern
Location:	Tulare County, south of Sequoia National Park, south-central California
Driving Time:	Bakersfield—1 hour; Los Angeles—3.5 hours
Difficulty:	Class IV–V+; Class IV paddle rafting experience required

Trip Length: 18 miles (29 km)
Trip Options: Paddle raft, oar raft; two and three days
Season: April–July
Cost: $400–$550

The remarkable Kern River, only a few hours from Los Angeles, is one of California's premier whitewater rivers. Fed by the snowmelt of Mount Whitney, highest peak in the contiguous forty-eight states, the Kern, unlike most Sierra waters, flows north-to-south instead of east-to-west for 100 of its 165 miles (264 km). Kern River's four outfitters offer nearly 60 miles (96 km) of exciting whitewater and beautiful Sierra mountain scenery between Sequoia National Park and Bakersfield.

The Forks of the Kern, formed by the confluence of the Little Kern and the main Kern, is rated by whitewater experts as one of the most technically demanding runs in California. The Forks, as the river is called by outfitters, has a gradient of 60 feet per mile, creating numerous Class IV–V+ rapids and waterfalls, many of which must be scouted and, during high water, sometimes must be portaged.

Access to the Forks of the Kern is almost as difficult as its whitewaters. The put-in, at the confluence of the Little Kern and the main Kern, requires a 3-mile (5-km) steep hike into the ravine. All food and river equipment is transported by pack animals, and each guest carries his or her personal items.

Skilled oarsman guides raft through Vortex Rapid on California's Class IV–V+ Forks of the Kern. Photo by Curt Smith.

Section:	Johnsondale to Kernville (upper)
Location:	Kern and Tulare counties, north of Kernville, south-central California
Driving Time:	Bakersfield—1 hour; Los Angeles—3 hours
Difficulty:	Class III–IV+; Class IV paddle rafting experience required
Trip Length:	20 miles (32 km) or less
Trip Options:	Paddle raft, oar raft; one and two days
Season:	May–July
Cost:	$90–$140 one day; $200–$300 two days

The upper Kern River, between Johnsondale Bridge and River Kern Beach at the top of Lake Isabella Reservoir, although slightly less demanding than the Forks run, still has plenty of exciting whitewater of varying difficulty. The Class III–IV Limestone run above Fairview Dam is just a warm-up for the whitewater in the dam's tailwaters. The 17 miles (27 km) from the dam to Kernville includes the Fairview and Goldledge, or Thunder Run stretches, which offer numerous Class III-V rapids. Some outfitters now offer family and first-timer float trips through Class II–III Powerhouse, Big Daddy, and Ewings rapids beginning just above Kernville.

Section:	Lake Isabella to Democrat Beach (lower)
Location:	Kern County, east of Bakersfield, south-central California
Driving Time:	Bakersfield—1 hour; Los Angeles—3 hours
Difficulty:	Class III–IV
Trip Length:	19 miles (30 km) or less
Trip Options:	Paddle raft, oar raft; one and two days
Season:	May–October
Cost:	$90–$135; $225–$275 two days

The lower Kern River whitewater stretch through the Greenhorn Mountain canyons to the Central Valley's floor begins just below Lake Isabella. Although its rapids are not as intense and technically difficult as either the Forks or upper Kern runs, it offers excellent Class III–IV rapids and superb scenery.

Whereas outfitters commonly promote the 19-mile (30-km) lower Kern as a two-day trip with overnight camping, one-day trips on either the Miracle Run or Big Water sections are also popular. Favorite rapids on the first-day Miracle Run include Class III–IV rapids Wallow Rock, Hoppopitamus, and Miracle. On the second day, for overnight river runners, the Big Water Run includes the lower Kern's most challenging rapids: White Maidens' Walkaway, Silver Staircase, Powerful Possum, and Sundown Falls. Most rapids in this section are rated Class III–IV with the exception of Royal Flush (Class V+), which is normally portaged.

Kern River Outfitters

Chuck Richards' Whitewater
Box W.W. Whitewater
Lake Isabella, CA 93240
(800) 624–5950
(619) 379–4444

Kern River Tours
P.O. Box 3444
Lake Isabella, CA 93240
(619) 379–4616

Outdoor Adventures
P.O. Box 1149
Pt. Reyes Station, CA 94956–9900
(800) 323–4234
(415) 663–8300

Whitewater Voyages
P.O. Box 20400
El Sobrante, CA 94820–0400
(800) 488–7238
(510) 222–5994

SACRAMENTO RIVER (UPPER), CALIFORNIA

Section:	Sims Flat to Dog Creek
Location:	Siskiyou and Shasta counties near Dunsmuir, northern California
Driving Time:	Sacramento—3 hours
Difficulty:	Class III–IV
Trip Length:	14 miles (22 km); 35 miles (56 km) multiday
Trip Options:	Paddle raft, oar raft; one to three days
Season:	April–June
Cost:	$60–$80; $180–$220 two days

Just below northern California's snowcapped Mount Shasta, and parallel to Interstate 5, the upper Sacramento River features nearly fifty rapids during its 35-mile (56-km) descent from Box Canyon Dam north of Dunsmuir to Shasta Reservoir. The favored whitewater run on the upper Sacramento is the 14-mile (22-km) Class III–IV upper-canyon trip from Sims Flat to Dog Creek near Shasta Lake. These beautiful canyons contain numerous rapids with pool-drop rapids.

In most years, the upper Sacramento can be rafted only in the spring. Early reservations are recommended because the season is short and the number of raft trips is limited.

Sacramento River (Upper) Outfitters

Tributary Whitewater Tours
20480 Woodbury Dr.
Grass Valley, CA 95949
(916) 346–6812

Wilderness Adventures
19504 Statton Acres Rd.
Lakehead, CA 96051
(916) 238–8121

Turtle River Rafting Company
P.O. Box 313
Mt. Shasta, CA 96067
(800) 726–3223
(916) 926–3223

SALMON RIVER, CALIFORNIA

Sections:	Forks of Salmon to Somes Bar, which includes the Nordheimer (upper) and Butler Creek (lower) sections
Location:	Siskiyou County, east of Orleans, northern California
Driving Time:	Eureka—2 hours; Medford—3 hours
Difficulty:	Class III–V; Class IV rafting experience required by most outfitters on the Nordheimer (upper) section
Trip Length:	18–21 miles (29–34 km)
Trip Options:	Paddle raft, oar raft, paddle/oar raft; one and two days
Season:	April–July
Cost:	$95–$115; $240–$325 two days

The Wild and Scenic California Salmon, so referred to by river outfitters to avoid confusion with the famed Idaho Salmon River, is one of northern California's finest Class IV–V whitewater stretches for thrill-seekers. After a deceptively easy start near the community of Forks of the Salmon in the Klamath National Forest, northeast of Eureka, the Salmon drops into an incredibly beautiful and rugged gorge with vertical granite walls decorated by hanging ferns, wildflowers, and sparkling waterfalls. Snowmelt waters from the Trinity Alps passing over and through large boulder gardens generate more than fifty exciting rapids that include Class IV runs. Also in this stretch are three dynamic Class V rapids: Cascade, Last Chance, and Freight Train.

Outfitters normally run one-day trips on both the upper and lower sections of the Salmon. On two-day trips, the 10-mile (16-km) Class III–IV or Butler Creek (lower) section, is frequently used as a preparatory run to the more difficult Class IV–V Nordheimer (upper) section.

Rafters must not take the California Salmon lightly. Its steep gradient exceeds that of the main Tuolumne. Most outfitters require rafters to be at least sixteen years old and have Class IV rafting experience.

Salmon River Outfitters

The Adventure Center
40 N. Main St.
Ashland, OR 97520
(800) 444–2819
(503) 488–2819

All-Outdoors Adventure Trips
2151 San Miguel Dr.
Walnut Creek, CA 94596
(800) 247–2387
(510) 932–8993

ARTA River Trips
Star Route 73
Groveland, CA 95321
(800) 323–2782
(209) 962–7873

Electric Rafting Company
P.O. Box 3456
Eureka, CA 95501
(707) 826–2861

O.A.R.S.
P.O. Box 67
Angels Camp, CA 95222
(800) 346–6277
(209) 736–4677

Noah's World of Water
P.O. Box 11
Ashland, OR 97520
(800) 858–2811
(503) 488–2811

Turtle River Rafting Company
P.O. Box 313
Mt. Shasta, CA 96067
(916) 926–3223

Whitewater Voyages
P.O. Box 20400
El Sobrante, CA 94820–0400
(800) 488–7238
(510) 222–5994

Wilderness Adventures
19504 Statton Acres Rd.
Lakehead, CA 96051
(916) 238–8121

TRINITY RIVER (UPPER AND LOWER), CALIFORNIA

Sections: Pigeon Point to Big Flat (upper); Hawkins Bar to Willow Creek (lower)
Location: Trinity County, west of Weaverville, northern California
Driving Time: Eureka—1.5 hours; Sacramento—5 hours
Difficulty: Class II–III+ (upper); I–II (lower)
Trip Length: Upper—13 miles (21 km); lower—6 miles (9 km)
Trip Options: Paddle raft, oar raft; half-day, one to five days
Season: April–October
Cost: $45–$60, $90–$120 two days (upper)

The upper Trinity's Hayden Flat and Pigeon Point runs, which parallel California Route 299 west of Weaverville, offer an excellent introduction to whitewater rafting in the Salmon–Trinity Alps Wilderness and the Trinity National Forest. Single-day and multiday trips of varying lengths enable families, senior citizens, and the disabled to enjoy the mountain scenery and exciting, but not too difficult, rapids.

Near the town of Willow Creek, the lower Trinity River offers a gentle Class I–II whitewater adventure for children and timid first-time rafters. Drifting on mild currents, rafters pass sandy beaches, table rocks, and inviting swimming holes in the narrow canyons of Fish Fang Gorge.

Regular water releases from Lewiston Dam, in the Whiskeytown Shasta-Trinity National Recreation Area, usually ensure ample water levels for rafting throughout the summer.

Trinity River (Upper and Lower) Outfitters

Big Foot Outdoor Company
P.O. Box 729
Willow Creek, CA 95573
(916) 629–2263

Kimtu Outdoor Adventures
P.O. Box 938
Willow Creek, CA 95573
(916) 629–3843

TRINITY RIVER (BURNT RANCH GORGE), CALIFORNIA

Section: Burnt Ranch Gorge
Location: Trinity County near Burnt Ranch, northern California
Driving Time: Eureka—1.5 hours; Sacramento—5 hours
Difficulty: Class IV–V; Class IV paddle raft experience required
Trip Length: 9 miles (14 km)
Trip Options: Paddle raft, oar raft; one day
Season: May–August
Cost: $120–$140

The most spectacular stretch of the Trinity River, near the tiny town of Burnt Ranch, is known as Burnt Ranch Gorge. First commercially rafted in 1983, many professional outfitters had previously considered this Class IV–V section unrunnable. Today, with self-bailing paddle rafts and more experienced guides, outfitters regularly schedule trips through the highly technical waters of the nearly 2,000-foot-deep gorge.

Whitewater experts rate the 9-mile (14-km) Burnt Ranch Gorge as one of California's most challenging commercial rafting trips. Five Class IV–IV+ rapids within the first 2.5 miles (4 km) are a prerequisite to the seven Class V–V+ rapids that follow: Upper, Middle, and Lower Burnt Ranch falls, Hennessy Falls, Origami, Table Rock, and Gray Falls.

Water releases from Lewiston Dam provide some of the very best summer-season Class V rafting in the state. Only experienced and physically fit rafters are permitted on the Trinity's Burnt Ranch Gorge whitewater trip.

Trinity River (Burnt Ranch Gorge) Outfitters

Beyond Limits Adventures
P.O. Box 215
Riverbank, CA 95367
(800) 234–7238 (California only)
(209) 529–7655

Whitewater Voyages
P.O. Box 20400
El Sobrante, CA 94820–0400
(800) 488–7238
(510) 222–5994

Tributary Whitewater Tours
20480 Woodbury Dr.
Grass Valley, CA 95949
(916) 346–6812

KLAMATH RIVER (UPPER), CALIFORNIA/OREGON

Section:	Hell's Corner Gorge
Location:	Klamath County, southwest of Klamath Falls in southern Oregon, and Siskiyou County, northern California
Driving Time:	Medford—1 hour
Difficulty:	Class IV–V; Class IV paddle raft experience recommended
Trip Length:	17 miles (27 km)
Trip Options:	Paddle raft, oar raft; one and two days
Season:	May–September
Cost:	$90–$115; $200–$250 two days

The upper Klamath, between the John Boyle Powerhouse near Klamath Falls, in southern Oregon, and Copco Lake in northern California, features the 200-mile-long (320 km) river's most exciting and challenging whitewater. It is little wonder that so many of central California's outfitters include the Upper Klamath on their list of river selections.

The moderate Class II–III waters at the beginning of the upper Klamath trip are used to practice maneuvering rafts and hone paddling skills. Once the river enters the volcanic Hell's Corner Gorge, the river is transformed into a very challenging and demanding Class IV+ whitewater stretch with more than forty major rapids and waterfalls. During one 6-mile (9-km) stretch, the river's gradient averages 85 feet per mile. Many of these rapids are known by colorful western names: Old Hooch, Gunsmoke, Stageline, Branding Iron, Wild Card, Jackass, Ambush, and Ol' Bushwacker.

Hell's Corner Gorge is well known for its consistent year-round water flows. Many outfitters accordingly promote the gorge trip as California and Oregon's best all-season Class IV+ trip. While river guides do their best to help rafters enjoy the beautiful scenery, abundant wildlife, and quaint nineteenth-century cabins and ranches in the gorge, this is not always an easy task due to the demanding nature of the trip.

Klamath River (Upper) Outfitters

The Adventure Center
40 N. Main St.
Ashland, OR 97520
(800) 444–2819
(503) 488–2819

Adventure Connection
P.O. Box 475
Coloma, CA 95613
(800) 556–6060
(916) 626–7385

Cascade River Runners
P.O. Box 86
Klamath Falls, OR 97601
(503) 883–6340

Noah's World of Water
P.O. Box 11
Ashland, OR 97520
(800) 858–2811
(503) 488–2811

Turtle River Rafting Company
P.O. Box 313
Mt. Shasta, CA 96067
(800) 726–3223
(916) 926–3223

Whitewater Voyages
P.O. Box 20400
El Sobrante, CA 94820–0400
(800) 488–7238
(510) 222–5994

Wilderness Adventures
19504 Statton Acres Rd.
Lakehead, CA 96051
(916) 238–8121

KLAMATH RIVER (LOWER), CALIFORNIA

Section:	Happy Camp to Ti Bar
Location:	Del Norte County, northern California
Driving Time:	Eureka—2.5 hours; Medford—2 hours
Difficulty:	Class II–III
Trip Length:	35 miles (56 km) or less
Trip Options:	Paddle raft, oar raft, paddle/oar raft, inflatable kayak; half-day, one to five days
Season:	April–October
Cost:	$50–$85 one day, $110–$185 two days, $250–$325

The lower Klamath gives families and first-time rafters an opportunity to enjoy either a single-day or multiday whitewater trip. The scenic river, with deep-wooded canyons and abundant wildlife, is protected by both California and National Wild and Scenic Rivers legislation.

Exciting Class II–III rapids alternating with quiet stretches offer a near-perfect blend of rafting, swimming, hiking, fishing, and relaxing on the trip beginning at Happy Camp. Its flow, along with that of the upper Klamath, is dam-controlled; it has consistently reliable water levels throughout the summer.

Rafting enthusiasts seeking a Klamath adventure that combines both the upper and lower sections should ask outfitters for information about a five- or six-day river extravaganza.

Klamath River (Lower) Outfitters

Electric Rafting Company
P.O. Box 3456
Eureka, CA 95501
(707) 826–2861

Klamath River Outfitters
92520 Highway 96
Somes Bar, CA 95568
(800) 552–6284
(916) 469–3322

O.A.R.S.
P.O. Box 67
Angels Camp, CA 95222
(800) 346–6277
(209) 736–4677

Orange Torpedo Trips
P.O. Box 1111
Grants Pass, OR 97526
(800) 635–2925
(503) 479–5061

Turtle River Rafting Company
P.O. Box 313
Mt. Shasta, CA 96067
(800) 726–3223
(916) 926–3223

The Rogue River in southern Oregon was one of America's first Wild and Scenic Rivers. Photo by Nancy Jane Reid.

CHAPTER 9

■ ■ ■

Pacific Northwest States

Melting snows in the Cascade Mountains and spring rains tumbling through steep valleys at lower elevations are the source of almost all recreational whitewater activity in Washington and Oregon. While most of Washington's many fine whitewater rafting trips are challenging one-day adventures, there are several excellent beginning-level trips for families.

Five rivers rushing down the eastern slopes of the Cascades give rafters the advantage of the warmer and drier climate of eastern Washington:

- The Wenatchee River creates the state's most popular commercial raft trip, with powerful waves that attract mostly adventure-seeking guests in the spring. Families can also enjoy the Wenatchee during lower and warmer early-summer whitewaters.
- The Methow River's large and powerful waves excite both beginning and experienced rafters.
- The Tieton attracts thousands of rafting enthusiasts each September, when water releases from Rim Rock Dam result in exciting and continuous Class II–III+ rapids.
- The White Salmon and Klickitat rivers, popular Class III–IV tributaries of the Columbia, offer big whitewater and family trips.

Western Washington has a number of exciting whitewater rivers:

- Four rivers in the North Cascades—the Nooksack, Suiattle, Sauk, and Skagit— provide an excellent choice of Class II–IV whitewater thrills within three hours of Seattle. The Skagit, easiest of these, offers summertime family and youth rafting trips and a popular eagle-watching float trip each winter.
- The Skykomish, close to Seattle, is the state's most technically demanding commercial whitewater trip, with plenty of excitement for experienced rafters.
- The Elwha River, a very scenic and fun river on the northern Olympic Peninsula, and the Hoh River, whose mild waters pass through the famed Olympic rain forest, will delight nature lovers of all ages.

The following are some favorite Oregon whitewater rivers:

- The well-known Rogue River in southern Oregon serves up multiday rafting and half- and one-day family-oriented trips. Nearby, the Illinois River, an infrequently run Rogue tributary, unquestionably offers one of the most outstanding wilderness river experiences anywhere.

Pacific Northwest States

Pacific Northwest States
River Comparison

	Difficulty	Min. Age	H	D	M	Season	P	O	K
Washington									
Wenatchee	//	12	X			Apr–Jul	X	X	
Methow	//	12	X	X		May–Jun	X	X	
Tieton	//	12	X			September	X	X	
White Salmon	//	12	X			Apr–Sep	X	X	
Klickitat	//	14	X			Apr–Jun	X	X	
Nooksack (North Fork)	//	14	X			Jul–Sep	X	X	
Suiattle	//	12	X			May–Aug	X	X	
Sauk	//	14	X			May–Jul	X	X	X
Skagit									
Upper	/	6	X			Jul–Sep	X	X	X
Lower	/	6	X			Dec–Feb	X	X	
Skykomish	//	16	X			Mar–Jul	X	X	
Elwha	/	4	X			Apr–Sep	X	X	
Hoh	/	None	X			Apr–Jul	X	X	
Oregon									
Rogue (Wild)	//	7		X		May–Oct	X	X	X
Rogue (Recreation)	/	4	X	X	X	Apr–Sep	X	X	X
Illinois	//	12		X		Mar–May	X	X	
North Umpqua	//	10		X	X	May–Sep	X	X	X
McKenzie									
Upper	//	10	X			May–Sep	X	X	
Lower	/	6	X			May–Sep	X	X	
Deschutes (Upper)	/	6	X			May–Sep	X	X	
Deschutes (Lower)	//	8		X	X	Apr–Oct	X	X	
Grande Ronde	/	4		X	X	Apr–Jul	X	X	

/   Beginner—Easy whitewater. Fun for everyone.

//   Intermediate—Moderate whitewater.
No previous rafting experience is necessary.

///   Advanced—Difficult whitewater.
Previous Class IV paddle rafting experience is recommended or required.

H—Half-Day Trip, D—Day Trip, M—Multiday Trip
P—Paddle Raft, O—Oar Raft, K—Inflatable Kayak

- The North Umpqua, which flows through scenic southern Oregon forests, continues to be a popular river for rafts and inflatable kayaks.
- The McKenzie River, a scenic tributary of western Oregon's Willamette River, provides exciting family raft trips within a drive of two and a half hours from Portland.
- The Deschutes River in central Oregon, the state's most popular river, offers both single-day and multiday trips through semi-arid canyons.
- The Grande Ronde, whose moderate waters flow through the Blue Mountains in northeast Oregon to the Snake River along the Washington-Idaho border, is considered the perfect multiday river trip for families with young children.

WENATCHEE RIVER, WASHINGTON

Section:	Leavenworth to Cashmere or Monitor
Location:	Chelan County near Cashmere, eastern Washington
Driving Time:	Seattle—2.5 hours; Spokane—3.5 hours
Difficulty:	Class II–III, IV
Trip Length:	15–21 miles (24–34 km)
Trip Options:	Paddle raft, oar raft; one day
Season:	April–July
Cost:	$55–$75

The Wenatchee River, lifeblood of its famous apple-growing region, is Washington's most popular rafting trip. Roller-coaster whitewater action, big waves, and usually sunny spring weather can be enjoyed by novice and experienced rafters. Exciting Class II–III+ rapids like Boulder Bend, Rock 'n Roll, Gorilla Falls, Drunkard's Drop, and Snowblind provide plenty of thrills as the Wenatchee winds its way between apple orchards and small towns adjacent to U.S. Highway 2.

The Wenatchee River trip is not all whitewater excitement. Quiet stretches of the river, interspersed between its fine rapids, allow rafters to enjoy the varied scenery and even engage in water fights.

When springtime water levels lower and temperatures rise, usually in June and early July, the Wenatchee's outfitters welcome families. Children as young as eight may raft with parents during this reduced water period.

Visitors to the Wenatchee River should allow enough time either before or after their raft trip to sample some of the fine apple products from local roadside markets. A visit to the neo-Bavarian shops and restaurants in Leavenworth is also recommended.

Outfitters listed on page53.

METHOW RIVER, WASHINGTON

Section:	McFarland Creek to Pateros
Location:	Okanogan County northwest of Brewster, eastern Washington
Driving Time:	Seattle—4 hours; Spokane—3 hours
Difficulty:	Class III–IV
Trip Length:	17 miles (27 km)
Trip Options:	Paddle raft, oar raft; one and two days

Season: May–June
Cost: $55–$75

Whitewater enthusiasts seeking big-wave action, rather than technical rock and boulder rapids, will find the Methow, in eastern Washington's Okanogan National Forest, a springtime utopia.

The Methow is best known for a superb stretch of whitewater in Black Canyon, which has become a favorite of guides and adventurous rafters. Fortunately for rafting guests, there are nearly 8 miles (13 km) of Class I–II rapids to hone paddling skills before the steep-walled Class IV Black Canyon. Here, for nearly 6 miles (9 km), huge waves, big holes, and powerful hydraulics provide a fantastic and memorable whitewater ride.

Although outfitters normally run the 17-mile (26-km) Methow as a single-day trip, multiday camping adventures are available. While rafters can usually expect warm and sunny springtime weather on the Methow, its cold North Cascades waters necessitate wet suits.

Wenatchee River and Methow River Outfitters

All Rivers Adventures
Wenatchee Whitewater
P.O. Box 12
Cashmere, WA 98815
(800) 743–5628
(509) 782–2254

Blue Sky Outfitters
P.O. Box 124
Pacific, WA 98047
(800) 228–7238 (WA only)
(206) 931–0637

Cascade Adventures
1202 E. Pike St. Suite 1142
Seattle, WA 98122
(800) 723–8386
(206) 323–5485

Downstream River Runners
12112 N.E. 195th
Bothell, WA 98011
(800) 234–4644
(206) 483–0335

North Cascades River Expeditions
P.O. Box 116
Arlington, WA 98223
(800) 634–8433
(206) 435–9548

Northern Wilderness River Riders
P.O. Box 2887
Woodinville, WA 98072
(206) 448–7238

Orion Expeditions
2366 E. Eastlake Ave.
Seattle, WA 98102
(800) 553–7466
(206) 322–9130

River Recreation
13-211th Place SE
Redmond, WA 98053
(206) 392–5899

Rivers Incorporated
P.O. Box 2092
Kirkland, WA 98083
(206) 822–5296

Wildwater River Tours
P.O. Box 3623
Federal Way, WA 98063–3623
(800) 522–9453
(206) 939–2151

TIETON RIVER, WASHINGTON

Section: Tieton Dam to Windy Point
Location: Yakima County, west of Naches, south-central Washington
Driving Time: Portland—3 hours; Seattle—3 hours
Difficulty: Class II–III+; paddle rafting experience recommended
Trip Length: 13 miles (21 km)
Trip Options: Paddle raft, oar raft; one day
Season: September
Cost: $45–$65

The Tieton River, a mere trickle in the summer, roars with excitement and thousands of boaters each September when the dam gates of Rimrock Lake are opened to provide additional water to the Yakima Valley and the salmon run up the Yakima River. The swift-flowing Tieton drops at rates exceeding 50 feet a mile in a stretch flowing over countless stair-step ledges. While most of the river's numerous technical drops are individually only Class II–III+, the continuous nature of the rapids and its steep gradient makes it closer to a Class IV run.

Outfitters recommend experienced rafting guests as there is little time for training novices. Because of the Tieton's extreme popularity and short season, usually two weekends each September, it is essential that prospective rafters make early reservations.

Located southeast of Mount Rainier, the Tieton whitewater run parallels U.S. Highway 12 for 13 miles (21 km) from Tieton Dam to Windy Point Campground near Naches.

Tieton River Outfitters

All Rivers Adventures
Wenatchee Whitewater
P.O. Box 12
Cashmere, WA 98815
(800) 743–5628
(509) 782–2254

North Cascades River Expeditions
P.O. Box 116
Arlington, WA 98223
(800) 634–8433
(206) 435–9548

Blue Sky Outfitters
P.O. Box 124
Pacific, WA 98047
(800) 228–7238 (WA only)
(206) 931–0637

Northern Wilderness River Riders
P.O. Box 2887
Woodinville, WA 98072
(206) 448–7238

Downstream River Runners
12112 NE 195th
Bothell, WA 98011
(800) 234–4644
(206) 483–0335

Orion Expeditions
2366 E. Eastlake Ave.
Seattle, WA 98102
(800) 553–7466
(206) 322–9130

River Recreation
13-211th Place SE
Redmond, WA 98053
(206) 392–5899

Rivers Incorporated
P.O. Box 2092
Kirkland, WA 98083
(206) 822–5296

Wildwater River Tours
P.O. Box 3623
Federal Way, WA 98063–3623
(800) 522–9453
(206) 939–2151

WHITE SALMON RIVER, WASHINGTON

Section:	BZ Corners to Northwestern Lake
Location:	Klickitat County near Trout Lake, south-central Washington
Driving Time:	Portland—1.5 hours; Seattle—4.5 hours
Difficulty:	Class III–IV
Trip Length:	7 miles (13 km)
Trip Options:	Paddle raft, paddle/oar raft; half-day
Season:	April–September
Cost:	$40–$45

The White Salmon River, a National Wild and Scenic River in south-central Washington, has exciting whitewaters that match its well-deserved scenic designation. At the beginning of the trip, rafts must be lowered by a cable system 135 feet down a vertical cliff to the river. Rafters hike to the river on a switchback trail.

The White Salmon's technical Class III rapids—Grasshopper, Shark's Fin, Corkscrew, Waterspout, and Stairstep Falls—are at the bottom of a narrow gorge with steep lava cliffs. Following the canyon's intense rapids, one may relax and enjoy the calmer waters and scenic pastoral surroundings before reaching the last major rapid and whitewater highlight, Husum Falls. Outfitters do not run this Class V falls.

The White Salmon, located on the dry eastern crest of Washington's southern Cascades, is fed by glacier melt and numerous springs as it flows from the slopes of 12,278-foot Mount Adams to the Columbia River near the town of White Salmon. The White Salmon has long been a popular river stretch for canoe and kayak races, which are held as part of the Husum Days celebration each July. During July and August, when the White Salmon's waters are both lower and warmer, outfitters offer family raft trips that include all of the same rapids—including a walk around Husum Falls—as in the early season. Children as young as five years old are welcome.

White Salmon River Outfitters

AAA Rafting
P.O. Box 203
Husum, WA 98623
(800) 866–7238
(509) 493–2511

White Water Adventures
38 NW Lake
White Salmon, WA 98672
(800) 366–2004
(509) 493–3121

Phil Zoller's Guide Service
1244 Highway 141
White Salmon, WA 98672
(509) 493–2641

KLICKITAT RIVER, WASHINGTON

Section:	Yakima Indian Reservation boundary to Leidl Bridge
Location:	Yakima and Klickitat counties near Glenwood, south-central Washington
Driving Time:	Seattle—5 hours; Portland—2 hours
Difficulty:	Class III–IV; rafting experience recommended
Trip Length:	15 miles (24 km)
Trip Options:	Paddle raft, paddle/oar raft; one day
Season:	April–June
Cost:	$70–$85

The Klickitat River, like the White Salmon River 30 miles (48 km) to its west, flows southward into the Columbia River Gorge. Its beautiful scenery, within dramatic basalt canyons typical of the Columbia Plateau, is a significant part of the wilderness river experience. Because of the difficult access to the Klickitat, however, its excellent whitewater and breathtaking beauty can only be viewed from the river. Scrub oak and pine trees cling precariously from the spectacular 200-foot columnar basalt cliffs of the lower gorge. Scenic Wonder Falls, a natural freshwater spring erupting from the basalt wall and cascading about 40 feet to the river, is a unique attraction of the Klickitat.

Although most of the Klickitat's more technical rapids—Rattler, Diamondback, Hatchery Drop, and Borde—are in the first half of the trip, fairly continuous Class II–II+ whitewater fills the remainder of the ride.

Some outfitters offer the Klickitat as a two-day overnight trip or a Klickitat-White Salmon combination two-day trip.

Klickitat River Outfitters

NCAT Whitewater
P.O. Box 6263
Kennewick, WA 99336
(800) 827–6228

Phil Zoller's Guide Service
1244 Highway 141
White Salmon, WA 98672
(509) 493–2641

White Water Adventure
38 NW Lake
White Salmon, WA 98672
(800) 366–2004
(509) 493–3121

NOOKSACK RIVER, WASHINGTON

Section:	Douglas Fir Camp to Maple Falls (North Fork)
Location:	Whatcom County, east of Bellingham, western Washington
Driving Time:	Seattle—2.5 hours; Vancouver—1.5 hours
Difficulty:	Class II–III

Trip Length:	8 miles (13 km)
Trip Options:	Paddle raft, oar raft; one day
Season:	July–September
Cost:	$50–$75

Western Washington's North Fork of the Nooksack River is the state's northernmost raft trip. The source of the Nooksack's challenging whitewater is the glacier slopes of the North Cascades, so its best whitewater occurs in mid-to-late summer, after most other Cascade Mountains rivers are too low for rafting.

Outfitters normally begin the 8-mile (13-km) North Fork Nooksack trip at the Douglas Fir Camp about 2 miles (3 km) east of Glacier, a popular lodging village for skiers at Mount Baker. The Nooksack's seven or eight Class III rapids are all located within the first 3 miles (5 km) of the run. Downstream, less intense Class II rapids and flat stretches provide rafters the opportunity to enjoy views of the impressive snowcapped Mount Baker and the scenic farmlands of central Whatcom County.

Nooksack River Outfitters

Blue Sky Outfitters
P.O. Box 124
Pacific, WA 98047
(800) 228–7238 (WA only)
(206) 931–0637

Northern Wilderness River Riders
P.O. Box 2887
Woodinville, WA 98072
(206) 448–7238

Downstream River Runners
12112 NE 195th
Bothell, WA 98011
(800) 234–4644
(206) 483–0335

SUIATTLE RIVER, WASHINGTON

Section:	Rat Trap Bridge to Sauk River
Location:	Snohomish and Skagit counties near Darrington, western Washington
Driving Time:	Seattle—2 hours
Difficulty:	Class I–III
Trip Length:	13 miles (21 km)
Trip Options:	Paddle raft, oar raft; one day
Season:	May–August
Cost:	$55–$75

The Suiattle River, a National Wild and Scenic tributary of the Sauk River, is an excellent trip for persons wanting a relatively mellow introduction to whitewater. The lower 13 miles (21 km) of the Suiattle River are not intimidating or strenuous. All of its whitewater, with the exception of the Class III Coyote Crossing and Hurricane Rapids, is fairly easy Class I–II+. Its wilderness forest scenery, which on a clear day includes the 10,541-foot snowcapped Glacier Peak, is incredibly beautiful.

The Suiattle starts in the melting ice of Glacier Peak in the Glacier Peak Wilderness Area and flows through Mount Baker National Forest to the Sauk River north of Darrington. Braided channels, gravel bars, and fallen alder trees often change channel courses during high water. The Suiattle's cold waters, which still carry a large volume of glacial silt, necessitate wet suits.

Suiattle River Outfitters

Blue Sky Outfitters
P.O. Box 124
Pacific, WA 98047
(800) 228–7238 (WA only)
(206) 931–0637

Downstream River Runners
12112 NE 195th
Bothell, WA 98011
(800) 234–4644
(206) 483–0335

North Cascades River Expeditions
P.O. Box 116
Arlington, WA 98223
(800) 634–8433
(206) 435–9548

Northern Wilderness River Riders
P.O. Box 2887
Woodinville, WA 98072
(206) 448–7238

Orion Expeditions
2366 E. Eastlake Ave.
Seattle, WA 98102
(800) 553–7466
(206) 322–9130

River Recreation
13-211th Place SE
Redmond, WA 98053
(206) 392–5899

Rivers Incorporated
P.O. Box 2092
Kirkland, WA 98083
(206) 822–5296

Wildwater River Tours
P.O. Box 3623
Federal Way, WA 98063–3623
(800) 522–9453
(206) 939–2151

SAUK RIVER, WASHINGTON

Section: White Chuck Campground to Darrington
Location: Snohomish County, southeast of Darrington, western Washington
Driving Time: Seattle—2 hours
Difficulty: Class II–III, IV
Trip Length: 10 miles (16 km)
Trip Options: Paddle raft, paddle/oar raft, inflatable kayak; one day
Season: May–July
Cost: $65–$75

The silt-laden waters of the middle Sauk River, between its confluence with the White Chuck and Suiattle rivers near Darrington, is rapidly becoming one of western Washington's more popular whitewater rafting trips. The heavily forested banks of the river and views of Cascade foothills, seen on the lower portion of the trip, provide a gorgeous backdrop to the Sauk River trip.

The Sauk provides ample opportunity for all paddlers to improve their navigational skills on the not-too-difficult boulder-filled Class II rapids; Class III Alligator Drop, Whirlpool, Popeye, and Sue; and the Class III–IV Jaws. Early-season rafters often return after summertime water levels become too low for rafting and test their paddling skills on inflatable-kayak trips.

While Glacier Peak, the origin of the Sauk's glacial waters, cannot be seen from the river, but its cold waters most certainly can be felt. Wet suits are a must.

Sauk River Outfitters

Downstream River Runners
12112 NE 195th
Bothell, WA 98011
(800) 234–4644
(206) 483–0335

Orion Expeditions
2366 E. Eastlake Ave.
Seattle, WA 98102
(800) 553–7466
(206) 322–9130

North Cascades River Expeditions
P.O. Box 116
Arlington, WA 98223
(800) 634–8433
(206) 435–9548

SKAGIT RIVER, WASHINGTON

Section:	Newhalem to Copper Creek (upper)
Location:	Whatcom and Skagit counties near Marblemount, western Washington
Driving Time:	Seattle—2.5 hours
Difficulty:	Class I–II, III
Trip Length:	9 miles (14 km)
Trip Options:	Paddle raft, oar raft, inflatable kayak; one day
Season:	July–September
Cost:	$45–$60

The upper Skagit River, adjacent to North Cascades National Park in western Washington, is a very scenic whitewater opportunity for venturesome first-time rafters. Except for a half-mile section of whitewater that includes the Class III rapids Jack-the-Ripper and Wavy Gravy, the upper Skagit has a low gradient and easy Class I–II rapids. The Skagit's thickly forested banks and frequent views of North Cascades mountain peaks create a memorable river environment.

The flow of the upper Skagit, controlled by water releases from Seattle City Light's Ross, Diablo, and Gorge dams, generally has adequate water for rafting from midsummer until early fall. Its mostly Class I–II rapids have made it the favorite summertime trip for children and early teenage rafting groups. While the Skagit's whitewaters are easy, they are also very cold. Wet suits are almost always required.

Section:	Marblemount to Rockport (lower)
Location:	Skagit County near Rockport, western Washington
Driving Time:	Seattle—2 hours

Difficulty:	Class I
Trip Length:	8 miles (13 km)
Trip Options:	Paddle raft, oar raft; half-day
Season:	December–February
Cost:	$45–$60

Between Marblemount and Rockport on the lower Skagit River, outfitters offer half-day winter float trips from December to February for wildlife enthusiasts who wish to see bald eagles. Migrating south from Alaska and Canada, more than three hundred eagles now congregate in the Skagit River Bald Eagle Natural Area, adjacent to Washington Route 20, to feed on the river's spawning salmon. Sightings of the magnificent and endangered birds are frequent because the eagles have become accustomed to seeing river rafts. Children as young as six years are welcome. Everyone is encouraged to bring a camera and a telephoto lens.

Skagit River Outfitters

Blue Sky Outfitters
P.O. Box 124
Pacific, WA 98047
(800) 228–7238 (WA only)
(206) 931–0637

Downstream River Runners
12112 NE 195th
Bothell, WA 98011
(800) 234–4644
(206) 483–0335

Midwinter float trips on the Wild and Scenic Skagit River in Washington's North Cascades enable passengers to photograph bald eagles. Photo by Lorrie North.

North Cascades River Expeditions
P.O. Box 116
Arlington, WA 98223
(800) 634–8433
(206) 435–9548

Wildwater River Tours
P.O. Box 3623
Federal Way, WA 98063–3623
(800) 522–9453
(206) 939–2151

Orion Expeditions
2366 E. Eastlake Ave.
Seattle, WA 98102
(800) 553–7466
(206) 322–9130

SKYKOMISH RIVER, WASHINGTON

Section:	Index to Big Eddy
Location:	Snohomish County near Gold Bar, western Washington
Driving Time:	Seattle—1.5 hours
Difficulty:	Class III–V; paddle raft experience highly recommended
Trip Length:	8 miles (13 km)
Trip Options:	Paddle raft, oar raft; one day
Season:	March–July
Cost:	$55–$75

The exciting Skykomish, or "Sky," River is considered by most Washington outfitters to be the state's premier whitewater trip for thrill-seekers. Starting below Sunset Falls in the shadow of the nearly-6,000-foot Mount Index, the Skykomish is respected for its well-known Class V Boulder Drop Rapids with its Airplane Turn, the preferred route at most water levels. Numerous other technical Class III–IV rapids—such as Marbleshoot, Lunch Hole, and little and big Déjà Vu—and a thickly forested Cascade Mountains setting add to this spectacular river experience. On clear days, rafters will enjoy superb views of the area's big peaks: Mount Index, Baring, Persis, and Merchant. The Skykomish River is included in Washington's Scenic Rivers System.

The Skykomish whitewater run, located approximately 45 miles (72 km) east of Everett, is the nearest whitewater rafting opportunity to the cities of Seattle, Tacoma, and Everett. It flows immediately adjacent to U.S. Highway 2 and the Great Northern Railway tracks between the small towns of Index and Gold Bar.

Skykomish River Outfitters

Blue Sky Outfitters
P.O. Box 124
Pacific, WA 98047
(800) 228–7238 (WA only)
(206) 931–0637

Cascade Adventures
1202 E. Pike St., Suite 1142
Seattle, WA 98122
(800) 723–8386
(206) 323–5485

Downstream River Runners
12112 NE 195th
Bothell, WA 98011
(800) 234-4644
(206) 483-0335

Orion Expeditions
2366 E. Eastlake Ave.
Seattle, WA 98102
(800) 553-7466
(206) 322-9130

North Cascades River Expeditions
P.O. Box 116
Arlington, WA 98223
(800) 634-8433
(206) 435-9548

River Recreation
13-211th Place SE
Redmond, WA 98053
(206) 392-5899

Northern Wilderness River Riders
P.O. Box 2887
Woodinville, WA 98072
(206) 448-7238

Wildwater River Tours
P.O. Box 3623
Federal Way, WA 98063-3623
(800) 522-9453
(206) 939-2151

ELWHA RIVER, WASHINGTON

Section:	Altaire Campground to Highway 101 and the Elwha Resort
Location:	Clallam County, west of Port Angeles, northwest Washington
Driving Time:	Seattle—3.5 hours
Difficulty:	Class I–II
Trip Length:	6 miles (9.5 km)
Trip Options:	Paddle raft, oar raft; half-day
Season:	April–September
Cost:	$30–$35

The Elwha River, which originates in the snowcapped mountains of Olympic National Park, offers rafters an excellent opportunity to experience the thrill of whitewater rafting and enjoy a small portion of the park's famed beauty and serenity. In addition to the ferns and wildflowers that adorn the Elwha's forested environs, rafters often see eagles, hawks, osprey, deer, and even Roosevelt elk during the early spring. Impressive views of the park's Carrie Glacier can also be seen from the river.

Elwha's friendly Class I–II rapids on the 6-mile (9.5-km) raft trip take about two hours and may be enjoyed by anyone. The Park's sole concessionaire is well prepared to host families, seniors, and the disabled.
Outfitter listed on page 63.

HOH RIVER, WASHINGTON

Section:	Oxbow Canyon
Location:	Jefferson County, south of Forks, northwest Washington
Driving Time:	Seattle—4.5 hours
Difficulty:	Class I
Trip Length:	6 miles (9.5 km)
Trip Options:	Paddle raft, oar raft; half-day

| Season: | April–July |
| Cost: | $30–$35 |

The picturesque Hoh River, flowing westward from Olympic National Park to the scenic Pacific coastline, provides an extraordinary opportunity to float quietly through a portion of the famous moss- and fern-covered Olympic peninsula rain forest where annual rainfalls often exceed 120 inches.

The first half of the Hoh trip meanders through a wide valley with breathtaking views of snowcapped mountains including Mount Olympus, the park's highest peak. This section is home to bald eagles, river otter, Roosevelt elk, and other wildlife.

The second half of the float trip traverses the lush forests of Oxbow Canyon. Here, large coniferous and deciduous trees loom over the river, bringing shade and quiet time for relaxation. Morning and afternoon trips can be enjoyed by guests of all ages.

Elwha River and Hoh River Outfitter

Olympic Raft and Guide Service
464 Highway 101 West
Port Angeles, WA 98362
(206) 452–1443

ROGUE RIVER (WILD), OREGON

Section:	Wild
Location:	Josephine and Curry counties, west of Grants Pass, southwest Oregon
Driving Time:	Medford—.5 hour; Portland—4.5 hours
Difficulty:	Class III–IV
Trip Length:	35 miles (56 km)
Trip Options:	Paddle raft, oar raft, paddle/oar raft, dory and inflatable kayak; three to five days
Season:	May–October
Cost:	$330–$700

It is little wonder that when Congress began protecting the nation's rivers under the Wild and Scenic Rivers Act in 1968, southern Oregon's pristine Rogue River became one of the first chosen. The Rogue includes not just first-class whitewater, but heavily forested canyons with abundant wildlife, wildflowers, and fascinating folklore.

The Rogue River originates near Crater Lake National Park, and along its 140-mile (224-km) course cuts through numerous coastal-range canyons to the Pacific Coast at Gold Beach. Popular three- to five-day raft trips are run through the Rogue's Wild Section in the Siskiyou Mountains between Grave Creek, 5 miles north of Galice, and Foster Bar, north of Agness.

Rogue's Wild Section includes the famed Mule Creek Canyon (Class IV) and many excellent Class III–III+ rapids, such as Grave Creek, Tyee, Wildcat, Black Bar Falls, Slim Pickins, Coffee Pot, Blossom Bar, and Devil Stairs. Class V Rainie Falls, on the first day of the trip, must be portaged. Rogue's canyons are also home to deer, bears, otters, mink, ospreys, bald eagles, and dozens of other bird species. Along with the thrill of whitewater rapids, there is sufficient time for rafters to hike and explore abandoned gold mines, cabins, and Indian grounds.

In an effort to preserve the wilderness experience of the Rogue, the Bureau of Land Management allows only three or four outfitters per day to begin trips at Grave Creek. Customers may choose between oar and paddle rafts, and even inflatable kayaks when water levels are low. Additionally, one chooses between trips offering comfortable lodge accommodations or riverside tent camping.

Although outfitters recommend early reservations to ensure the dates of your choice, it is often possible to book trips on fairly short notice.

Rogue River (Wild) Outfitters

ARTA River Trips
Star Route 73
Groveland, CA 95321
(800) 323–2782
(209) 962–7873

Briggs Rogue River Guide Service
2750 Cloverlawn Dr.
Grants Pass, OR 97527
(800) 845–5091
(503) 476–2941

ECHO: The Wilderness Company
6529 Telegraph Ave.
Oakland, CA 94609–1113
(800) 652–3246
(510) 652–1600

O.A.R.S.
P.O. Box 67
Angels Camp, CA 95222
(800) 346–6277
(209) 736–4677

Orange Torpedo Trips
P.O. Box 1111
Grants Pass, OR 97526
(800) 635–2925
(503) 479–5061

Outdoor Adventures
P.O. Box 1149
Pt. Reyes Station, CA 94956–9900
(800) 323–4234
(415) 663–8300

Ouzel Outfitters
P.O. Box 827
Bend, OR 97709
(800) 788–7238
(503) 385–5947

River Adventure Float Trips
P.O. Box 841
Grants Pass, OR 97526
(503) 476–6493

Rogue River Raft Trips
8500 Galice Rd.
Merlin, OR 97532–9799
(800) 826–1963
(503) 476–3825

Rogue Wilderness
P.O. Box 1647
Grants Pass, OR 97526
(800) 336–1647
(503) 479–9554

ROGUE RIVER (RECREATION), OREGON

Section: Recreation
Location: Josephine County near Grants Pass, southwest Oregon
Driving Time: Medford—.5 hour; Portland—4.5 hours
Difficulty: Class I–II
Trip Length: 14 miles (22 km) or less

Trip Options: Paddle raft, oar raft, inflatable kayak; two hours, half-day, one day, and two days

Season: April–September

Cost: $20 two hours; $35 half-day; $45–$50 one day; $225 two days

Just upstream from the Wild Section of the Rogue River, the Hellgate Recreation Section of the Rogue offers an ideal introduction to whitewater rafting. With a guide-escorted trip, families, senior citizens, and inexperienced rafters can enjoy the impressive Hellgate Canyon between Hog Creek, some 15 miles (24 km) downstream from Grants Pass, and Grave Creek, the put-in for the Wild Section.

Hellgate Canyon, with easy Class I–II rapids such as Dunn Riffle, Galice Chute, Rocky Riffle, Chair Riffle, Almeda, Argo, and Wooldridge, can be enjoyed by paddle or oar raft or by inflatable kayak. Either half- or one-day trips are excellent for those lacking either the time or money for the multiday Rogue trips. Vacationers can usually book these trips on short notice.

Rogue River (Recreation) Outfitters

Orange Torpedo Trips
P.O. Box 1111
Grants Pass, OR 97526
(800) 635–2925
(503) 479–5061

Rogue Wilderness
P.O. Box 1647
Grants Pass, OR 97526
(800) 336–1647
(503) 479–9554

ILLINOIS RIVER, OREGON

Section: Miami Bar to Oak Flat

Location: Josephine County, west of Grants Pass, southwest Oregon

Driving Time: Medford—1.5 hours; Portland—6 hours

Difficulty: Class IV–V; rafting experience is recommended

Trip Length: 40 miles (64 km)

Trip Options: Paddle raft, oar raft; three and four days

Season: March–May

Cost: $400–500

The Illinois River, a National Wild and Scenic tributary of the Rogue River, is hidden in the remote canyons of southwest Oregon near the Pacific Ocean and the California–Oregon border. Its isolation provides for a truly outstanding multiday wilderness river experience, with first-growth Port Orford cedar forests, lush ferns, and the abundant wildlife that inhabits the rugged hills of the Siskiyou National Forest.

The rapids of the Illinois are as exciting as the river is beautiful. Most of its Class IV rapids—Pine Flat, Prelude, Let's Make a Deal, Submarine Rock, and Green Wall (Class V)—are in the canyon section, usually rafted on the second day of the three- or four-day trip.

The biggest drawback of the Illinois is its short rafting season. Its watershed, though rugged and remote, lacks sufficient elevation to hold the winter snows required for sustained late-spring and early-summer river running. Persons interested in rafting the Illinois River should make early reservations with outfitters as there are a limited number of trips each spring.

ARTA River Trips
Star Route 73
Groveland, CA 95321
(800) 323–2782
(209) 962–7873

Illinois River Outfitters

Rogue Wilderness
P.O. Box 1647
Grants Pass, OR 97526
(800) 336–1647
(503) 479–9554

NORTH UMPQUA RIVER, OREGON

Section:	Wild and Scenic
Location:	Douglas County, east of Roseburg, southern Oregon
Driving Time:	Medford—2 hours; Portland—4 hours
Difficulty:	Class II–III+
Trip Length:	30 miles (48 km) or less
Trip Options:	Paddle raft, oar raft, inflatable kayak; one to three days
Season:	May–September
Cost:	$55–$80 one day; $200–$500 multiday

The North Umpqua River provides whitewater enthusiasts an excellent opportunity to challenge exciting Class II–III+ rapids in the heart of southern Oregon's Umpqua National Forest. Oregon Route 138 allows outfitters several options for either one-day or multiday raft trips along the North Umpqua. The most popular one-day paddling excursion is a 16-mile (26-km) trip from Boulder Flat to Gravel Bin.

North Umpqua's often continuous whitewaters have one Class IV and numerous technical Class III+ pool-drop rapids—including Pinball (IV), Bridged Rock, and Amazon Queen—that are fairly steep and exciting, and yet forgiving. Flat stretches between many of the rapids give ample time for relaxation and swimming. In addition to paddle-raft trips, inflatable kayak trips are popular during the low-water summer months.

The North Umpqua is one of Oregon's most popular late-spring/early-summer whitewater rivers. Its easy access to Roseburg and Interstate 5, and its excellent rapids easily accessible to out-of-state visitors, contribute to its high percentage of repeat customers.

North Umpqua River Outfitters

Orange Torpedo Trips
P.O. Box 1111
Grants Pass, OR 97526
(800) 635–2925
(503) 479–5061

Oregon Whitewater Adventures
660 Kelly Blvd.
Springfield, OR 97477
(503) 746–5422

Oregon Ridge & River Excursions
P.O. Box 495
Glide, OR 97443
(503) 496–3333

Ouzel Outfitters
P.O. Box 827
Bend, OR 97709
(800) 788–7238
(503) 385–5947

Wild Water Adventures
P.O. Box 249
Creswell, OR 97426
(800) 289–4534
(503) 895–4465

MCKENZIE RIVER, OREGON

Sections: Paradise Campground to Blue River (upper); Blue River to Helfrich Landing (lower)
Location: Lane County, east of Eugene, west-central Oregon
Driving Time: Portland—2.5 hours
Difficulty: Class II–III+ (upper); II–III (lower)
Trip Length: Upper—14 miles (22 km); Lower—13 miles (20 km)
Trip Options: Paddle raft, oar raft; one day
Season: May–September
Cost: $40–$65

The McKenzie River, one of west-central Oregon's most beautiful rivers, is ideal for first-time river runners and families as well as experienced rafters wanting superb whitewater. The McKenzie is easily accessible along Oregon Route 126 for almost the entire 90-mile (144-km) course of the river, which runs between Clear

Paddle rafters pass through Martin's Rapid on McKenzie River east of Eugene. Photo courtesy of Wild Water Adventures Oregon.

Lake in the western Cascades and its confluence with the Willamette River at Eugene.

Whitewater raft trips on both the upper and lower sections of the McKenzie are strikingly beautiful and exciting, yet not too difficult. Between Paradise Campground and Blue River, the slightly more technical upper McKenzie is highlighted by fairly continuous Class II–III rapids—including Paradise Rock, Plunger, Old Pushy, Big Fish, The Slammer, and Phil's Rock Garden—that require a surprising amount of coordinated raft movements by paddlers.

Downriver, the lower McKenzies provides many Class II rapids, such as Clover Point, upper and lower Eagle Rock, Bear Creek, and Brown's Hole, plus the Class III Martin's. The rapids blend nicely with many additional miles of easy Class I–II waters, which allow rafters time to enjoy the superb scenery of the Willamette National Forest.

McKenzie River Outfitters

Jim's Oregon Whitewater
 (upper section only)
56324 McKenzie Hwy.
McKenzie Bridge, OR 97413
(503) 822–6003

Kloch's Water Works
P.O. Box 60
Waterville, OR 97489
(503) 726–9039

McKenzie River Adventures
 (upper section only)
P.O. Box 567
Sisters, OR 97759
(904) 677–2033
(503) 822–3806

Oregon Whitewater Adventures
660 Kelly Blvd.
Springfield, OR 97477
(503) 746–5422

Ouzel Outfitters (upper section only)
P.O. Box 827
Bend, OR 97709
(800) 788–7238
(503) 385–5947

Wild Water Adventures
P.O. Box 249
Creswell, OR 97426
(800) 289–4534
(503) 895–4465

DESCHUTES RIVER (UPPER), OREGON

Section:	Upper Deschutes River
Location:	Deschutes County, central Oregon, west of Bend
Driving Time:	Portland—3 hours
Difficulty:	Class II–IV
Trip Length:	3 miles (5 km)
Trip Options:	Paddle raft, oar raft; 2.5 hours
Season:	May–September
Cost:	$25–$30

The Deschutes River, originating on the eastern slopes of the Cascade Mountains between Crater Lake and Bend, flows for nearly 240 miles (384 km) northward to the Columbia River, providing much-needed water to adjacent central Oregon's farm and range lands. During this course, its moderate waters offer half-day, one-day, and multiday rafting trips that are suitable for first-time river runners, families, senior citizens, and outdoor lovers who want to enjoy a scenic river in an arid environment.

A 3-mile (5-km) stretch of the upper Deschutes River, about eight miles west of Bend, is becoming an increasingly popular vacation interlude for summertime visitors to central Oregon. This segment, which contains mostly Class II–IV rapids, is enjoyed by all guests. Families with children as young as age seven are welcome.

Albeit brief, the short upper Deschutes experience offers both the serenity of a unique desert lava canyon and the thrill of exciting whitewater. After nearly a mile of relatively flat water, rafters enter a quarter-mile stretch of Class IV rapids known as Big Eddy. Here, guides help paddle-rafters maneuver through a series of technical rapids created by an old lava flow. Below, the river mellows into a mostly Class II section before the take-out located just above Lava Falls.

Because of the frequency of the Deschutes River daily whitewater trips—as many as six are run by each of the river's three licensed commercial outfitters—reservations are normally not required. The entire trip, including round-trip shuttle from Bend, takes about two and one-half hours.

Deschutes River (Upper) Outfitters

Hunter Expeditions
P.O. Box 346
Bend, OR 97709
(503) 389–8370

Sun Country Tours
P.O. Box 771
Bend, OR 97709
(503) 593–2161
(503) 382–6277

Inn of the Seventh Mountain
P.O. Box 1207
Bend, OR 97709
(800) 452–6810
(503) 382–8711

DESCHUTES RIVER (LOWER), OREGON

Section:	Warm Springs to Columbia River
Location:	Jefferson, Wasco, and Sherman counties, south of The Dalles, north-central Oregon
Driving Time:	Portland—2.25 hours
Difficulty:	Class II–III+, IV
Trip Length:	13 miles (21 km), one day; 98 miles (157 km) multiday
Trip Options:	Paddle raft, oar raft; one to three days
Season:	April–October
Cost:	$50–$75 one day; $175–$340 two and three days

The lower Deschutes River, a National Wild and Scenic River and State Scenic Waterway Recreation Area, includes the 98 miles (157 km) between the Warm Springs Indian Reservation and the river's confluence with the Columbia River near The Dalles. Very popular single-day whitewater trips as well as multiday float trips are offered by outfitters on the lower Deschutes.

The one-day trip is an enjoyable 13-mile (20-km) family-oriented adventure between Harpham Flat and Sherars Falls. Officially known as segment II, this popular whitewater stretch contains the lively splashes of nearly a dozen Class III+ rapids, including Wapinitia, Box Car, Oar Springs, upper and lower Elevator, and Osborne.

During the slower-paced, multiday raft trips, guests have ample time to enjoy the steep, scenic basalt canyons which are home to a wide variety of desert flora and fauna.

Deschutes River (Lower) Outfitters

CJ Lodge
P.O. Box 130
Maupin, OR 97037
(503) 395–2404

Deschutes River Adventures
P.O. Box 371
Maupin, OR 97037
(800) 723–8464
(503) 395–2238

Deschutes U-Boat
P.O. Box 144
Maupin, OR 97037
(503) 395–2503

Ewing's Whitewater
P.O. Box 427
Maupin, OR 97037
(800) 538–7238
(503) 395–2697

Ouzel Outfitters
P.O. Box 827
Bend, OR 97709
(800) 788–7238
(503) 385–5947

River Drifters Whitewater Tours
13570 NW Lakeview Dr.
Portland, OR 97229
(800) 972–0430
(503) 645–6264

GRANDE RONDE RIVER, OREGON/WASHINGTON

Sections: Minam to Troy; Troy to confluence with Snake River
Location: Wallowa County, northeast of La Grande, northeast Oregon; Asotin County, south of Clarkston, southeast Washington
Driving Time: Boise—3.5 hours; Portland—5 hours
Difficulty: Class I–II+
Trip Length: Minan to Troy—44 miles (70 km); Troy to confluence of Snake River—45 miles (72 km)
Trip Options: Paddle raft, oar raft, dory; one to five days
Season: April–July
Cost: $55 half-day; $85–$90 one day; $220–$450 multiday

The Grande Ronde River, which winds through the wild conifer forest canyons of the Blue Mountains in northeastern Oregon to the Snake River in southeastern Washington, is a perfect multiday river trip for families. Its friendly Class I–II+ waters are easy and fun.

While the Grande Ronde's most popular raft or float excursion is the three-day, 44-mile (70-km) section between Minam and Troy in northeast Oregon, many prefer the five-day trip that continues an additional 45 miles (72 km) to

Heller's Bar near the river's confluence with the Snake River. Half-day and one-day trips are also available upon request. Raft trips are usually run only between mid-April and mid-July, when temperatures and water levels are at their best.

The Grande Ronde's diverse environs are rich in history, wildlife, and natural beauty. Chief Joseph and the Nez Perce Indians wintered on these lower stretches because of the mild winters and abundant wildlife. Even today, rafters commonly see Rocky Mountain elk, bighorn sheep, bears, deer, ospreys, and bald eagles in the river's spectacular gorges and forests.

Grande Ronde River Outfitters

Anderson River Adventures
Route 2, Box 192-H
Milton-Freewater, OR 97862
(800) 624–7583
(503) 558–3629

Tildon's River Tours
P.O. Box 893
Elgin, OR 97827
(503) 437–9270

Northwest Dories
P.O. Box 216
Altaville, CA 95221
(209) 736–0805

Oar-guided raft prepares to enter Pistol Creek Rapid on Middle Fork of Idaho's Salmon River. Photo by Robert Winslow.

CHAPTER 10

■ ■ ■

Northern Rocky Mountain States

Prior to the popularization of whitewater rafting more than two decades ago, only the hardiest of outdoor adventurers were able to enjoy the remote and primitive mountain wilderness of the northern Rocky Mountain states. Today, however, dozens of rafting outfitters provide safe access to hundreds of miles of wilderness canyons in Idaho, Montana, and Wyoming.

In addition to spectacular alpine scenery, rafters of wilderness rivers are frequently treated to views of bears, whitetail deer, elk, moose, mule deer, Rocky Mountain bighorn sheep, mountain goats, cougars, coyotes, and foxes.

The famed main Salmon River of central Idaho, its renowned Middle Fork tributary, and the lower Salmon offer more than 230 miles (368 km) of exceptional wilderness rafting adventure through six national forests, the incredible Frank Church—River of No Return Wilderness, and the Sawtooth National Recreation Area. In recent years outfitters on the upper main Salmon near Sun Valley have also popularized half-day and one-day raft trips. Other whitewater trips beckon in northern and central Idaho:

- Hell's Canyon, the last major whitewater stretch of the lengthy Snake River, features a Class III–IV multiday trip through North America's deepest canyon.
- The Lochsa River, route of the early nineteenth-century explorers Lewis and Clark, and the nearby Selway River, of early Indian fame, are superb multiday wilderness whitewater trips for hardy rafters.
- In southwest Idaho, less than an hour's drive north of Boise, three forks of the Payette River provide whitewater enthusiasts with nearly 80 miles (128 km) of Class II, III, and IV one-day rafting opportunities.

Most of Montana's recreation whitewater is located near its two popular national parks, Glacier and Yellowstone:

- Near Glacier, the Flathead River's Middle and North Forks and the Lower Flathead provide half-day, one-day, and multiday rafting through the beautiful wilderness mountains of northwest Montana.
- Near Yellowstone, the Gallatin, Madison, Yellowstone, Stillwater, and Shoshone rivers provide summer visitors with excellent beginning and intermediate whitewater trips. Family trips are available on the more moderate sections.
- Near Missoula, the Blackfoot and Clark Fork rivers feature exciting Class II–III whitewater in the mid-to-late summer.

In Wyoming, float trips on the Snake River in Grand Teton National Park and float and whitewater trips in the upper Snake canyons just south of the park attract some 150,000–200,000 rafters each year.

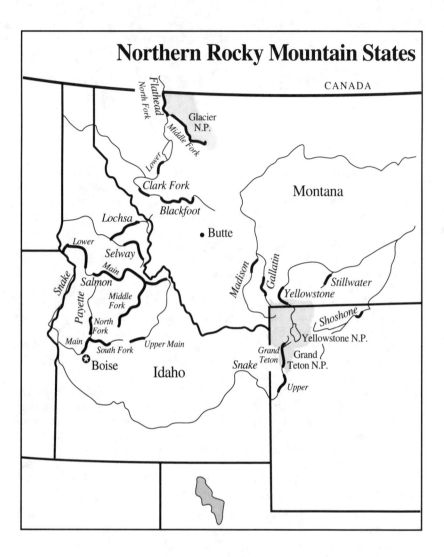

Northern Rocky Mountain States

CANADA

North Fork
Flathead

Glacier
N.P.

Middle Fork

Lower

Montana

Clark Fork

Blackfoot

Lochsa

• Butte

Lower

Selway

Madison

Gallatin

Main

Stillwater

Salmon

Yellowstone

Snake

Payette

Middle Fork

North Fork

Shoshone

Main

South Fork *Upper Main*

Yellowstone N.P.

✪ Boise

Idaho

Grand Teton

Grand
Teton N.P.

Snake

Upper

Northern Rocky Mountain States
River Comparison

	Difficulty	Min. Age	H	D	M	Season	P	O	K	D
Idaho										
Salmon (Middle Fork)	⁄ ⁄	6			✗	May–Sep	✗	✗	✗	✗
Salmon (Main)	⁄ ⁄	6			✗	Jun–Oct	✗	✗	✗	✗
Salmon (Lower)	⁄ ⁄	6			✗	Jul–Oct	✗	✗	✗	✗
Salmon (Upper Main)	⁄	4	✗	✗		May–Sep	✗	✗	✗	
Snake (Hells Canyon)	⁄ ⁄	6			✗	May–Oct	✗	✗	✗	✗
Lochsa	⁄ ⁄	16			✗	May–Jul	✗	✗		
Scenic Float	⁄	4	✗	✗		Jul–Aug	✗	✗		
Selway	⁄ ⁄	12			✗	Jun–Jul	✗	✗		
Payette										
North Fork	⁄ ⁄	15	✗			May–Sep	✗	✗		
South Fork	⁄ ⁄	6	✗	✗	✗	May–Sep	✗	✗		
Main	⁄ ⁄	6	✗	✗		May–Sep	✗	✗		
Montana										
Flathead (Middle Fork)										
Lower	⁄ ⁄	6	✗	✗		May–Sep	✗	✗		
Upper	⁄ ⁄	12			✗	Jun–Jul	✗	✗		
Flathead (North Fork)	⁄	4			✗	Jun–Aug	✗	✗		
Flathead (Lower)	⁄	6	✗			Jun–Aug	✗	✗		
Clark Fork	⁄ ⁄	8		✗		Jul–Sep	✗	✗	✗	
Blackfoot	⁄ ⁄	6		✗	✗	May–Jul	✗	✗	✗	
Gallatin	⁄	6	✗	✗		Jun–Aug	✗	✗		
Madison	⁄	6		✗		Jun–Aug	✗			
Yellowstone	⁄	6	✗	✗		May–Sep	✗	✗		
Stillwater	⁄	6	✗			May–Aug	✗	✗	✗	
Wyoming										
Shoshone	⁄	4	✗			May–Sep	✗	✗		
Snake (Grand Teton)	⁄	4	✗			May–Sep	✗			
Snake (Upper)	⁄	6	✗	✗		May–Sep	✗	✗		

⁄   Beginner—Easy whitewater. Fun for everyone.

⁄ ⁄   Intermediate—Moderate whitewater.
No previous rafting experience is necessary.

⁄ ⁄ ⁄   Advanced—Difficult whitewater.
Previous Class IV paddle rafting experience is recommended or required.

H—Half-Day Trip, D—Day Trip, M—Multiday Trip
P—Paddle Raft, O—Oar Raft, K—Inflatable Kayak, D—Dory

SALMON RIVER (MIDDLE FORK), IDAHO

Section: Boundary or Indian Creek to main Salmon River
Location: Custer and Lemhi counties, east-central Idaho
Driving Time: Boise—2 hours
Difficulty: Class III–IV+
Trip Length: 80 or 105 miles (128 or 168 km)
Trip Options: Paddle raft, oar raft, inflatable kayak, dory; five and six days
Season: May–September
Cost: $800–$1,600

The Middle Fork of the Salmon, considered the crown jewel of the National Wild and Scenic Rivers system by the U.S. Forest Service, provides one of the world's premier multiday wilderness river experiences. Between Boundary Creek, north of Stanley in east-central Idaho, and its confluence with the main Salmon River near Cache Bar, the Middle Fork flows through the heart of the 2.4-million-acre Frank Church—River of No Return Wilderness and traverses portions of the Challis, Payette, and Salmon national forests.

More than eighty exciting rapids are in the Middle Fork, including many Class III–IV rapids, such as Velvet Falls, Waterwheel, Pistol Creek, Tappan Falls, Haystack, Porcupine, Redside, Rubber, Hancock, and Jumpoff. The pristine river is graced with excellent campsites, most adjacent to crystal-clear streams and rapids. Rafting trips allow time both mornings and evenings to hike, visit, read, or relax. Although Middle Fork rafting begins in May, families, seniors, and first-time rafters are advised to schedule trips during the lower flows and warmer waters of July and August.

The Middle Fork trip begins in an alpine environment about a two-hour drive north of Sun Valley. Its elevation, nearly 6,000 feet at the put-in, accounts for the variety of wildlife. During spring and early-summer trips, rafters commonly see deer, elk, bighorn sheep, mountain goats, and bears. Other wildlife sometimes seen are mink, lynx, cougars, bobcats, coyotes, foxes, porcupines, badgers, beavers, martens, otters, muskrats, and skunks. Fishing for the Middle Fork's salmon, steelhead, and cutthroat, rainbow, and Dolly Varden trout is excellent.

Salmon River (Middle Fork) Outfitters

ARTA River Trips
Star Route 73
Groveland, CA 95321
(800) 323–2782
(209) 962–7873

Canyons Incorporated
P.O. Box 823
McCall, ID 83638
(208) 634–4303

Don Hatch River Expeditions
P.O. Box 1150
Vernal, UT 84078
(800) 342–8243
(801) 789–4316

ECHO: The Wilderness Company
6529 Telegraph Ave.
Oakland, CA 94609–1113
(800) 652–3246
(510) 652–1600

Hughes River Expeditions
P.O. Box 217
Cambridge, ID 83610
(208) 257–3477

Mackay Bar Wilderness River Trips
3190 Airport Way
Boise, ID 83705
(800) 635–5336
(208) 344–1881

Middle Fork Rapid Transit
160 Second St. West
Twin Falls, ID 83301
(800) 342–9728
(208) 734–7890

Middle Fork River Company
401 Lewis St., Box 54
Sun Valley, ID 83353
(800) 232–8588
(208) 726–8888

Middle Fork River Expeditions
P.O. Box 199
Stanley, ID 83278
(208) 774–3659
(206) 324–0364 (winter)

Middle Fork River Tours
P.O. Box 2368
Ketchum, ID 83340
(800) 445–9738
(208) 726–5666

Norman H. Guth Company
P.O. Box D
Salmon, ID 83467
(208) 756–3279

Outdoor Adventures
P.O. Box 1149
Pt. Reyes Station, CA 94956–9900
(800) 323–4234
(415) 663–8300

River Odysseys West (ROW)
P.O. Box 579
Coeur d'Alene, ID 83816–0579
(800) 451–6034
(208) 765–0841

Rocky Mountain River Tours
P.O. Box 520
Eagle, ID 83616
(208) 345–2400

Sevy Guide Service
P.O. Box 24
Stanley, ID 83278
(208) 744–2200

SALMON RIVER (MAIN), IDAHO

Section: Main
Location: Lemhi and Idaho counties, north-central Idaho
Driving Time: Boise—4.5 hours
Difficulty: Class III–IV
Trip Length: 80 miles (128 km)
Trip Options: Paddle raft, oar raft, inflatable kayak, dory; four to five days
Season: June–October
Cost: $650–$1000

The main Salmon, or legendary River of No Return, originates in the Sawtooth and Salmon River mountains of central and eastern Idaho. No fewer than five national forests constitute its watershed as it collects the waters of many tributaries, including the Middle Fork, and cuts the second-deepest gorge in North America in its journey across central Idaho.

During its nearly 80-mile (128-km) trip through the remote granite canyons of central Idaho, the main Salmon drops 1,000 feet, creating more than forty memorable rapids. Its most difficult and impressive rapids include Salmon Falls, Bailey, Split Rock, Big Mallard, Elk Horn, and Chittam.

Forested hills, sandy beaches, crystal-clear sidestreams, adventure trails, ranches, and abandoned homesteads add to the river experience. Like the Middle Fork, the main Salmon offers a good chance to see big animals. Each spring and fall, deer, elk, bighorn sheep, mountain goats, and bears are commonly seen during their migrations between winter and summer ranges.

Many families and seniors enjoy the main Salmon each year. Reservations for the warmer July and August months are recommended.

Salmon River (Main) Outfitters

Action Whitewater Adventures
P.O. Box 1634
Provo, UT 84603
(800) 453–1482
(801) 375–4111

ARTA River Trips
Star Route 73
Groveland, CA 95321
(800) 323–2782
(209) 962–7873

Barker-Ewing Raft Trips
P.O. Box 3032
Jackson, WY 83001
(800) 448–4202
(307) 733–1000

Canyons Incorporated
P.O. Box 823
McCall, ID 83638
(208) 634–4303

ECHO: The Wilderness Company
6529 Telegraph Ave.
Oakland, CA 94609–1113
(800) 652–3246
(510) 652–1600

Holiday River Expeditions
P.O. Box 86
Grangeville, ID 83530
(208) 983–1518
(208) 983–2299

Mackay Bar Wilderness River Trips
3190 Airport Way
Boise, ID 83705
(800) 635–5336
(208) 344–1881

Northwest Dories
P.O. Box 216
Altaville, CA 95221
(209) 736–0805

Salmon River Outfitters
P.O. Box 307
Columbia, CA 95310
(209) 532–2766

Silver Cloud Expeditions
P.O. Box 1006
Salmon, ID 83467
(208) 756–6215

SALMON RIVER (LOWER), IDAHO

Section: Whitebird to the Heller Bar on the Snake River
Location: Idaho and Nez Perce counties, north-central Idaho

Driving Time:	Boise—3.5 hours
Difficulty:	Class I–III
Trip Length:	52 miles (83 km)
Trip Options:	Paddle raft, oar raft, paddle/oar raft, inflatable kayak, dory; three to five days
Season:	July–October
Cost:	$700–$1,300

The last 52 miles (83 km) of the Salmon River, before its confluence with the Snake River, is known as the lower Salmon. While perhaps not as wild or remote as the Middle Fork or main Salmon, the lower Salmon contains exciting white-water and beautiful canyon scenery. The flatter stretches of the lower Salmon are excellent for hiking, relaxing, swimming, and fishing.

Four canyons—Green, Cougar, Snowhole, and Blue—have the lower Salmon's best rapids. These include the Class III–rated Snowhole, Half and Half, China, Devil's Slide, Sluice Box, Checkerboard, and the Needle. During July and August, many families and senior citizens enjoy the exciting whitewater and arid-canyon scenery.

Lower Salmon rafting trips also include an additional 20 miles (32 km) or more of the Snake River below Hell's Canyon, along the Idaho-Oregon border. The take-out for the lower Salmon raft trip is Heller Bar on the Snake River in Washington.

Salmon River (Lower) Outfitters

Barker River Trips
2124 Grelle
Lewiston, ID 83501
(208) 743–7459

Northwest Dories
P.O. Box 216
Altaville, CA 95221
(209) 736–0805

Holiday River Expeditions
P.O. Box 86
Grangeville, ID 83530
(208) 983–1518
(208) 983–2299

Northwest Voyageurs
P.O. Box 373
Lucile, ID 83542
(800) 727–9977
(208) 628–3021

Hughes River Expeditions
P.O. Box 217
Cambridge, ID 83610
(208) 257–3477

River Odysseys West (ROW)
P.O. Box 579
Coeur d'Alene, ID 83816–0579
(800) 451–6034
(208) 765–0841

SALMON RIVER (UPPER MAIN), IDAHO

Section:	Redfish Lake Creek to Slate Creek
Location:	Custer County, north of Sun Valley, south-central Idaho
Driving Time:	Boise—2.5 hours
Difficulty:	Class II–III+
Trip Length:	35 miles (56 km) or less

Trip Options: Paddle raft, oar raft, inflatable kayak; half-day, one day
Season: May–September
Cost: $50–$75

About a ninety-minute drive north of Sun Valley, an alpine stretch of the upper main Salmon is one of Idaho's most popular whitewater trips. Here the Salmon headwaters, although much smaller than the famed River of No Return section, provide summer visitors to Sun Valley/Stanley-area resorts an exciting, yet not too difficult, opportunity to experience the thrills of rafting.

Outfitters specialize in various types of river trips. These include paddle trips where each guest helps control the raft under the direction of a guide; oar-guided rafts for families with young children, senior citizens, and the disabled; and inflatable kayaks for the adventuresome, with each guest following the guide through the rapids. Outfitters welcome anyone above the age of four to share this exciting Salmon River adventure.

Trips begin near Stanley, Idaho, in the Sawtooth National Recreation Area. The Salmon's rapids and currents are ideal for practicing newly learned paddling techniques. Many first-time rafters catch whitewater fever and return year after year to enjoy the Salmon River's special allure.

Wooden dories, similar to those used by explorer John Wesley Powell, are popular in the Grand Canyon and on Idaho's Salmon River. Photo courtesy of Northwest Dories.

Salmon River (Upper Main) Outfitters

The River Company
P.O. Box 2329
Sun Valley, ID 83353
(800) 398–0346
(208) 726–8890

Two-M River Outfitters
P.O Box 163
Sun Valley, ID 83353
(208) 838–2422 (summer)
(208) 726–8844

Triangle C Ranch Whitewater
P.O. Box 69
Stanley, ID 83278
(208) 774–2266

White Otter Outdoor Adventures
P.O. Box 2733
Ketchum, ID 83340
(208) 726-4331

SNAKE RIVER (HELLS CANYON), IDAHO/OREGON

Section: Hells Canyon Dam to Pittsburg Landing or Heller Bar
Location: Idaho and Nez Perce counties, west of Grangeville, north-central Idaho
Driving Time: Boise—2.5 hours
Difficulty: Class III–IV
Trip Length: 32 or 83 miles (51 or 133 km)
Trip Options: Paddle raft, oar raft, inflatable kayak, dory; three to six days
Season: May–October
Cost: $550–$1,000

The Snake River's Hells Canyon provides a multiday rafting experience that compares with those of the renowned Grand Canyon and the Middle Fork and main Salmon River. The Snake River carves its course through North America's deepest canyon, Hells Canyon, averaging nearly 6,600 feet. The spectacular gorge creates a most impressive border between Oregon's Wallowa and Idaho's Seven Devils mountains.

Most of the Snake's largest rapids, including Wildsheep, Granite Falls, Waterspout, and Rush Creek, come during the first 30 miles (48 km) below Hell's Canyon Dam. These rapids, while fairly difficult during early-year high-water levels, mellow during the summer. Many families and senior citizens safely enjoy the Snake River raft trip between July and September.

Hells Canyon is far more than a whitewater adventure. The canyon is rich in historic homesteads and cabins, ancient Indian ruins, and excellent petroglyphs and pictographs. It has abundant wildlife, which includes Rocky Mountain bighorn sheep, goats, mule deer, black bears, and birds of prey.

In addition to the popular 83-mile (133-km) scenic Snake River raft trip between Hells Canyon Dam and Heller Bar, some 32 miles (51 km) above Lewiston, outfitters offer several shorter trips. It is possible to raft Hells Canyon from the dam to Pittsburg Landing, or to put in at Pittsburg Landing and raft to Heller Bar.

The Snake River in Hells Canyon is a National Wild and Scenic River. It is "Wild" from Hells Canyon Dam to Pittsburg Landing, which is 32 miles (51 km), and "Scenic" from Pittsburg Landing to Heller Bar, which is 51 miles (82 km). The entire river trip is included in the Hells Canyon National Recreation Area and the Wallowa-Whitman National Forest.

Snake River (Hells Canyon) Outfitters

Hells Canyon Adventures
P.O. Box 159
Oxbow, OR 97840
(800) 422–3568
(503) 785–3352

Holiday River Expeditions
P.O. Box 86
Grangeville, ID 83530
(208) 983–1518
(208) 983–2299

Hughes River Expeditions
P.O. Box 217
Cambridge, ID 83610
(208) 257–3477

Northwest Dories
P.O. Box 216
Altaville, CA 95221
(209) 736–0805

Northwest Voyageurs
P.O. Box 373
Lucile, ID 83542
(800) 727–9977
(208) 628–3021

River Odysseys West (ROW)
P.O. Box 579
Coeur d'Alene, ID 83816–0579
(800) 451–6034
(208) 765–0841

LOCHSA RIVER, IDAHO

Section:	Lolo Pass to Lowell
Location:	Idaho County, northeast of Grangeville, north-central Idaho
Driving Time:	Missoula—2.5 hours; Spokane—4 hours
Difficulty:	Class III–IV+; paddle rafting experience recommended
Trip Length:	14–60 miles (22–96 km)
Trip Options:	Paddle raft, oar raft; half-day and one day, two and three days
Season:	May–July; July–August (scenic floats)
Cost:	$20–$35 half-day; $75–$100 one day; $220–$300 multiday

The Indians named the river Lochsa, meaning "rough water," and today these same turbulent waters create one of Idaho's best multiday recreational whitewater challenges. More than twenty-five major rapids—such as Grim Reaper, Lochsa Falls, Bloody Mary, Horsetail Falls, and Ten Pin Alley—are rated Class III–IV+. The Lochsa is considerably more difficult than the Salmon River; it should be undertaken only by active paddlers in good physical shape.

The Lochsa, part of the Clearwater Wild and Scenic River system, parallels U.S. Highway 12 from just below Lolo Pass to Lowell, where it meets the Selway River to form the Clearwater River. During years of average snowpack, outfitters normally run two- and three-day trips between late May and early July. Half-day and one-day scenic float trips are available through Labor Day weekend on the lower Lochsa near Lowell.

Lochsa River Outfitters

Glacier Raft Company
P.O. Box 218
West Glacier, MT 59936
(800) 332–9995
(406) 888–5454

Holiday River Expeditions
P.O. Box 86
Grangeville, ID 83530
(208) 983–1518
(208) 983–2299

Lewis & Clark Trail Adventures
P.O. Box 9051
Missoula, MT 59801
(406) 728–7609

Three Rivers Resort
HCR 75, Box 61
Kooskia, ID 83539
(208) 926–4430

River Odysseys West (ROW)
P.O. Box 579
Coeur d'Alene, ID 83816–0579
(800) 451–6034
(208) 765–0841

SELWAY RIVER, IDAHO

Section:	Paradise Creek to Selway Falls
Location:	Idaho County, east of Grangeville, north-central Idaho
Driving Time:	Missoula—2.5 hours; Spokane—4 hours
Difficulty:	Class III–IV+
Trip Length:	45 miles (72 km)
Trip Options:	Paddle raft, oar raft, paddle/oar raft; three to five days
Season:	June–July
Cost:	$900–$1,000

The Selway River canyon, in the Selway-Bitterroot Wilderness Area near the Idaho–Montana border, is one of the premier multiday river experiences in the northern Rockies. Unlike the Salmon River with numerous daily trips, rafting access to the remote and secluded Selway is very limited. The U.S. Forest Service issues only one launch per day during the seventy-eight-day rafting season. Only sixteen of these launch dates are available for guided commercial rafting trips.

For those fortunate enough to raft the Selway, one of the first rivers protected by the National Wild and Scenic Rivers Act, the experience is unforgettable. For up to five days, rafters navigate exciting Class II–IV rapids, such as Galloping Gertie, Washer Woman, Goat Creek, Ham, Double Drop, Ladle, Puzzle Creek, and Wolf Creek. Take-out is just above the Class VI Selway Falls. In the quiet pools between the exciting whitewater, much time remains to enjoy the varied wildlife and forest scenery.

Selway River Outfitters

ARTA River Trips
Star Route 73
Groveland, CA 95321
(800) 323–2782
(209) 962–7873

Northwest River Company
P.O. Box 403
Boise, ID 83701
(208) 344–7119

Elwood Masoner's Whitewater Adventures
P.O. Box 184
Twin Falls, ID 83303
(208) 733–4548

PAYETTE RIVER, IDAHO

Section: North Fork (Cabarton to Smith Ferry)
Location: Valley County, south of McCall, southwest Idaho
Driving Time: Boise—1.5 hours
Difficulty: Class III–IV
Trip Length: 9.5 miles (15 km)
Trip Options: Paddle raft, oar raft; one day
Season: May–September
Cost: $40–$75

Three forks of southwest Idaho's Payette River—the North, South, and Main— provide whitewater enthusiasts nearly 80 miles (128 km) of superb Class II–IV rafting opportunities within a one-hour drive of Boise. Commercially rafted are a 10-mile (16-km) section of the North Fork, some 60 miles (96 km) of the South Fork and, immediately after the confluence of the two forks, 9 miles (14 km) of the main Payette.

Rafting on the Cabarton section of the North Fork, a very popular summer- time Class III–IV trip adjacent to Idaho Route 55, is made possible by controlled- water releases from Cascade Reservoir by Idaho Power. There are several easy rapids on which first-time rafters can perfect newly learned paddling skills before the North Fork's biggest whitewaters, the Class III–IV Tressel Rapid and Howard's Plunge.

Section: South Fork (canyon and lower)
Location: Boise County, north of Boise, southwest Idaho
Driving Time: Boise—1.5 hours
Difficulty: Class III–IV (upper), II–III (Old Swirley Canyon), II–III+ (lower canyon)
Trip Length: Upper—15 miles (24 km); Old Swirley Canyon—14 miles (24 km); Lower canyon—7 miles (11 km)
Trip Options: Paddle raft, oar raft; multiday (upper), one day (Old Swirley Canyon), half-day (lower canyon)
Season: May–September
Cost: $40 half-day; $80–$85 one day; $190–$230 two day

The Payette's best whitewater challenges are found in the canyons and gorges of its South Fork. The narrow, steep-walled Old Swirley Canyon run has mostly Class III pool-drop rapids, but it does have four technical Class IV rapids—S- turn, Blackadar's Drop, Little Falls, and Surprise—as well as a mandatory portage around the 40-foot, Class VI Big Falls. Although an adjacent county road allows take-out just below Little Falls, some one-day and all multiday South Fork rafting trips include the breathtaking Class III Old Swirley Canyon. The South Fork also has several refreshing hot springs.

Downstream, the last 5 miles (8 km) of the lower South Fork, before its conflu- ence with the North Fork, is one of Idaho's most popular whitewater runs. Well known as the site of the annual Payette Whitewater Rodeo, the lower run has fairly continuous and exciting Class II–III+ rapids. Prior to the South Fork's confluence with the main Payette, Staircase Rapid (a long Class III–IV rapid) will adequately test the skills of paddle rafters. Some rafters take advantage of the relatively short length of the whitewater trip and run the Staircase section twice in one day.

Section:	Main—Banks to Horseshoe Bend
Location:	Boise County, north of Boise, southwest Idaho
Driving Time:	1 hour
Difficulty:	Class I–III
Trip Length:	9 miles (14 km)
Trip Options:	Paddle raft, oar raft; half-day and one day
Season:	May–September
Cost:	$20–$30 half-day; $40–$50 one day

The very popular main Payette, created by the confluence of the North and South forks, offers an excellent introduction to whitewater rafting for families and inexperienced paddlers. This beautiful whitewater river is also a favorite with large groups. Guide-escorted half- and one-day raft trips start at the town of Banks. Nearly 4 miles (6 km) of easy Class I–II rapids at the beginning of the trip give paddle rafters ample time to practice their skills before Class III-rated Mike's Hole. The main Payette's two other Class III rapids, Mixmaster and AMF, are located just prior to the Beehive Bend take-out for half-day trips.

On morning and afternoon trips, outfitters allow time for swimming and relaxing. For those wishing to scout the river prior to their trip, Idaho Route 55 parallels the main Payette's entire whitewater run.

Payette River Outfitters

Bear Valley River Company
HC 76, Box 1000
Banks, ID 83602
(208) 793–2272

Cascade Raft Company
P.O. Box 6
Garden Valley, ID 83622
(800) 292–7238
(208) 462–3292

Headwaters Raft Company
P.O. Box 1
Banks, ID 83602
(800) 876–7238
(208) 793–2348

Idaho Whitewater Unlimited
1042 E. Ustick
Meridian, ID 83642
(208) 888–3008

FLATHEAD RIVER (MIDDLE FORK), MONTANA

Section:	Essex to confluence with North Fork (lower)
Location:	Flathead County, southern boundary of Glacier National Park, northwest Montana
Driving Time:	Kalispell—.75 hour; Missoula—2.5 hours
Difficulty:	Class II–III+ (lower)
Trip Length:	7–15 miles (11–24 km)
Trip Options:	Paddle raft, oar raft; half-day and one day
Season:	May–September
Cost:	$20–$30 half-day; $30–$60 one day

The lower Middle Fork of the Flathead River, which flows between U.S. Highway 2 and the southern boundary of Glacier National Park, provides a popular whitewater rafting opportunity for park visitors. Guests on either half-day or one-day trips will likely get wet in many of the Flathead's fine Class III rapids—Tunnel, Bone Crusher, Jaws, Narrows, CBT, and Pumphouse. Everyone will also enjoy viewing the scenic mountains and forests of the adjacent park and Flathead Range. Both trips end near Glacier Park's west entrance.

Section:	Shafer Meadows to Essex (upper)
Location:	Flathead County, southeast of Glacier National Park, northwest Montana
Driving Time:	Kalispell—.75 hour; Missoula—3 hours
Difficulty:	Class II–IV+
Trip Length:	35 miles (56 km)
Trip Options:	Paddle raft, oar raft; four to six days
Season:	June–July
Cost:	$675–$875

The upper Middle Fork of the Flathead River, accessible only by air, horse, or foot, is one of Montana's wildest wilderness waterways. Raft trips, beginning at Shafer Meadows near the Continental Divide, present some of the state's finest alpine wilderness river environment. Immediately below the Schafer Meadows put-in, the river passes through the Great Bear Wilderness, home to grizzly bears, elk, deer, moose, mountain goats, waterfowl, and birds of prey.

The Middle Fork offers very challenging whitewater, with Class III–IV rapids providing ample excitement for enthusiasts. All multiday trips on the upper Middle Fork allow time for fishing, hiking, and relaxing.

Flathead River (Middle Fork) Outfitters

Glacier Raft Company
P.O. Box 218
West Glacier, MT 59936
(800) 332–9995
(406) 888–5454

Wild River Adventures
P.O. Box 272
West Glacier, MT 59936
(800) 826–2724
(406) 387–9453

Great Northern Whitewater
P.O. Box 278
West Glacier, MT 59936
(800) 735–7897
(406) 387–5340

Wilderness River Outfitters
P.O. Box 871
Salmon, ID 83467
(800) 252–6581
(208) 756–8959

Montana Raft Company
P.O. Box 535
West Glacier, MT 59936
(800) 521–7238
(406) 888–5466

FLATHEAD RIVER (NORTH FORK), MONTANA

Section: Canadian border to confluence with Middle Fork
Location: lathead County, western border of Glacier National Park, northwest Montana
Driving Time: Kalispell—.75 hour; Missoula—3 hours
Difficulty: Class I–II
Trip Length: 60 miles (96 km)
Trip Options: Paddle raft, oar raft; two and three days
Season: June–August
Cost: $150–$275

The North Fork of the Flathead River float trip is part of America's Wild and Scenic Rivers system. During its southward flow from British Columbia, the North Fork creates the western boundary of Montana's Glacier National Park and offers impressive views of the park's most beautiful peaks. For nearly 60 miles (96 km), from the put-in near the Canada–United States border to its confluence with the Middle Fork, the easy Class I–II waters and slow pace of the North Fork enable rafters to relax and fully enjoy the wilderness river experience.

It is recommended that families and seniors schedule North Fork Flathead trips during the warmer months of July and August.

Flathead River (North Fork) Outfitters

Glacier Raft Company
P.O. Box 218
West Glacier, MT 59936
(800) 332–9995
(406) 888–5454

Wild River Adventures
P.O. Box 272
West Glacier, MT 59936
(800) 826–2724
(406) 387–9453

FLATHEAD RIVER (LOWER), MONTANA

Section: Kerr Dam
Location: Flathead Indian Reservation, Lake County, south of Polson, western Montana
Driving Time: Kalispell—1.5 hours; Missoula—1.5 hours
Difficulty: Class II–III+
Trip Length: 8 miles (13 km)
Trip Options: Paddle raft, oar raft; half-day
Season: June–August
Cost: $30

The lower Flathead River, which begins near Polson at the south end of Flathead Lake, provides an exciting, yet relatively easy, half-day introduction to whitewater rafting. With the exception of four Class III rapids—The Ledge, Pinball, Eagle Wave, and Buffalo—its rapids are Class I–II. The river is especially popular with families, seniors, and first-time rafters. Paddle trips give everyone an opportunity to improve navigation skills.

The lower Flathead, being dam-controlled, is usually raftable throughout the summer season. Morning and afternoon trips normally take about three hours. Reservations are recommended, but same-day raft trips are usually possible.

The scenic lower Flathead, on the Flathead Indian Reservation, is home to many birds of prey and waterfowl.

Flathead River (Lower) Outfitter

Glacier Raft Company
P.O. Box 218
West Glacier, MT 59936
(800) 332–9995
(406) 888–5454

CLARK FORK RIVER, MONTANA

Section:	Alberton Gorge
Location:	Mineral County, northwest of Missoula, western Montana
Driving Time:	Missoula—.75 hour
Difficulty:	Class II–III
Trip Length:	12 miles (19 km)
Trip Options:	Paddle raft, oar raft, inflatable kayak; one day
Season:	July–September
Cost:	$25–$40

Alberton Gorge, on the Clark Fork River, is one of western Montana's best white-water rafting stretches during late summer. The later runoff of the eastern slopes of the Bitterroot Range provides the Clark Fork with water when most other rivers are nearing their water-level low. The gorge's exciting Class II–III rapids—Fang, Boateater, Tumbleweed, Trip Bridges, Cliffside, and Rest Stop—are ideal for both beginning and intermediate rafters.

Although Interstate 90 parallels the entire gorge, the highway can seldom be seen. The Clark Fork's mountain canyons provide habitat to wildlife including deer, bears, ospreys, hawks, turkey vultures, and eagles.

Outfitters listed on page 89.

BLACKFOOT RIVER, MONTANA

Section:	Middle
Location:	Missoula County, east of Missoula, western Montana
Driving Time:	Missoula—.5 hour
Difficulty:	Class II–III
Trip Length:	12–30 miles (19–48 km)
Trip Options:	Paddle raft, oar raft, inflatable kayak; one to three days
Season:	May–July
Cost:	$25–$40; $85 two days

Less than a half-hour-drive east of Missoula, the middle Blackfoot River provides an ideal introduction to whitewater rafting for families, senior citizens, and first-time rafters. The trip passes through beautiful pine-forested rocky gorges. Its relatively easy Class II–III rapids alternate with quiet stretches of the river that permit relaxing, fishing, and swimming.

Most one-day raft trips on the Blackfoot cover about 12 miles (19 km). Two-day trips with overnight camping normally travel about 30 miles (48 km).

Clark Fork River and Blackfoot River Outfitters

Lewis & Clark Trail Adventures
P.O. Box 9051
Missoula, MT 59801
(406) 728–7609

Rocky Mountain Whitewater
1905 Ola Drive
East Missoula, MT 59802
(406) 728–2984

GALLATIN RIVER, MONTANA

Section:	Karst to Squaw Creek
Location:	Gallatin County near Yellowstone National Park, southwest Montana
Driving Time:	Bozeman—1 hour
Difficulty:	Class II–III, IV
Trip Length:	8 miles (13 km)
Trip Options:	Paddle raft, oar raft; half-day, one day
Season:	June–August
Cost:	$29–$35 half-day; $53–$65 one day

The put-in for whitewater rafting on the Gallatin is just north of Yellowstone National Park. Deep in the Gallatin Canyon, alongside U.S. Highway 191, Class III+ rapids, such as Show Stopper, House Rock, and The Mad Mile, highlight a stretch of almost continuous whitewater.

Rafting guests on the Gallatin have their choice of half- and one-day raft trips. Half-day trips, which run three times a day, include most of the river's best whitewater. Full-day trips have a more leisurely pace, and lunch is served. Oar-guided raft trips during the summer are suggested for families and seniors. Scenic float trips on calmer stretches of the Gallatin are also available.

Gallatin River Outfitters

Adventures Big Sky Rafting
P.O. Box 160001
Big Sky, MT 59716
(406) 995–2324

Yellowstone Raft Company
P.O. Box 46
Gardiner, MT 59030
(800) 858–7781
(406) 848–7777

MADISON RIVER, MONTANA

Section:	Bear Trap Canyon
Location:	Madison County, west of Bozeman, southwest Montana
Driving Time:	Bozeman—1.5 hours
Difficulty:	Class II–IV
Trip Length:	9 miles (14 km)
Trip Options:	Oar raft; one day
Season:	June–August
Cost:	$75–$90

The Madison River's majestic Bear Trap Canyon, about an hour's drive northwest of Yellowstone National Park, contains one of Montana's finest white-water stretches. Unlike the Gallatin or Yellowstone raft trips, no roads and few signs of civilization are seen from the river. Raft trips, which begin near the Madison Dam powerhouse below Ennis Lake, are usually run at a leisurely enough pace for rafting guests to appreciate the beauty of the 1,500-foot-canyon, its plentiful wildlife, and its challenging whitewater.

Bear Trap Canyon's whitewater includes three major rapids: White Horse, Kitchen Sink, and Green Wave. On warm summer days, outfitters permit both swimming and tubing.

Madison River Outfitter

Yellowstone Raft Company
P.O. Box 46
Gardiner, MT 59030
(800) 858–7781
(406) 848–7777

YELLOWSTONE RIVER, MONTANA

Sections:	Paradise Valley and Yankee Jim Canyon
Location:	Park County near Gardiner, north of Yellowstone National Park, southwest Montana
Driving Time:	Bozeman—1.5 hours
Difficulty:	Class II–III
Trip Length:	8–25 miles (13–40 km)
Trip Options:	Paddle raft, oar raft; half-day, one day
Season:	May–September
Cost:	$17–$30 half-day; $35–$60 one day

The historic Yellowstone River is an almost 680-mile (1,088-km) free-flowing tributary of the Missouri River. It is rafted just north of Yellowstone National Park's Mammoth Hot Springs entrance in southwest Montana. For some 25 miles (40 km) below the Gardiner put-in, the exciting Class II–III waters of upper Paradise Valley and Yankee Jim Canyon attract of thousands of rafters to the same canyons that were visited by early Indians and trappers.

The outfitter offers both half- and full-day raft trips on the Yellowstone. Full-day trips, which cover nearly 17 miles (27 km), allow time for relaxation and swimming. Visitors with less time can consider two- to three-hour trips. There is still plenty of whitewater and time enough to enjoy the beautiful scenery. Either paddle- or oar-guided raft trips on the Yellowstone are an excellent introduction to whitewater for families, senior citizens, and other first-time rafters. When requested, the outfitter offers scenic float trips on calmer stretches.

Yellowstone River Outfitter

Yellowstone Raft Company
P.O. Box 46
Gardiner, MT 59030
(800) 858–7781
(406) 848–7777

STILLWATER RIVER, MONTANA

Section: Stillwater Canyon
Location: Stillwater County, near Absarokee, south-central Montana
Driving Time: Billings—1 hour
Difficulty: Class II–III
Trip Length: 11–17 miles (17.5–27 km)
Trip Options: Paddle raft, oar raft, inflatable kayak; half-day
Season: May-August
Cost: $15–$25

The Stillwater River was inappropriately named by the famed explorers Lewis and Clark, who saw only its gentle confluence with the Yellowstone River. From its headwaters, which form near Yellowstone National Park among Montana's highest mountain peaks, to the Yellowstone near Columbus, the Stillwater continues to gain volume and intensity.

Rafters ride the highest volume section of the Stillwater River, where a one-sided canyon creates a series of waves and whitewater rapids. Rolling hills and canyons dominate on the left bank while typical Montana farm and ranch lands occupy the right. Back upstream, the snowcapped Absaroka-Beartooth Mountains are frequently in view.

From mid-May until August, rafters may enjoy the Stillwater's exciting Class II–III rapids in paddle rafts, oar rafts, or inflatable kayaks. Half-day trips are available both mornings and afternoons.

Stillwater River Outfitter

Beartooth Whitewater
P.O. Box 781
Red Lodge, MT 59068
(406) 446–3142

SHOSHONE RIVER, WYOMING

Section: Canyon
Location: Park County, west of Cody, northwest Wyoming
Driving Time: Billings—2 hours
Difficulty: Class I–II
Trip Length: 6 or 13 miles (9.5 or 21 km)
Trip Options: Paddle raft, oar raft; half-day
Season: May–September
Cost: $14–$23

Just an hour's drive east of Yellowstone National Park, the beautiful Shoshone River offers visitors a perfect introduction to whitewater rafting. Shoshone's easy Class II–III rapids, adjacent to Wyoming routes 14/16 in beautiful Red Rock Canyon, can be enjoyed by almost anyone. Seniors and families with small children are welcome as scheduled releases from Buffalo River Reservoir make water levels very predictable.

Outfitters offer daily two-hour trips on a six-mile (9.5-km) section of the river and half-day trips on a 13-mile (21-km) section. Both trips traverse Red Rock Canyon and end in Cody.

The Shoshone River and the town of Cody are rich in Indian and Wild West history and folklore. The banks of the river served as sacred burial grounds for the Shoshone tribe. Today the town's main attraction is the Buffalo Bill Historical Center, whose museums commemorate the art and culture of the American West.

Shoshone River Outfitters

River Runners of Cody
P.O. Box 845
Cody, WY 82414
(307) 527–7238

Wyoming River Trips
P.O. Box 1541
Cody, WY 82414
(307) 587–6661

SNAKE RIVER (GRAND TETON), WYOMING

Section:	Pacific Creek to Moose Village
Location:	Grand Teton National Park, north of Jackson, northwest Wyoming
Driving Time:	Idaho Falls—2 hours; Salt Lake City—5.5 hours
Difficulty:	Class I–II
Trip Length:	10 miles (16 km)
Trip Options:	Oar raft; two-hour
Season:	May–September
Cost:	$12–$30

A scenic float trip on the upper Snake River in Grand Teton National Park provides a close-up look at majestic mountains and birds of prey.

One of the more memorable ways for visitors to enjoy the awesome beauty of Grand Teton National Park is a float trip on the Snake River. Beneath the majestic Teton mountains, the mellow Snake River is the only avenue for seeing many of Jackson Hole's forests and meadows that provide secluded habitat to beavers, otters, bears, moose, eagles, and ospreys.

Below Jackson Lake, from mid-May until mid-September, the park's licensed rafting outfitters offer 10-mile (16-km) daily float trips which include optional deli or picnic lunch, supper floats, and sunrise and evening wildlife trips.

Snake River outfitters have few passenger restrictions. Almost anyone above the age of four can enjoy the river. Outfitters welcome families, senior citizens, and the disabled. While it is almost always possible to join a raft trip on short notice, reservations at least a day or two in advance are recommended.

Snake River (Grand Teton) Outfitters

Barker-Ewing Float Trips
P.O. Box 100
Moose, WY 83012
(800) 365–1800
(307) 733–1800

Fort Jackson Float Trips
P.O. Box 1176
Jackson, WY 83001
(800) 735–8430
(307) 733–2583

Grand Teton Lodge Company
P.O. Box 250
Moran, WY 83013
(307) 543–2811

O.A.R.S.
P.O. Box 67
Angels Camp, CA 95222
(800) 346–6277
(209) 736–4677

Solitude Float Trips
P.O. Box 112
Moose, WY 83012
(307) 733–2871

Triangle X Float Trips
National Park Float Trips
Osprey Float Trips
Moose, WY 83012
(307) 733–5500
(307) 733–2183

SNAKE RIVER (UPPER), WYOMING

Sections:	Canyons
Location:	Lincoln County, south of Jackson, northwest Wyoming
Driving Time:	Idaho Falls—1.5 hours; Salt Lake City—5.5 hours
Difficulty:	Class II–III
Trip Length:	8 and 16 miles (13 and 26 km)
Trip Options:	Paddle raft, oar raft; half-day, one day
Season:	May–September
Cost:	$25–$35 scenic or whitewater section; $50–$55 scenic float/whitewater combination

Approximately 20 miles (32 km) south of Grand Teton National Park, the Snake River affords vacationers two 8-mile (13-km) rafting choices. The first, near Hoback Junction, is a scenic float trip along the quiet waters of the Snake that enables guests to relax and enjoy the mountain scenery. In addition to daytime trips, several outfitters offer morning and evening floats so visitors have a better chance to see much of the wildlife common to the region.

Downstream, from West Table Creek to Sheep Gulch north of Alpine Junction, the upper Snake River canyon offers a more lively 8-mile (13 km) introduction to whitewater rafting. Class II–III rapids—Main Line, Three Oar-deal, Kahuna, Lunch Counter, Rope, Champagne, and Cottonwood—are not difficult and can be enjoyed by families, seniors, and first-time rafters.

Snake River (Upper) Outfitters

Barker-Ewing River Trips
P.O. Box 3032
Jackson, WY 83001
(800) 448–4202
(307) 733–1000

Dave Hansen Whitewater
P.O. Box 328
Jackson, WY 83001
(307) 733–6295

Jackson Hole Whitewater
P.O. Box 3695
Jackson, WY 83001
(800) 648–2602
(307) 733–1007

Lewis and Clark River Expeditions
P.O. Box 720
Jackson, WY 83001
(800) 824–5375
(307) 733–4022

Lone Eagle Expeditions
P.O. Box 952
Jackson, WY 83001
(800) 321–3800
(307) 733–1090

Mad River Boat Trips
P.O. Box 2222
Jackson, WY 83001
(800) 458–7238
(307) 733–6203

Sands Whitewater
P.O. Box 696
Wilson, WY 83014
(800) 358–8184
(307) 733–4410

Snake River Park Whitewater
Box 14A Star Route
Jackson, WY 83001
(307) 733–7078

Colorado

Colorado, world famous for its magnificent mountain environment and winter skiing, also receives widespread acclaim for its outstanding whitewaters during the spring and summer. In most years, these noteworthy waters attract more than a half million rafters. Nearly two dozen rafting trips include an excellent variety of half-day, one-day, and multiday raft trips suitable for the adventurous, families, seniors, and the disabled. Many of the more popular trips are easily accessible from the state's well-known parks, resorts, and other vacation centers.

The Arkansas River, from Twin Lakes below Independence Pass in south-central Colorado to Canon City, is one of the West's most popular whitewater rivers. Families, seniors, first-time rafters, and experienced rafters all will enjoy one or more sections of the river—The Numbers, Browns Canyon, Salida-Cotopaxi, Cotopaxi-Parkdale, and the Royal Gorge. Outfitters offer a wide variety of one-day, half-day, and shorter trips.

Only two other whitewater stretches in Colorado are not part of the mighty Colorado River's drainage system. The Cache la Poudre River run, through an intermediate-level canyon northeast of Rocky Mountain National Park, has exciting whitewater throughout the summer. The North Platte, another tributary of the South Platte in the Missouri River drainage, has challenging and exciting alpine whitewaters only during the spring.

Five of Colorado's popular whitewater stretches are in the central Rockies, near the all-season Aspen and Vail resort areas. Outfitters provide half-day, one-day, and multiday raft trips for families and first-time rafters on the moderate waters of the upper Colorado beginning near Kremmling and the middle Colorado at Glenwood Springs. The Eagle, Blue, and Roaring Fork, three tributaries of the upper Colorado, also have relatively easy whitewater sections for new paddlers in very scenic canyons.

In southwest Colorado, rafting occurs on alpine streams and the rivers of the Colorado plateau. The Gunnison River system, which joins the Colorado at Grand Junction, has rafting trips of varying difficulty on two of its tributaries (the Taylor and Lake forks), the upper Gunnison, and Gunnison Gorge immediately below the famed Black Canyon of the Gunnison. Likewise, the upper San Juan River offers popular family rafting trips through two scenic canyons near Pagosa Springs during the late spring and summer months. Each spring, both the Piedra and upper Animas rivers in the San Juan Mountains provide some of the state's best Class V waters. The moderate lower Animas at Durango provides daily rafting trips for families and first-time rafters throughout much of the summer. The Dolores River, which runs parallel to the Colorado–Utah border, offers several excellent multiday trip options.

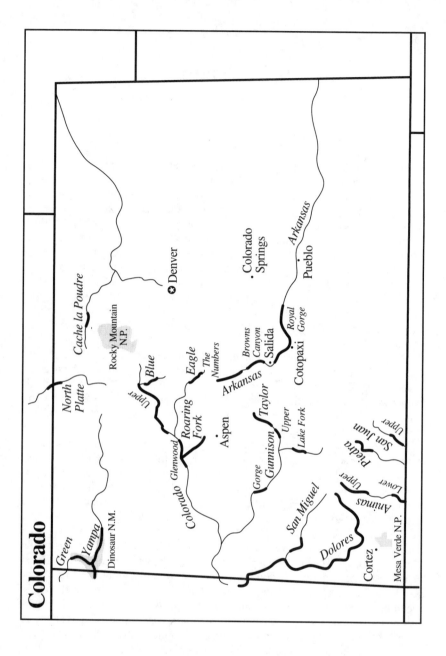

Colorado

Colorado
River Comparison

	Difficulty	Min. Age	H	D	M	Season	P	O	K
South-Central Colorado									
Arkansas									
The Numbers	/ / /	14	✗			May–Jul	✗		
Browns Canyon	/ /	10	✗	✗		May–Sep	✗	✗	✗
Salida-Cotopaxi	/	6	✗	✗		May–Sep	✗	✗	✗
Cotopaxi-Parkdale	/	8	✗	✗		May–Sep	✗	✗	✗
Royal Gorge	/ /	12	✗			May–Sep	✗	✗	
North-Central Colorado									
Cache la Poudre	/ /	12	✗	✗		May–Jul	✗	✗	
North Platte	/ /	12		✗	✗	May–Jul	✗	✗	
Blue	/	8	✗			May–Jul	✗	✗	
Eagle	/	8	✗	✗		May–Jul	✗	✗	
Colorado (Upper)									
Gore Canyon	/	8	✗	✗		May–Sep	✗	✗	
State Bridge	/	8	✗	✗	✗	May–Sep	✗	✗	
Roaring Fork	/ /	12	✗	✗		May–Jul	✗	✗	
Colorado (Glenwood)									
Glenwood Canyon	/	6	✗	✗		Jun–Sep	✗	✗	
Shoshone Run	/ /	16	✗			Jun–Jul	✗	✗	
Southwestern Colorado									
Taylor	/ /	12	✗	✗		May–Sep	✗	✗	
Gunnison (Upper)	/	None	✗			May–Sep	✗	✗	
Gunnison (Lake Fork)	/ /	12	✗			May–Jul	✗		
Gunnison (Gorge)	/	8		✗	✗	May–Sep	✗	✗	
San Juan (Upper)									
Mesa Canyon	/	5	✗			Apr–Jun	✗	✗	
Montezuma Canyon	/	3		✗		Jul–Aug	✗	✗	
Piedra	/ / /	16	✗	✗		May–Jul	✗	✗	
Animas (Upper)	/ / /	16		✗		May–Jul	✗	✗	
Animas (Lower)	/	6	✗	✗		May–Aug	✗	✗	
San Miguel	/	6	✗	✗		May–Jul	✗	✗	
Dolores	/ /	10		✗	✗	Apr–Jun	✗	✗	✗
Northwest Colorado–Northeast Utah									
Yampa and Green									
Dinosaur National Monument	/ /	10		✗		May–Jun	✗	✗	
Lodore Canyon	/	10		✗		May–Aug	✗	✗	
Whirlpool Canyon	/	10		✗		May–Aug	✗	✗	
Split Mountain Gorge	/	None	✗			Jun–Sep	✗	✗	✗

/   Beginner—Easy whitewater. Fun for everyone.

/ /   Intermediate—Moderate whitewater.
No previous rafting experience is necessary.

/ / /   Advanced—Difficult whitewater.
Previous Class IV paddle rafting experience is recommended or required.

H—Half-Day Trip, D—Day Trip, M—Multiday Trip
P—Paddle Raft, O—Oar Raft, K—Inflatable Kayak

Rafters paddle under suspension footbridge in the Arkansas River's towering Royal Gorge.

Finally, in northwest Colorado, the Green and Yampa rivers unveil the majestic canyon splendor of Dinosaur National Monument on popular multiday raft trips. Outfitters also offer excellent one-day family raft trips through Split Mountain Gorge, one of Dinosaur's three spectacular canyons.

ARKANSAS RIVER, COLORADO

Section:	The Numbers
Location:	Chaffee County, north of Buena Vista, south-central Colorado
Driving Time:	Colorado Springs—2 hours; Denver—3 hours
Difficulty:	Class III–IV+; paddle rafting experience highly recommended
Trip Length:	12 miles (19 km)
Trip Options:	Paddle raft; one day
Season:	May–July
Cost:	$70–$80

The Numbers—one through six—above Buena Vista is the uppermost section of the Arkansas commonly rafted by professional outfitters. Its continuous Class III–IV+ rapids are also some of the river's most technical and demanding. Not all Arkansas outfitters run the Numbers, and it can only be rafted at certain water levels. Rafters must be in excellent physical condition and have had previous Class IV whitewater experience. Most outfitters require rafters to be at least eighteen years old.

Section:	Browns Canyon
Location:	Chaffee County, south of Buena Vista, south-central Colorado
Driving Time:	Colorado Springs—2 hours; Denver—3 hours
Difficulty:	Class II–III+
Trip Length:	12–21 miles (19–34 km)
Trip Options:	Paddle raft, oar raft, inflatable kayak; half-day and one day
Season:	May–September
Cost:	$20–$35

The Arkansas River's most-favored section is granite-walled Browns Canyon, a few miles south of Buena Vista. This relatively easy 12-mile (19-km) adventure has exciting, yet not intimidating, whitewater. Numerous large boulders and a gradient of almost 40 feet per mile create dozens of exciting and somewhat technical Class III+ rapids such as Zoom Flume, Pinball, Big Drop, Staircase, Widowmaker, Siedell's Suckhole, and Twin Falls.

Section:	Salida-Cotopaxi
Location:	Fremont County, southeast of Salida, south-central Colorado
Driving Time:	Colorado Springs—2 hours
Difficulty:	Class II–III
Trip Length:	11-23 miles (18-37 km)
Trip Options:	Paddle raft, oar raft, inflatable kayak; half-day and one day
Season:	May–September
Cost:	$20–$30 half day; $40–$60 one day

The Salida-Cotopaxi section of the Arkansas is a particular favorite of senior citizens and families with young children. Guided oar rafts allow passengers ample time to enjoy the impressive canyon scenery and beautiful views of the 14,000-foot Sangre de Cristo Mountains. The section's exciting, but not difficult, Class II–III rapids—Bear and Badger creeks, Tin Cup, Red Rocks, and Cottonwood—should frighten no one. Outfitters offer two-hour, half-day, and all-day trips.

Section: Cotopaxi-Parkdale
Location: Fremont County, west of Canon City, south-central Colorado
Driving Time: Colorado Springs—1.5 hours; Denver—2.5 hours
Difficulty: Class II–III
Trip Length: 10–22 miles (16–35 km)
Trip Options: Paddle raft, oar raft, inflatable kayak; half-day and one day
Season: May–September
Cost: $20–$30 half day; $40–$60 one day

The Cotopaxi-Parkdale stretch of the Arkansas River features a superb blend of canyon scenery and moderate whitewater. This section's Class III rapids—Maytag, Devils Hole, Wake Up, Three Rock Falls, and Spike Buck Falls—are not as difficult those of the downstream Royal Gorge; they are nevertheless exciting and challenging for beginning and intermediate-level rafters. Either Cotopaxi-Parkdale or Browns Canyon is a recommended prerequisite for the Class III–IV+ Royal Gorge.

Section: Royal Gorge
Location: Fremont County, west of Canon City, south-central Colorado
Driving Time: Colorado Springs—1.25 hours; Denver—2.25 hours
Difficulty: Class III–IV+; paddle rafting experience recommended
Trip Length: 9–19 miles (14–30 km)
Trip Options: Paddle raft, oar raft; one day
Season: May–September
Cost: $70–$80

The Royal Gorge is the Arkansas River's most unusual whitewater canyon trip. Nearly one thousand feet below the world's highest suspension bridge, steep pool-drops, large waves, and numerous demanding Class IV-IV+ rapids—Sunshine Falls, Sledgehammer, the Narrows, Wall Slammer, Boateater, and Corner Pocket—create a truly extraordinary whitewater trip. The overall canyon river experience is made even more memorable by the historic river-level railroad, an inclined railway, and the remnants of the early-century water flume.

Arkansas River Outfitters

American Adventure Expeditions
P.O. Box 1549
Buena Vista, CO 81211
(800) 288–0675
(719) 395–2409

Arkansas River Tours
Four Corners Rafting
P.O. Box 1032
Buena Vista, CO 81211
(800) 321–4352
(800) 332–7238

Arkansas Valley Expeditions
P.O. Box 100
Salida, CO 81201
(800) 833-7238
(719) 539-6669

Dvorak's Kayak/Rafting Expeditions
17921 Hwy. 285
Nathrop, CO 81236
(800) 824-3795
(719) 539-6851

Echo Canyon River Expeditions
45000 U.S. Hwy. 50 West
Canon City, CO 81212
(800) 748-2953
(719) 275-3154

Moondance River Expeditions
310 W. First St.
Salida, CO 81201
(719) 539-2113

Noah's Ark Whitewater Rafting
P.O. Box 850
Buena Vista, CO 81211
(719) 395-2158

Rocky Mountain Outdoor Center
10281 Hwy. 50
Howard, CO 81233
(800) 255-5784
(719) 942-3213

Rocky Mountain Tours
P.O. Box 3031
Buena Vista, CO 81211
(800) 551-5140
(719) 395-4101

Whitewater Voyageurs
P.O. Box 346
Poncha Springs, CO 81242
(800) 255-2585
(719) 539-7618

Wilderness Aware
P.O. Box 1550
Buena Vista, CO 81211
(800) 462-7238
(719) 395-2112

CACHE LA POUDRE RIVER, COLORADO

Section:	Canyon
Location:	Larimer County, west of Fort Collins, north-central Colorado
Driving Time:	Denver—2 hours
Difficulty:	Class III–IV
Trip Length:	15 miles (24 km)
Trip Options:	Paddle raft, oar raft; half-day and one day
Season:	May–July
Cost:	$25–$35 half-day; $50–$75 one day

Colorado's Cache la Poudre, tumbling from the snowcapped peaks of Rocky Mountain National Park, is an exceptionally beautiful and exciting tributary of the North Platte. Long known for its beauty, this river in Roosevelt National Forest became the state's first National Wild and Scenic River.

While the upper stretches of the Cache la Poudre are well known for their many fine kayak runs, whitewater rafting trips begin less than 20 miles (32 km) west of Fort Collins. Adjacent to Colorado Route 14, almost continuous whitewater with numerous technical rapids, powerful hydraulics, and steep drops—such as the Class IV+ Mishawaka and Pineview Falls—leave little time to fully appreciate the river canyon's towering spires and sheer cliffs.

The river's easy access enables outfitters to offer a number of different half-day and one-day raft trips. Most popular are half-day runs that include Mishawaka and Pineview falls and family-oriented trips that start below the falls.

Cache la Poudre River Outfitters

A Wanderlust Adventure
P.O. Box 976
Laporte, CO 80535–0976
(800) 745–7238
(303) 484–1219

Rapid Transit Rafting
P.O. Box 4095
Estes Park, CO 80517
(800) 367–8523
(303) 586–8852

A-1 Whitewater
317 Stover St.
Fort Collins, CO 80524
(303) 224–3379

Rocky Mountain Adventures
P.O. Box 1989
Fort Collins, CO 80522
(800) 858–6808
(303) 493–4005

NORTH PLATTE RIVER, COLORADO/WYOMING

Section:	Northgate Canyon
Location:	Jackson County, north-central Colorado; Carbon County, south-central Wyoming
Driving Time:	Denver—2.5 hours
Difficulty:	Class III–IV
Trip Length:	14–20 miles (22–32 km)
Trip Options:	Paddle raft, oar raft; one and two days
Season:	May–mid July
Cost:	$55–$70 one day; $150–$200 two days

North Platte River rafting is done in high-altitude mountain valleys near the river's headwaters in north-central Colorado. About an hour and a half's drive northeast of Steamboat Springs, the North Platte flows northwest through the scenic alpine wilderness of Northgate Canyon into southern Wyoming, creating a premier whitewater adventure.

Although North Platte outfitters promote the river as an intermediate-level raft trip, narrow Northgate Canyon's steep gradient and boulder-strewn channels contain significant whitewater during late spring and early summer. Several Class III–IV rapids, such as Windy Hole, the Narrows, and Stovepipe, can be very challenging to paddle rafters.

The North Platte's rafting season begins after the snowmelt, when outfitter vehicles can reach the 8,000-foot-elevation Routt Access put-in, and normally lasts until mid-July. While outfitters run many two-day raft trips through the canyon from the Routt Access near Walden to Bennett Peak in Medicine Bow National Forest near Saratoga, Wyoming, a shorter 14-mile (22-km), one-day trip is the most popular. As the mountain waters mellow near the end of the rafting season, many outfitters offer leisurely float trips through the Routt and Medicine Bow national forests in southern Wyoming.

North Platte River Outfitters

A-1 Whitewater
317 Stover St.
Fort Collins, CO 80524
(303) 224–3379

Dvorak's Kayak/Rafting Expeditions
17921 Hwy. 285
Nathrop, CO 81236
(800) 824–3795
(719) 539–6851

Rapid Transit Rafting
P.O. Box 4095
Estes Park, CO 80517
(800) 367–8523
(303) 586–8852

Raven Adventure Trips
P.O. Box 108
Granby, CO 80446
(800) 332–3381
(303) 887–2141

Rocky Mountain Adventures
P.O. Box 1989
Fort Collins, CO 80522
(800) 858–6808
(303) 493–4005

Whitewater Odyssey
P.O. Box 2186
Evergreen, CO 80439
(303) 674–3637

Wilderness Aware
P.O. Box 1550
Buena Vista, CO 81211
(800) 462–7238
(719) 395–2112

BLUE RIVER, COLORADO

Section: Silverthorne to Columbine Landing or Green Mountain Reservoir

Location: Summit County, northwest of Dillon, north-central Colorado

Driving Time: Denver—1.5 hours

Difficulty: Class II–III

Trip Length: 8 miles (13 km)

Trip Options: Paddle raft, oar raft; half-day

Season: May–July

Cost: $25–$50

While much of the Blue River's flow, between its source near Breckenridge and its confluence with the upper Colorado River near Kremmling, has been quieted by the construction of Dillon Dam and Green Mountain Reservoir, rafting is possible from Silverthorne to the reservoir during a few weeks each spring and early summer.

The most popular whitewater stretch is an 8-mile (13-km) run paralleling U.S. Highway 9 from Silverthorne to Columbine Landing about 8 miles upriver from the Green Mountain Reservoir. This run features 6 miles (9.5 km) of rather easy Class I–II whitewater, which can be used as practice for new paddlers for the final 2 miles (3 km) of fairly continuous Class II–III waters.

Morning or afternoon trips on the Blue are convenient for those driving from

Denver or the central-Colorado mountain resorts. Due to the short season and unpredictability of water flows, it is advisable to check with outfitters a day or two prior to scheduled trips.

Blue River Outfitters

The Adventure Company
P.O. Box 3876
Breckenridge, CO 80424
(800) 497–7238
(303) 453–0747

KODI Rafting & Bikes
P.O. Box 1215
Breckenridge, CO 80424
(800) 525–9624
(303) 453–2194

Joni Ellis River Tours
P.O. Box 764
Dillon, CO 80435
(800) 477–0144
(303) 468–1028

Performance Tours
P.O. Box 7305
Breckenridge, CO 80424
(800) 328–7238
(303) 453–0661

Keystone Resort
P.O. Box 38
Keystone, CO 80435
(800) 451–5930
(303) 468–4130

EAGLE RIVER, COLORADO

Sections:	Upper and lower
Location:	Eagle County, near Eagle, north-central Colorado
Driving Time:	Denver—2 hours
Difficulty:	Class III–IV+ (upper); II–III+ (lower)
Trip Length:	Upper—8 miles (13); lower—12 miles (19 km)
Trip Options:	Paddle raft, oar raft; half-day and one day
Season:	May–July
Cost:	$25–$40 half-day; $40–$60 one day

The Eagle River, a free-flowing tributary of the upper Colorado, originates high in the central Rockies' Tennessee Pass, a few miles north of the historic mining town of Leadville. For most of its 60-mile (96-km) northwesterly journey to the Colorado at Dotsero, the Eagle parallels U.S. Highway 24. Its diverse course through narrow canyons, over steep drops, and down Eagle Valley features fine whitewater, peerless alpine scenery, and assorted high-altitude wildlife.

Two excellent whitewater rafting trips are available during the short late-spring and early-summer season. Beginning west of Minturn, the Class III–IV+ upper Eagle offers an exciting half-day ride for adventurous rafters. Immediately downriver, the more popular lower Eagle provides a mellower yet still exciting Class II–III+ whitewater run suitable for families and first-time rafters. Outfitters offer half-day and one-day trips on the lower section, which ends just upriver from the town of Eagle.

Eagle River Outfitters

Colorado River Runs
Star Route, Box 32
Bond, CO 80423
(800) 826–1081
(303) 653–4292

Raftmeister
P.O. Box 1805
Vail, CO 81658
(800) 274–0636
(303) 476–7238

Nova Guides
P.O. Box 2018
Vail, CO 81658
(303) 949–4232

Timberline Tours
P.O. Box 131
Vail, CO 81658
(800) 831–1414
(303) 476–1414

COLORADO RIVER (UPPER), COLORADO

Sections: Gore Canyon and State Bridge
Location: Grand and Eagle counties between Kremmling and Dotsero, north-central Colorado
Driving Time: Denver—2.5 hours
Difficulty: Class II–III+
Trip Length: Lower Gore Canyon to State Bridge—14 miles (22 km); State Bridge to Dotsero—44 miles (70 km)
Trip Options: Paddle raft, oar raft; half-day, one and two days
Season: May–September
Cost: $20–$45 half-day; $30–$60 one day, $100–$150 multiday

The upper stretches of the legendary Colorado River, west of its Rocky Mountain National Park source, feature some of Colorado's finest and most popular beginning-level whitewater trips for families, first-time rafters, and large groups. In the beautiful high forests and steep canyons of the Gore Range, the upper Colorado is rafted and floated for nearly 58 miles (92 km) between Kremmling and Interstate 70 near Dotsero.

Upper Colorado outfitters offer a wide variety of relatively easy raft trips ranging in length from a half-day to three days. The most popular are half-day and one-day family trips on a 14-mile (22-km) Class I–II+ run from the Pumphouse in Lower Gore Canyon past Radium to State Bridge. Multiday trips with overnight camping continue downstream through scenic valleys and ranch lands for as much as 44 miles (70 km). Multiday trips have ample time for relaxing, swimming, hiking, and fishing.

Colorado River (Upper) Outfitters

Colorado River Runs
Star Route, Box 32
Bond, CO 80423
(800) 826–1081
(303) 653–4292

Joni Ellis River Tours
P.O. Box 764
Dillon, CO 80435
(800) 477–0144
(303) 468–1028

Keystone Resort
P.O. Box 38
Keystone, CO 80435
(800) 451–5930
(303) 468–4130

Rapid Transit Rafting
P.O. Box 4095
Estes Park, CO 80517
(800) 367–8523
(303) 586–8852

Mad Adventures
P.O. Box 650
Winter Park, CO 80482
(800) 451–4844
(303) 726–5290

Raven Adventure Trips
P.O. Box 108
Granby, CO 80446
(800) 332–3381
(303) 887–2141

Nova Guides
P.O. Box 2018
Vail, CO 81658
(303) 949–4232

Timberline Tours
P.O. Box 131
Vail, CO 81658
(800) 831–1414
(303) 476–1414

Raftmeister
P.O. Box 1805
Vail, CO 81658
(800) 274–0636
(303) 476–7238

Raft guide demonstrates proper paddle-raft technique during pre-trip orientation.

ROARING FORK RIVER, COLORADO

Sections: Upper and lower
Location: Pitkin, Eagle, and Garfield counties, northwest of Aspen, north-central Colorado
Driving Time: Denver—3 hours
Difficulty: Class III–IV (upper); II–III (lower)
Trip Length: Upper—12 miles (19 km); lower—14 miles (22 km)
Trip Options: Paddle raft, oar raft; half-day, one day
Season: May–July
Cost: $40–$55

The Roaring Fork gives late-spring and early-summer visitors to Aspen and Snowmass a convenient opportunity to experience challenging and exciting whitewater. The 60-mile (96-km) Roaring Fork, which starts near 12,000-foot Independence Pass, drops very quickly down the Rockies to the aspen-forested Roaring Fork Valley. Almost 30 miles (48 km) of its length can be rafted between Aspen and its confluence with the Colorado River at Glenwood Springs.

Outfitters run trips on the upper and lower sections of the Roaring Fork. The more difficult upper-fork trip, from Woody Creek Bridge (about a 15-minute drive northwest of Aspen) to the Frying Pan River, is a fast-flowing Class III–IV half-day run during normal spring runoff. Its numerous rocks and boulders create thrilling mazelike rapids and chutes, such as Toothache and Old Snowmass Hole.

Cemetery Run, the Roaring Fork's milder lower section, extends from Carbondale to the Colorado River at Glenwood Springs. Other than Cemetery Rapids, an exciting Class III stretch, most of its rapids are Class I–II+. Outfitters welcome families with children as young as eight years during summertime low-water runs. Some outfitters combine a portion of the Cemetery Rapids trip with the Colorado River below Glenwood Springs.

Roaring Fork River Outfitters

Blazing Paddles Raft Adventures
P.O. Box 2127
Aspen, CO 81612
(800) 282–7238
(303) 925–5651

Colorado Riff Raft
P.O. Box 4949
Aspen, CO 81612
(800) 759–3939
(303) 925–5405

Rock Gardens Rafting
1308 County Road 129
Glenwood Springs, CO 81601
(303) 945–6737

COLORADO RIVER (GLENWOOD), COLORADO

Sections: Glenwood Canyon and Shoshone Run
Location: Garfield County near Glenwood Springs, north-central Colorado
Driving Time: Denver—3 hours

Difficulty:	Class I–II+ (Glenwood Canyon); Class III–IV+ (Shoshone Run)
Trip Length:	Glenwood Canyon—10 miles (16 km); Shoshone Run—2 miles (3 km)
Trip Options:	Paddle raft, oar raft; half-day and one day
Season:	June–September
Cost:	$40–$50

The most frequently rafted section of the Colorado River is a 10-mile (16-km) stretch paralleled by Interstate 70 near Glenwood Springs in north-central Colorado. During normal summertime water levels, almost anyone older than six may enjoy fairly easy half-day and one-day trips through the spectacular Class II+ Glenwood Canyon above Glenwood Springs. Also available to rafters is the option of continuing an even milder river trip from Glenwood Springs toward New Castle.

Rafting the middle Colorado is very popular with summer visitors to Glenwood Springs. Usually neither reservations nor previous rafting experience are necessary. Several outfitters have sales offices in the vicinity of the town's motels and the popular hot springs.

Glenwood Canyon offers a big-water bonus for teenagers and adults. Just above the Grizzly Creek put-in, the Shoshone section of the Colorado provides rafters with an extra 2 miles (3 km) of action-packed whitewater. Six challenging Class III–IV rapids—including the Superstitions, The Wall, Tombstone, and Maneater—become a dynamic preface to the much-easier waters of the Glenwood Canyon trip that follows. During springtime high waters, outfitters have a sixteen-year age minimum on the Shoshone section.

Colorado River (Glenwood) Outfitters

Blazing Paddles Raft Adventures
P.O. Box 2127
Aspen, CO 81612
(800) 282–7238
(303) 925–5651

Blue Sky Adventures
P.O. Box 1566
Glenwood Springs, CO 81602
(303) 945–6605

Colorado Riff Raft
P.O. Box 4949
Aspen, CO 81612
(800) 759–3939
(303) 925–5405

Raftmeister
P.O. Box 1805
Vail, CO 81658
(800) 274–0636
(303) 476–7238

Rock Gardens Rafting
1308 County Road 129
Glenwood Springs, CO 81601
(303) 945–6737

Timberline Tours
P.O. Box 131
Vail, CO 81658
(800) 831–1414
(303) 476–1414

Whitewater Rafting
P.O. Box 2462
Glenwood Springs, CO 81602
(303) 945–8477

TAYLOR RIVER, COLORADO

Section:	Taylor Park Reservoir to Almont
Location:	Gunnison County, northeast of Gunnison, southwest Colorado
Driving Time:	Grand Junction—2.5 hours
Difficulty:	Class III–IV (upper), I–II (lower)
Trip Length:	5 and 13 miles (8 and 21 km) or less
Trip Options:	Paddle raft, oar raft; half-day and one day
Season:	May–September
Cost:	$25–$30 half-day; $55–$60 one day

The Taylor River, which meets the East River at Almont to create the upper Gunnison River, has carved one of Colorado's most impressive alpine canyons. Large herds of elk and bighorn sheep that winter in the Almont Triangle Game Refuge are often seen from the river in the spring.

Water releases from Taylor Park Reservoir generally permit sufficient water for rafting throughout the summer. The Class III–IV rapids of the Taylor's forested upper section—The Slot, Sneaky Pete's, Generator Alley, The Squeeze, and Suckhole—start below Lottis, some 4 miles (6.5 km) below the dam. The narrow channel and regulated flow create an excellent whitewater run.

Downstream, the easier Class I–II lower Taylor between Harmels and Almont is an ideal river adventure for families and first-time rafters. Outfitters offering half-day trips on the lower Taylor will accommodate rafters of any age.

Outfitters listed on page 110.

GUNNISON RIVER (UPPER), COLORADO

Section:	Almont
Location:	Gunnison County, north of Gunnison, southwest Colorado
Driving Time:	Grand Junction—2.5 hours; Colorado Springs—3 hours
Difficulty:	Class I–II
Trip Length:	10 miles (16 km)
Trip Options:	Paddle raft, oar raft; half-day
Season:	May–September
Cost:	$12–$18 half-day

The upper Gunnison River, created by the merger of the Taylor and East rivers, offers very easy Class I–II waters just north of Gunnison. The river, which parallels Colorado Route 135 from Almont to Gunnison, passes through farmlands and rolling hills graced with large cottonwood trees.

Although outfitters promote the upper Gunnison as an ideal introductory trip for seniors and families with young children, everyone will enjoy the pastoral beauty of the Gunnison Valley.

Outfitters listed on page 110.

GUNNISON RIVER (LAKE FORK), COLORADO

Section:	Lower canyons
Location:	Hinsdale and Gunnison counties, north of Lake City, southwest Colorado

Driving Time:	Grand Junction—2.5 hours
Difficulty:	Class III–IV+; paddle rafting experience is recommended
Trip Length:	16 miles (26 km)
Trip Options:	Paddle raft; one day
Season:	May–July
Cost:	$65

The Lake Fork, one of the Gunnison's many fine tributaries, offers superb whitewater just south of the Curecanti National Recreation Area near Gunnison. Spring runoff on the Lake Fork of the Gunnison River, which flows northward out of the San Juan Mountains, generates fair technical whitewater—dropping at a rate of 50 feet per mile—through spectacular canyons as it makes its final descent to the quiet waters of the Blue Mesa Reservoir. Surprise—Big Drop and Rattlesnake are just a few of the many rapids that will challenge all paddle rafters.

Because of the swiftness of the Lake Fork flow, outfitters offer the same 8-mile (13-km) trip twice in one day. Immediately after lunch, rafters are shuttled back to the original put-in to begin a second run.

Outfitters prefer that customers have previous experience and are at least twelve years old.

Taylor River and Gunnison River (Upper and Lake Fork) Outfitters

Scenic River Tours
703 W. Tomichi
Gunnison, CO 81230
(303) 641–3131

Three Rivers Outfitting
P.O. Box 339
Almont, CO 81210
(303) 641–1303

GUNNISON RIVER (GORGE), COLORADO

Section:	Gunnison Gorge
Location:	Montrose and Delta counties, north of Black Canyon of the Gunnison National Monument, southwest Colorado
Driving Time:	Grand Junction—1 hour
Difficulty:	Class II–III+
Trip Length:	14 miles (22 km)
Trip Options:	Paddle raft, oar raft; one to three days
Season:	May–September
Cost:	$125 one day; $285–$315 two days; $450–$475 three days

Southwest Colorado's Gunnison Gorge, immediately below Black Canyon of the Gunnison National Monument, is one of the state's finest wilderness river trips. The mood for the remote river adventure is set before the trip begins. Access to the gorge put-in is a 1-mile (1.5-km) hike from Chucker Trailhead down a side canyon. Pack horses carry the rafting equipment to the river.

The outstanding characteristics of the gorge are its magnificent canyon scenery, abundant wildlife, and fine whitewater. The canyon's sheer basalt and granite walls, although not as high as those of Black Canyon, are impressive. Peregrine falcons, bald eagles, bighorn sheep, ringtail cats, marmots, and river otters are part of the wildlife that inhabits Gunnison Gorge. The first 11 miles (18 km) of the 14-mile (22-km) gorge are interspersed with a number of fine Class III rapids, including Cable, The Squeeze, The Drops, and The Hall of the River King.

While the Gunnison Gorge can easily be rafted in a day, its pristine scenery, interesting side-canyon hiking, and excellent fishing are good reasons to make it a two- or three-day trip.

Gunnison River (Gorge) Outfitters

Dvorak's Kayak/Rafting Expeditions
17921 Hwy. 285
Nathrop, CO 81236
(800) 824-3795
(719) 539-6851

Telluride Outside
P.O. Box 685
Telluride, CO 81435
(800) 831-6230
(303) 728-3895

Gunnison River Expeditions
P.O. Box 315
Montrose, CO 81419
(303) 249-4441

Wilderness Aware
P.O. Box 1550
Buena Vista, CO 81211
(800) 462-7238
(719) 395-2112

SAN JUAN RIVER (UPPER), COLORADO

Section: Mesa Canyon
Location: Archuleta County, south of Pagosa Springs, southwest Colorado
Driving Time: Albuquerque—4 hours
Difficulty: Class I–III
Trip Length: 8 miles (13 km)
Trip Options: Paddle raft, oar raft; half-day
Season: Mid-April–June
Cost: $50–$55

The upper San Juan River's Mesa Canyon offers late spring and early summer vacationers in southwest Colorado an opportunity to experience small to moderate (Class I–III) whitewater rapids in a scenic wilderness environment. Most of the river trip is within the San Juan National Forest and the Southern Ute Indian Reservation.

Much of the emphasis of the Mesa Canyon river trip is on the scenic beauty of the wilderness area. As rafters float through mixed cottonwood and pine forests, they often see golden eagles, deer, elk, beavers, and bear. Bird-watchers are encourged to bring binoculars, as many side canyons are available for short hikes. Both morning and afternoon rafting trips are available.

Section: Montezuma Canyon
Location: Archuleta County, south of Pagosa Springs, southwest Colorado
Driving Time: Albuquerque—4 hours
Difficulty: Class I–II
Trip Length: 14 miles (22 km)

Trip Options: Paddle raft, oar raft; one day
Season: July–August
Cost: $63–$68

After the early summer waters of the upper San Juan River's Mesa Canyon become too low for rafting, raft trips are offered through Montezuma Canyon. Here, even easier Class I–II rapids enable virtually everyone a safe and enjoyable river float trip.

In addition to the scenic wilderness beauty of Montezuma Canyon, rafters will enjoy the historic abandoned railroad, ghost towns, and old homesteads of this area. There is ample time for swimming, relaxation, and hiking into one or more side canyons.

San Juan River (Upper) Outfitter

Pagosa Rafting Outfitters
P.O. Box 222
Pagosa Springs, CO 81147
(303) 731–4081

PIEDRA RIVER, COLORADO

Sections: Upper and lower box canyons
Location: Hinsdale and Archuleta counties between Pagosa Springs and Durango, southwest Colorado
Driving Time: Albuquerque—4 hours
Difficulty: Class IV–V; Class IV paddle rafting experience highly recommended
Trip Length: 22 miles (35 km)
Trip Options: Paddle raft, oar raft; one and two days
Season: May–July
Cost: $120–$130 one day; $250–$350 two days

The Piedra River, in southwest Colorado's San Juan Mountains, is one of the state's finest alpine rivers. Historically referred to as the "River of the Rock Wall," the Piedra is a very demanding river adventure. It should be considered only by experienced, physically fit rafters.

The Piedra's very narrow and steep upper and lower box canyons create several very technical Class IV-V drops. Outfitters normally run the 22-mile (35-km) Piedra raft trip in two days or a 14-mile (22-km) trip in one day. Its alpine mountain waters are always cold, and helmets and wet suits are required. Most trips include shuttles between the river and Durango or Pagosa Springs.

Animals including elk, mule deer, black bears, river otters, and the endangered peregrine falcon are frequently seen along the river's forested banks.

Piedra River Outfitters

Echo Canyon River Expeditions
45000 U.S. Hwy. 50 West
Canon City, CO 81212
(800) 748–2953
(719) 275–3154

Mountain Waters Rafting
P.O. Box 2681
Durango, CO 81302–2681
(800) 748–2507
(303) 259–4191

Pagosa Rafting Outfitters
P.O. Box 222
Pagosa Springs, CO 81147
(303) 731–4081

Peregrine River Outfitters
64 Ptarmigan Lane
Durango, CO 81301
(303) 385–7600

Wilderness Aware
P.O. Box 1550
Buena Vista, CO 81211
(800) 462–7238
(719) 395–2112

ANIMAS RIVER (UPPER), COLORADO

Section:	Upper
Location:	San Juan County, between Silverton and Durango, southwest Colorado
Driving Time:	Albuquerque—4 hours; Grand Junction—4 hours
Difficulty:	Class IV–V; paddle rafting experience highly recommended
Trip Length:	26 miles (42 km)
Trip Options:	Paddle raft, oar raft; two and three days
Season:	May–July
Cost:	$280–$320 (includes train ride from Durango); $400–$450 three days

The Animas River, located high in the snowcapped San Juan Mountains of southwest Colorado between Silverton and Durango, provides a challenging alpine whitewater trip for advanced paddlers and a relatively easy stretch for families and first-time rafters.

The upper Animas River, in southwest Colorado, is an exceptional alpine raft experience that includes outstanding whitewater and mountain scenery. Its southward course, which begins at Mineral Creek just outside the historic mining town of Silverton (elevation 9,230 feet), parallels the Durango and Silverton Narrow Gauge Railroad south for 26 miles (42 km).

During this exciting canyon course, the Animas drops an average of 85 feet per mile through dozens of Class III–IV and several Class V rapids. The intensity of the whitewater does not give the paddler much time to fully appreciate all of the many remnant footbridges, abandoned cabins, and spectacular views of the 13,000-foot mountain peaks.

The river trip ends in a unique manner near the small town of Rockwood. Outfitters have arranged with the Durango and Silverton Railroad to shuttle rafters and equipment to Durango on the afternoon train. Some outfitters also promote a three-day trip that includes a horseback ride through Cascade Canyon in the Weminuche Wilderness Area.

Because of the high altitude, rafting on the upper Animas normally does not begin until late May or early June. All outfitters require rafters to have paddled Class IV technical whitewater. Wet suits and helmets are always mandatory, and rafters must be at least sixteen years old.

Animas River (Upper) Outfitters

American Adventure Expeditions
P.O. Box 1549
Buena Vista, CO 81211
(800) 288–0675
(719) 395–2409

Mountain Waters Rafting
P.O. Box 2681
Durango, CO 81302–2681
(800) 748–2507
(303) 259–4191

Pagosa Rafting Outfitters
P.O. Box 222
Pagosa, CO 81147
(303) 731–4081

Peregrine River Outfitters
64 Ptarmigan Lane
Durango, CO 81301
(303) 385–7600

Telluride Outside
P.O. Box 685
Telluride, CO 81435
(800) 831–6230
(303) 728–3895

ANIMAS RIVER (LOWER), COLORADO

Section: Lower
Location: Durango, La Plata County, southwest Colorado
Driving Time: Albuquerque—4 hours, Grand Junction—4 hours
Difficulty: Class I–II, III
Trip Length: 5-12 miles (8-19 km)
Trip Options: Paddle raft, oar raft; one hour, two hours, half-day, and one day
Season: May–August
Cost: $10 one hour; $15–$25 two hours; $20–$30 half-day; $35–$45 one day

The lower Animas River offers an easy introduction to whitewater rafting. Animas River trips begin in downtown Durango, just a few blocks from the Durango-to-Silverton railroad station.

Class III Smelter Rapids, the largest rapid on the lower Animas, comes after a relaxing 2 miles (3 km) of Class I–II whitewater on the south side of Durango. As the raft trip proceeds south toward the Southern Ute Indian Reservation, old mine ruins, panoramic views of the southern Rockies, and occasional glimpses of wildlife add a long-remembered dimension to the family vacation.

Daily between Memorial Day and Labor Day, outfitters operate one- and two-hour trips and half-day and one-day excursions on the Animas. Although outfitter brochures recommend advance reservations, same-day raft trips are almost always possible. (Some outfitters have kiosks in Durango.) During summer's low-water levels, the Animas is an excellent rafting experience for families with young children.

Animas River (Lower) Outfitters

American Adventure Expeditions
P.O. Box 1549
Buena Vista, CO 81211
(800) 288–0675
(719) 395–2409

Durango Rivertrippers
720 Main Ave.
Durango, CO 81301
(303) 259–0289

Flexible Flyers
2344 C.R. 225
Durango, CO 81301
(303) 247–4628

Mountain Waters Rafting
P.O. Box 2681
Durango, CO 81302–2681
(800) 748–2507
(303) 259–4191

SAN MIGUEL RIVER, COLORADO

Section:	Placerville to Naturita Power Plant
Location:	San Miguel and Montrose counties, northwest of Telluride, southwest Colorado
Driving Time:	Grand Junction—3 hours
Difficulty:	Class II–III
Trip Length:	7 and 14 miles (11 and 22 km)
Trip Options:	Paddle raft, oar raft; half-day and one day
Season:	May–July
Cost:	$50 half-day; $90 one day

The San Miguel River, a major tributary of the Dolores River, starts high in the San Juan Mountains near the popular resort town of Telluride and flows northwest, without any major falls or rapids, to the Dolores some 70 miles (112 km) downstream. The constant dropping creates fairly continuous Class II–III whitewater action. Rafters are asked to help paddle the oar-guided raft when technical manuevers are required.

Most half- and one-day rafting trips begin below Placerville, some 25 miles (40 km) northwest of Telluride. Each morning and afternoon from late May until mid-August, virtually the whole family can enjoy the easy 7-mile (11-km) Class II–III trip. For those who want a longer river experience, a 14-mile (22-km), one-day trip that continues through the wilderness of Norwood Canyon is also available.

Wildlife along the San Miguel are plentiful. Guests are frequently treated to sights of eagles, hawks, dippers, Steller's jays, bears, deer, and elk.

San Miguel River Outfitter

Telluride Outside
P.O. Box 685
Telluride, CO 81435
(800) 831–6230
(303) 728–3895

DOLORES RIVER, COLORADO/UTAH

Sections:	Desert canyons
Location:	Montezuma, Dolores, San Miguel, Montrose and Mesa counties, southwest Colorado; Grand County, eastern Utah
Driving Time:	Grand Junction—3.5 hours
Difficulty:	Class II–III, IV
Trip Length:	185 miles (296 km) and less
Trip Options:	Paddle raft, oar raft, inflatable kayak; one to six days
Season:	April–June
Cost:	$70–$100 per day

In Colorado's southwest corner, the Dolores River flows southwest from the high San Juan Mountains before meandering north through impressive high-desert slickrock canyons before it meets the Colorado River northeast of Moab, Utah. The entire 185-mile (296-km) Dolores trip is the third longest multiday rafting adventure, after the Grand Canyon Colorado River and Texas Rio Grande River, in the Lower 48 states. Each spring, outfitters run a variety of multiday oar and paddle-raft trips through one or more of the five scenic desert-canyon sections: Ponderosa Gorge, Slickrock Canyon, Paradox Valley, Mesa Canyon, and Lower Gateway.

Ponderosa Gorge and Slickrock Canyon, the first two canyons, are the most commonly run stretches of the Dolores. Both are located in a semialpine transition zone between the San Juan Mountains and the Colorado plateau, below McPhee Dam. Ponderosa Gorge has the most difficult whitewater on the Delores, including the legendary Snaggletooth.

Most outfitters agree that the 58-mile (93-km) Slickrock Canyon section, between the towns of Slick Rock and Bedrock, is the most spectacular of the river's canyons. Its relatively easy Class II–III waters are overwhelmed by towering slickrock walls. Many grottoes and side canyons are garnished with magnificent prehistoric Indian pictographs.

Between Bedrock and Gateway, several Class II–III rapids provide ample time to relax and enjoy the diverse 45-mile (72-km) Paradox Valley and Mesa Canyon. After its confluence with the San Miguel River, the Dolores nearly doubles in size. At the rivers' confluence, the remnants of a decades-old hanging flume, which was used to transport water to the Lone Tree placer mine, can be seen nearly four hundred feet above the river.

Lower Gateway Canyon, the 30-mile (48-km) section of the Dolores before it meets the Colorado River in Utah, has both good whitewater and inspiring desert scenery. Stateline Rapid, a long and technical Class IV, is the highlight after many Class II–III rapids. Indian petroglyphs and pictographs adorn the canyon walls.

Dolores River Outfitters

Buffalo Joe River Trips
P.O. Box 1526
Buena Vista, CO 81211
(800) 356–7984
(719) 395–8757

Dvorak's Kayak/Rafting Expeditions
17921 Highway 285
Nathrop, CO 81236
(800) 824–3795
(719) 539–6851

O.A.R.S.
P.O. Box 67
Angels Camp, CA 95222
(800) 346–6277
(209) 736–4677

Rocky Mountain Adventures
P.O. Box 1989
Fort Collins, CO 80522
(800) 858–6808
(303) 493–4005

Peregrine River Outfitters
64 Ptarmigan Lane
Durango, CO 81301
(303) 385–7600

Telluride Outside
P.O. Box 685
Telluride, CO 81435
(800) 831–6230
(303) 728–3895

Wilderness Aware
P.O. Box 1550
Buena Vista, CO 81211
(800) 462–7238
(719) 395–2112

YAMPA AND GREEN RIVERS, COLORADO/UTAH

Section:	Dinosaur National Monument
Location:	Moffat County, within Dinosaur National Monument, northwest Colorado; Uintah County, northeast Utah
Driving Time:	Grand Junction—2.5 hours
Difficulty:	Class II–IV
Trip Length:	72 miles (115 km)
Trip Options:	Paddle raft, oar raft; three to five days
Season:	May–June
Cost:	$330–$600

The Yampa River rafting trip in Dinosaur National Monument is one of only two multiday trips that begin and end within a national park or monument in the Lower 48 states. For 46 miles (74 km) from its put-in at Deerlodge Park to its confluence with the Green River near Echo Park, the free-flowing Yampa River carves its way through spectacular 2,000-foot deep white Weber canyons.

Because of the premier beauty of the Dinosaur canyons, professional outfitters generally continue Yampa raft trips for 26 miles (42 km) onto the Green River and float an additional one to three days through Whirlpool Canyon and Split Mountain Gorge in the Utah portion of the national monument.

The Yampa is Colorado's last undammed major river. Its whitewater is best during May and June when its channel is swollen with runoff from upstream tributaries. During this time many Class III–IV rapids—such as Teepee, Big Joe, and the much-heralded Grand Canyon-size Warm Springs—are at their prime. More than sixty notable rapids challenge and delight Yampa rafters.

Rafters on the Yampa should allow an extra day either before or after their trip to visit the Dinosaur Quarry near Jensen at the southwest entrance to Dinosaur National Monument.

Sections:	Lodore Canyon, Whirlpool Canyon, and Split Mountain Gorge
Location:	Moffat County, northwest Colorado; and Uintah County near Vernal, northeast Utah
Difficulty:	Class II–III+ (Lodore Canyon); I–II (Whirlpool Canyon); II–III (Split Mountain Gorge)
Trip Length:	45 miles (72 km)
Trip Options:	Paddle raft, oar raft, inflatable kayak; three to five days (one day at Split Mountain Gorge)
Season:	May–September
Cost:	$400–$600 multiday; $45–$55 one day Split Mountain Gorge trip

Dinosaur National Monument's Green River provides 45 miles (72 km) of rafting through three magnificent canyons: Lodore, Whirlpool, and Split Mountain. Three- to five-day trips through the canyons afford rafters of almost any age the opportunity to enjoy the river's magnificent canyon scenery, wildlife, and relatively easy whitewater.

Green River rafting begins at the Lodore Ranger Station at the monument's north boundary. Shortly after put-in, the brilliant pre-Cambrian red sandstone walls of Lodore Canyon, called the Gates of Lodore, rise to nearly 2,500 feet as the river dramatically cuts through the Uintah Mountains. Most of Lodore's exciting Class II–III+ rapids—Disaster Falls, Triplet Falls, and Hells Half Mile—were named by John Wesley Powell and his brave explorers in 1869. Hikes into Lodore's interesting side canyons—Winnie Grotto, Rippling Brook, and Pot Creek—permit a close-up examination of Freemont Indian pictographs.

Immediately downriver from Lodore is Whirlpool Canyon, where the Green crosses from Colorado back into Utah. This colorful canyon, which begins at the Mitten Park Fault, south of Harpers Corner, is one of the monument's most beautiful canyons. Its easy whitewater (Class I–II) has recently become a favorite of disabled rafters.

Following Whirlpool is Split Mountain Gorge. In recent years this scenic canyon has become a very popular one-day rafting adventure. The 9.5-mile (14.5-km) passage through the gorge near Vernal, Utah, gives families, first-timers, and experienced rafters an excellent occasion to enjoy relatively easy whitewater in one of the Southwest's most impressive canyons.

Water releases from Flaming Gorge Dam normally permit outfitters to run trips through Dinosaur's canyons until late September. At most water levels outfitters allow teenage and adult rafters to choose between oar and paddle rafts or inflatable kayaks. Swimming in a few of the Green's rapids is also permitted.

Yampa and Green River Outfitters

Adrift Adventures
P.O. Box 192
Jensen, UT 84035
(800) 824–0150
(801) 789–3600

ARTA River Trips
Star Route 73
Groveland, CA 95321
(800) 323–2782
(209) 962–7873

Adventure Bound River Expeditions
2392 H Road
Grand Junction, CO 81505
(800) 423–4668
(303) 241–5633

Dinosaur River Expeditions
P.O. Box 3387
Park City, UT 84060
(800) 247–6197
(801) 649–8092

Don Hatch River Expeditions
P.O. Box 1150
Vernal, UT 84078
(800) 342–8243
(801) 789–4316

Holiday River Expeditions
544 East 3900 South
Salt Lake City, UT 84107
(800) 624–6323
(801) 266–2087

S'Plore
27 West 3300 South
Salt Lake City, UT 84115
(801) 481–4128

The Grand Canyon of the Colorado River is the grandest of all river trips. Photo by John Blaustein.

CHAPTER 12

■ ■ ■

Southwest States

America's Southwest States—Utah, Arizona, New Mexico, and Texas—are world famous for their unsurpassed canyonland beauty. Today, whitewater rafting provides access to these sandstone canyons, granite and basalt gorges, and arid deserts that previously could be seen only from overlooks and aircraft. The Southwest's menu of guided rafting adventures includes half-day, one-day, and multiday raft trips suitable for both the adventurous and the timid, the old and the young, and the disabled.

Utah's whitewater rafting trips are found on the middle Colorado and two of its tributaries, the Green and San Juan. Green River rafting trips through Dinosaur National Monument (see the Yampa and Green rivers in the Colorado chapter) and Desolation Canyon traverse some of the most rugged and unusual landscape in the United States. The Desolation-Gray canyons trip is a classic multiday adventure for anyone wanting superb scenery and nonintimidating whitewater. The final stretches of the San Juan River, in southeast Utah, contain unusual and colorful geologic formations and fairly easy rapids.

Middle Colorado River outfitters offer one- and two-day trips through the big waters of the impressive Westwater Canyon, popular one-day family trips in the Professor Valley-Fisher Towers canyons adjacent to Arches National Park, and multiday excursions through spectacular Canyonlands National Park.

Arizona's Grand Canyon of the Colorado rafting adventure is one of the grandest wilderness river experiences in the world. Some of the canyon's outfitters report that their trips are sold out a year or more in advance.

Some of the Southwest's lesser-known rafting trips are through the semiarid and arid lands of Arizona, New Mexico, and Texas. Central Arizona's Salt and Verde rivers offer late-winter and early-spring trips that often coincide with northward bird migrations.

New Mexico's three whitewater opportunities are located in the wild and scenic canyons near the charming old western town of Taos. One is a multiday trip through the Rio Chama's red and yellow sandstone canyons celebrated in the art of Georgia O'Keeffe. The second provides one- or two-day trips on the dynamic Class III–IV rapids of the Rio Grande's 800-foot-deep Taos Box. The third is the popular family Rio Grande trip on the Pilar, or Racecourse, section.

In Texas, year-round rafting on the Rio Grande, through the towering canyons of Big Bend National Park, is possible for nearly 300 miles (480 km) along the United States–Mexico border.

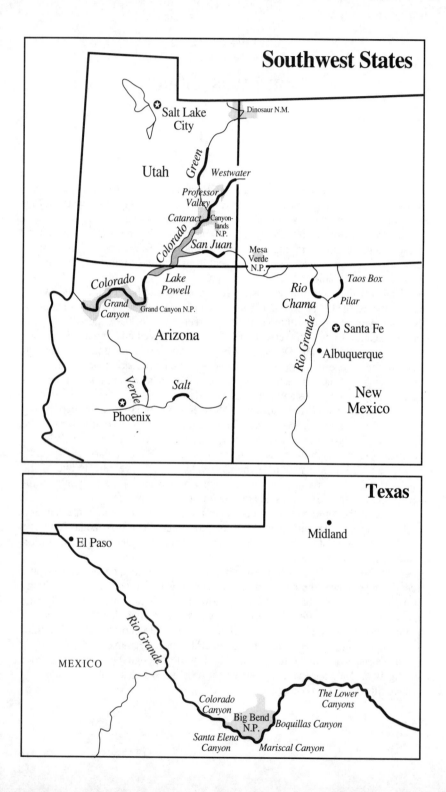

Southwest States
River Comparison

	Difficulty	Min. Age	H	D	M	Season	P	O	K	D	M
Utah											
Green	/	5			X	Apr–Oct	X	X	X		
Colorado (Westwater)	/ /	12		X	X	May–Sep	X	X	X		
Colorado (Cataract)	/ /	12			X	Apr–Oct	X	X			X
Colorado (Professor Valley)	/	5	X	X	X	May–Oct	X	X			
San Juan	/ /	10		X	X	Apr–Sep	X	X	X		
Arizona											
Colorado (Grand Canyon)	/ /	10			X	Apr–Oct	X	X		X	X
Salt	/ /	10		X	X	Feb–May	X	X	X		
Verde	/	10		X	X	Jan–Apr	X	X	X		
New Mexico											
Rio Chama	/	8			X	Apr–Aug	X	X			
Rio Grande											
Taos Box	/ /	12		X		Apr–Aug	X	X			
Pilar	/	6	X			Apr–Jul	X	X			
Texas											
Rio Grande (Big Bend)											
Colorado Canyon	/	4	X	X		Year-round	X	X			
Big Bend Canyons	/ /	5	X	X		Year-round	X	X			
Lower Canyons	/	6		X		Year-round	X	X			

/   Beginner—Easy whitewater. Fun for everyone.

/ /   Intermediate—Moderate whitewater.
    No previous rafting experience is necessary.

/ / /   Advanced—Difficult whitewater.
    Previous Class IV paddle rafting experience is recommended or required.

    H—Half-Day Trip, D—Day Trip, M—Multiday Trip
    P—Paddle Raft, O—Oar Raft, K—Inflatable Kayak, D—Dory,
      M—Motorized Raft

GREEN RIVER, UTAH

Section:	Desolation and Gray canyons
Location:	Uintah and Grand counties, east-central Utah
Driving Time:	Grand Junction—2 hours; Salt Lake City—3 hours
Difficulty:	Class II–III
Trip Length:	94 miles (150 km)
Trip Options:	Paddle raft, oar raft, inflatable kayak; three to six days
Season:	April–October
Cost:	$350–$800

In east-central Utah, less than 100 miles (160 km) downriver from Dinosaur National Monument, the Green River traverses two remote and beautiful wildernesses—Desolation and Gray canyons. These canyons, rich in ancient Indian art and abandoned homesteads, are vividly described in the journals of John Wesley Powell. Desolation Canyon is the only western river canyon to be listed as a Registered National Historic Landmark.

The Green is one of the Southwest's best rivers for learning basic boating skills in rafts or inflatable kayaks. None of its more than sixty Class II–III rapids are technically difficult. The river's rapids gradually increase in difficulty from rolling waves to rapids, such as Three Fords, Steer Ridge, and Coal Creek.

The relaxed pace of the Green River itinerary, and its enchanting environment, has prompted a number of special excursions, such as professional instructional seminars, gourmet meals, and concerts. Its relatively easy waters and sandy beaches have also made the Green a popular river for disabled rafters.

Outfitters listed on pages 125–126.

COLORADO RIVER (WESTWATER), UTAH

Section:	Westwater Canyon
Location:	Grand County, northeast of Moab, eastern Utah
Driving Time:	Grand Junction—1.5 hours; Salt Lake City—4 hours
Difficulty:	Class III–IV
Trip Length:	17-40 miles (27-64 km)
Trip Options:	Paddle raft, oar raft, motorized raft; one, two, and three days
Season:	May–September
Cost:	$100; $225–$300 two days; $375–$450 three days

Utah vacationers who want to experience a one- or two-day big-water raft trip in a beautiful Southwest canyon will find there is none better than the middle Colorado's Westwater. The diversity of Westwater's breathtaking sandstone and granite canyon walls and the challenge of its exciting whitewater make it one of the Southwest's classic short river trips. Eleven Class III–IV+ (Class V in high water) rapids, including Funnel Falls, The Steps, Last Chance, and Skull in the narrow Black Granite Gorge, excite both novice and experienced rafters.

Two-day trips, with overnight camping, are the most common Westwater excursion. The Bureau of Land Management does issue permits for a 17-mile (27-km) one-day trip to a limited number of outfitters. Westwater Canyon is located in eastern Utah's canyonlands, midway between Grand Junction, Colorado, and Moab, Utah.

Three-day trips on the middle Colorado begin with Horsethief and Ruby canyons downriver from Loma, Colorado. On this 25-mile (40-km) stretch, there is ample time to admire the river's spectacular sandstone canyon walls, explore its side canyons, or relax on its sandy beaches.

Outfitters listed on pages 125–126.

COLORADO RIVER (CATARACT), UTAH

Section:	Cataract Canyon
Location:	Garfield, Wayne, and San Juan counties, Canyonlands National Park, southeast Utah
Driving Time:	Grand Junction—2 hours; Salt Lake City—4 hours
Difficulty:	Class III–V
Trip Length:	96 miles (154 km) or less
Trip Options:	Paddle raft, oar raft, motorized raft; three to six days
Season:	April–October
Cost:	$450–$800

The Colorado River's Cataract Canyon, in spectacular Canyonlands National Park, offers a combination of relaxed floating and awesome whitewater that has changed little since it was first navigated and explored by John Wesley Powell in 1869.

While it is possible to reach Cataract through the scenic sandstone chasms of Labyrinth and Stillwater canyons on the Green River, outfitters put in for the Cataract trip on the middle Colorado, a few miles downstream from Moab. The first two or three days of the Cataract trip provide ample leisure time to enjoy the many cliff dwellings and petroglyphs of the ancient Anasazi Indian culture. There also are opportunities to hike, swim, fish, photograph, stare at the impressive canyon walls, or just do nothing.

Cataract's whitewater begins 4 miles (6.5 km) downstream from the confluence of the Green and Colorado rivers, deep within Canyonlands National Park. Hereafter, 26 major Class IV-V rapids, including Brown Betty, Mile Long, and The Big Drops—Little Niagara and Satan's Gut—excite rafters before they reach the quiet waters of Lake Powell above Glen Canyon Dam. In the spring, some of Cataract's rapids are larger than those of the Grand Canyon.

Although Canyonlands may not look hospitable to wildlife, flourishing in the arid habitat are desert bighorn sheep, mule deer, golden eagles, great horned owls, hawks, ravens, desert foxes, coyotes, bobcats, whiptail lizards, and kangaroo rats.

Green River and Colorado River (Westwater and Cataract) Outfitters

Adventure Bound River Expeditions
2392 H Road
Grand Junction, CO 81505
(800) 423–4668
(303) 241–5633

Adventure River Expeditions
P.O. Box 2133
Salt Lake City, UT 84110–2133
(800) 331–3324
(801) 943–0320

Holiday River Expeditions
544 East 3900 South
Salt Lake City, UT 84107
(800) 624–6323
(801) 266–2087

Western River Expeditions
7258 Racquet Club Dr.
Salt Lake City, UT 84121
(800) 453–7450
(801) 942–6669

Moki Mac River Expeditions
P.O. Box 21242
Salt Lake City, UT 84121
(800) 284–7280
(801) 268–6667

World Wide River Expeditions
153 East 7200 South
Midvale, UT 84047
(800) 231–2769
(801) 566–2662

Sheri Griffith River Expeditions
P.O. Box 1324
Moab, UT 84532
(800) 332–2439
(801) 259–8229

COLORADO RIVER (PROFESSOR VALLEY), UTAH

Section: Professor Valley
Location: Grand County, north of Moab, eastern Utah
Driving Time: Grand Junction—2 hours; Salt Lake City—4 hours
Difficulty: Class I–II+
Trip Length: 30 miles (48 km) or less
Trip Options: Paddle raft, oar raft, inflatable kayak; half-day, one and two days
Season: May–October
Cost: $25–$40

Professor Valley, or Fisher Towers, one of the middle Colorado's more scenic river stretches, is also one of its easiest. Its mild waters and proximity to Moab and to Canyonlands and Arches national parks make it a favorite half-, one- or two-day raft trip for children's groups, families, senior citizens, and persons with disabilities.

The Colorado flows gently through 30 miles (48 km) of red slickrock canyons, including the delicate spires and chimneys of Fisher Towers and the red buttes of Professor and Castle valleys. Rafters often see eagles, red-tailed hawks, deer, coyotes and desert foxes.

Colorado River (Professor Valley) Outfitters

Canyon Voyages
P.O. Box 416
Moab, UT 84532
(800) 488–5884
(801) 259–6007

Holiday River Expeditions
544 East 3900 South
Salt Lake City, UT 84107
(800) 624–6323
(801) 266–2087

North American River Expeditions
543 N. Main St.
Moab, UT 84532
(801) 259–5865

World Wide River Expeditions
153 East 7200 South
Midvale, UT 84047
(800) 231–2769
(801) 566–2662

Western River Expeditions
7258 Racquet Club Dr.
Salt Lake City, UT 84121
(800) 453–7450
(801) 942–6669

SAN JUAN RIVER, UTAH

Section:	Bluff to Lake Powell
Location:	San Juan County Utah near Bluff and Mexican Hat, southeast Utah
Driving Time:	Albuquerque—5.0 hours; Grand Junction—4 hours
Difficulty:	Class I–III
Trip Length:	84 miles (134 km) or less
Trip Options:	Paddle raft, oar raft, inflatable kayak; one, two, three, four, and six days
Season:	April–September
Cost:	$55–$75 one day; $200–$300 two days; $330–$650 three to five days

The San Juan River, a major tributary of the Colorado, has some of the Southwest's most unusual and beautiful geologic formations and some of its best Indian rock art and ruins. Its entire channel from Bluff to Lake Powell parallels the northern boundary of the huge Navajo Indian Reservation.

The first day or two of the four-to-six-day San Juan trip are spent leisurely floating the river's upper section between Bluff and Mexican Hat. After Mexican Hat, the lower San Juan passes through the Goosenecks, a deep, narrow canyon with towering walls of limestone, shale, and colorful sandstone.

Many veteran river runners claim that mile-for-mile the San Juan has more geologic diversity, Indian rock art, ancient ruins, and fossil outcrops than any other river in the West. The river's banks and side canyons have long been popular gathering places for anthropologists, archaeologists, geologists, photographers, and canyon lovers.

The San Juan's whitewater is fun, but not difficult. While paddle and oar rafts have long been the standard conveyance, many outfitters now encourage customers to navigate the river independently with inflatable kayaks and Sportyaks.

San Juan rafting usually runs from April until September or early October. In addition to the full Bluff to Lake Powell trip, outfitters also offer one- and two-day upper-canyon trips from Bluff to Mexican Hat and three- to five-day trips from Mexican Hat to Lake Powell.

San Juan River Outfitters

Adventure/Discovery Tours
403 W. Birch
Flagstaff, AZ 86001
(602) 774–1926

Arizona Raft Adventures
4050 E. Huntington Dr.
Flagstaff, AZ 86004
(800) 786–7238
(602) 526–8200

Holiday River Expeditions
544 East 3900 South
Salt Lake City, UT 84107
(800) 624–6323
(801) 266–2087

O.A.R.S.
P.O. Box 67
Angels Camp, CA 95222
(800) 346–6277
(209) 736–4677

Wild Rivers Expeditions
P.O. Box 118
Bluff, UT 84512
(800) 422–7654
(801) 672–2244

COLORADO RIVER (GRAND CANYON), ARIZONA

Sections: Lee's Ferry to Diamond Creek or Lake Mead
Location: Marble Canyon National Monument and Grand Canyon National Park, northern Arizona
Driving Time: Phoenix—4.5 hours
Difficulty: Class II–V
Trip Length: 87 to 225 miles (139–360 km)
Trip Options: Paddle raft, oar raft, motorized raft, dory; four to eighteen days
Season: April–October
Cost: $1,000–$2,000

Little has changed in the century and a quarter since John Wesley Powell and his brave companions first floated the Grand Canyon. Its sandstone and basalt walls render the same red, yellow, black, and brown hues; its turbulent waters, while less silt-laden because of the dams, are just as thrilling and exciting.

Between the placid waters of lakes Powell and Mead, the Grand Canyon has more than two hundred exciting and wild Class II, III, IV, and V rapids. Its powerful and technical Lava Falls and Crystal Rapids, rated two of the finest whitewater drops anywhere, capture the imagination of rafters and guides long before and after every river trip.

A Grand Canyon rafting experience includes much more than plunging through its rapids. On most trips only about four to five hours a day are spent on the river. Equal or greater time is available for exploring its colorful side canyons. Stops of varying length normally include the famous Vasey's Paradise, Redwall Cavern, Unkar Indian Ruins, the mouth of the Little Colorado, Shinumo Creek, Elves Chasm, Deer Creek Falls, Havasu Creek, and Fern Glen Grotto. While rafting and hiking, there is time for quiet meditation and for contemplating the magnificent canyon's rock formations, flora, and fauna.

Perhaps the most important decisions regarding the Grand Canyon adventure occur months before the rafting trip begins. Rafters must choose between oar and motorized rafts and between trips ranging from as few as four to as many as eighteen days. The classic Grand Canyon rafting trip is the seven- to thirteen-day 225-mile (360-km) trip from Lee's Ferry, near Page, Arizona, to Diamond Creek, below the Havasu Indian Reservation. Shorter trips may be run on either the upper or lower canyon sections. The 87-mile (139-km) upper trip from Lee's Ferry to Phantom Ranch requires a strenuous 9-mile (14-km) hike out to the canyon's south rim. The 138-mile (221-km) trip from Phantom Ranch to Diamond Creek requires the same trek—but fortunately in the downhill direction.

Commercial rafting trips through the Grand Canyon are normally run from early April until late October. Camping is required on all trips. The spring and fall months have comfortable daytime temperatures, but nighttime temperatures can drop into the forties or lower. Wet suits are normally worn during spring trips.

Rafting the Grand Canyon ranks as one of the world's truly outstanding wilderness experiences. The National Park Service, which regulates outfitters and launch dates, says about twenty-thousand customers are accommodated annually by the park's licensed rafting outfitters. Few of these outfitters have difficulty filling their allotted spaces for each launch permit. A significant percentage of rafting customers come from as far away as Germany, France, Great Britain, Australia, and Canada. Little wonder that reservations a year or more in advance are recommended.

Passengers on motorized raft enjoy the big waters of Grand Canyon's Crystal Rapids. Photo courtesy of Canyoneers/Gaylor L. Stavely.

Colorado River (Grand Canyon) Outfitters

Arizona Raft Adventures
4050 E. Huntington Dr.
Flagstaff, AZ 86004
(800) 786–7238
(602) 526–8200

Arizona River Runners
P.O. Box 47788
Phoenix, AZ 85068–7788
(800) 477–7238
(602) 867–4866

Canyon Explorations
P.O. Box 310
Flagstaff, AZ 86002
(800) 654–0723
(602) 774–4559

Canyoneers
P.O. Box 2997
Flagstaff, AZ 86003
(800) 525–0924
(602) 526–0924

Colorado River & Trail Expeditions
P.O. Box 57575
Salt Lake City, UT 84157–0575
(801) 261–1789

Expeditions
R.R. 4 Box 755
Flagstaff, AZ 86001
(602) 774–8176
(602) 779–3769

Grand Canyon Dories
P.O. Box 216
Altaville, CA 95221
(800) 877–3679
(209) 736–0805

Grand Canyon Expeditions
P.O. Box O
Kanab, UT 84741
(800) 544–2691
(801) 644–2691

O.A.R.S.
P.O. Box 67
Angels Camp, CA 95222
(800) 346–6277
(209) 736–4677

Outdoors Unlimited
6900 Townsend Winona Rd.
Flagstaff, AZ 86004
(800) 637–7238
(602) 526–4546

Sleight Expeditions
P.O. Box 40
St. George, UT 84771–0040
(801) 673–1200

Tour West Whitewater Adventures
P.O. Box 333
Orem, UT 84059
(800) 453–9107
(801) 225–0755

Western River Expeditions
7258 Racquet Club Dr.
Salt Lake City, UT 84121
(800) 453–7450
(801) 942–6669

SALT RIVER, ARIZONA

Section: Fort Apache Indian Reservation to Roosevelt Lake
Location: Gila County, northeast of Phoenix, east-central Arizona
Driving Time: Phoenix—2 hours
Difficulty: Class III–IV

Trip Length: 54 miles (86 km) or less
Trip Options: Paddle raft, oar raft, inflatable kayak; one to five days
Season: February–May
Cost: $75–$85 one day; $200–$500 multiday

The Salt River is born at the confluence of the White and Black rivers, below their headwaters in Arizona's White Mountains. West of U.S. Highway 60, north of Globe, the upper Salt carves a tumbling 54-mile (86-km) course through the granite gorges of the pristine Sonoran desert that includes the Fort Apache Indian Reservation, Tonto National Forest, and the Salt River Wilderness Canyon before reaching the quiet waters behind Theodore Roosevelt Dam. With passage of the Arizona Wilderness Act in 1984, approximately 35 miles (56 km) of the upper Salt, between Gleason Flat and the mouth of Pinal Creek, was incorporated into Salt River Wilderness Canyon.

During early-spring runoff, the upper Salt is more than just a scenic desert canyon river; Granite Gorge has several excellent Class III–IV+ rapids, including the exciting Eye of the Needle, Black Rock, Maze, and Quartzite Falls—a river-wide ledge that often requires lining or portaging. One- to five-day raft trips are run in the spring when the wildflowers of the Sonoran desert are at their best.

Salt River Outfitters

Desert Voyagers Guided
  Rafting Tours
P.O. Box 9053
Scottsdale, AZ 85203
(800) 222–7238
(602) 998–7238

Far Flung Adventures
P.O. Box 377
Terlingua, TX 79852
(800) 359–4138
(915) 371–2489

Salt River Rafting
7111 E. First St.
Scottsdale, AZ 85251
(800) 964–7238
(602) 941–4222

Worldwide Explorations
P.O. Box 686
Flagstaff, AZ 86002–0686
(800) 272–3353
(602) 774–6462

VERDE RIVER, ARIZONA
Section: Beasley Flats to Horseshoe Reservoir
Location: Yavapai County between Flagstaff and Phoenix, central Arizona
Driving Time: Phoenix—1.5 hours
Difficulty: Class II–III
Trip Length: 60 miles (96 km)
Trip Options: Paddle raft, oar raft, inflatable kayak; one to five days
Season: January–April
Cost: $90 one day; $160–$200 two days; $400–$600 four to six days

The Verde River, in 1984, became Arizona's first National Wild and Scenic River. Its refreshing waters and lush green vegetation, which serve as an oasis in the Sonoran desert for migratory birds, also make it a popular habitat for the bald eagle and other diverse wildlife including beavers, otters, and deer. Verde's January-to-April rafting season is the perfect time for both birdwatching and relaxing in the Southwest sun.

Although the upper Verde contains several Class III–IV rapids during high water, most of the river's relatively moderate Class II–III waters are ideal for both first-time rafters and senior citizens. In normal-water years, outfitters offer one-, two-, three-, and five-day rafting trips. Inflatable kayaks make it possible to extend the rafting season until early May.

Verde River Outfitters

Desert Voyagers Guided Rafting Tours
P.O. Box 9053
Scottsdale, AZ 85203
(800) 222–7238
(602) 998–7238

Worldwide Explorations
P.O. Box 686
Flagstaff, AZ 86002–0686
(800) 272–3353
(602) 774–6462

RIO CHAMA, NEW MEXICO

Section:	El Vado Dam to Big Eddy above Abiquiu Reservoir
Location:	Rio Arriba County, northwest of Espanola, northern New Mexico
Driving Time:	Albuquerque—2.5 hours
Difficulty:	Class II–III
Trip Length:	24–32 miles (38–51 km) or less
Trip Options:	Paddle raft, oar raft; two and three days
Season:	April–August
Cost:	$200–$350

Originating in the high San Juan Mountains of south-central Colorado, northern New Mexico's Rio Chama becomes a major tributary of the famed Rio Grande north of Espanola. Long recognized for its pristine canyon beauty, the Rio Chama, first protected by the state's Scenic and Pastoral Rivers System, recently was designated a National Wild and Scenic River. Its red and yellow sandstone canyons, celebrated in the art of Georgia O'Keeffe, are some of the Southwest's best for hiking and photography.

Chama Canyon, largest of the Rio Chama canyons, runs nearly 33 miles (49 km) from El Vado Dam to Abiquiu Reservoir. Most of its Class III rapids—Dark Canyon, Little Bridge, Skull Bridge, Gage Station, and Screaming Left Turn—are within 3 miles (5 km) of the Big Eddy take-out.

Chama's dam-controlled water flow makes it a very popular one- or two-day trip for families as well as anyone desiring a relaxing and scenic canyon trip. The canyon's campsites either are hidden among the ponderosa pines and fir or abut the beautiful sandstone walls. While the best rafting times are April through mid-June, water releases from the dam permit weekend trips in late July and August.

Outfitters listed on page 134.

RIO GRANDE, NEW MEXICO

Section: Taos Box (lower)
Location: Taos County near Taos, northern New Mexico
Driving Time: Albuquerque—2.5 hours
Difficulty: Class III–IV (Taos Box)
Trip Length: Taos Box—17 miles (27 km); Lower Gorge—5–12 miles (8–19 km)
Trip Options: Paddle raft, oar raft; one day
Season: April–August
Cost: $60–$90

In 1968, a 48-mile (77-km) section of the Rio Grande in northern New Mexico was among the first rivers to be included in the National Wild and Scenic Rivers system. Near the quaint northern New Mexico town of Taos, much of this protected Rio Grande affords a variety of popular whitewater opportunities for seasoned as well as young and inexperienced rafters.

During normal spring and early-summer water flows, the 17-mile (27-km) raft trip through the remote and majestic 800-foot-deep volcanic Taos Box is New Mexico's wildest whitewater ride. Its many dynamic Class III–IV+ rapids, which include Ski Jump, Powerline, and Rock Garden, provide a thrilling and wet day for adventurous rafters. The Taos Box is also noted for its natural hot springs and various birds, including eagles, geese, herons, and ducks.

Section: Pilar, or Racecourse (Lower Gorge)
Location: Taos and Rio Arriba counties, near Taos, northern New Mexico
Driving Time: Albuquerque—2 hours
Difficulty: Class I–III
Trip Length: 5 miles (8 km)
Trip Options: Paddle raft, oar raft; half-day
Season: April–July
Cost: $35–$45

A few miles downriver from the Taos Box and its confluence with the Rio Pueblo de Taos, Rio Grande rafting outfitters provide very popular half-day rafting trips on a more moderate section of the Lower Gorge. Commonly referred to as the Pilar, or Racecourse, section, this trip has been the sight of the annual Rio Grande Whitewater Races on Mother's Day weekends for more than twenty-five years.

During the 5-mile (8-km) trip through Rio Grande State Park, the canyon walls narrow to create fairly continuous Class II–III whitewater. The stretch includes the exciting Albert Falls, The Narrows, Big Rock, and Souse Hole Rapids.

Outfitters welcome families with children as young as six on both paddle- and oar-guided raft trips in the Lower Gorge.

Rio Chama and Rio Grande (Taos Box and Pilar) Outfitters

Far Flung Adventures
P.O. Box 377
Terlingua, TX 79852
(800) 359–4138
(915) 371–2489

Kokopelli Rafting Adventures
513 W. Cordova Rd.
Santa Fe, NM 87501
(800) 879–9035
(505) 983–3734

Los Rios River Runners
100 E. San Francisco St.
Santa Fe, NM 87501
(800) 338–6877
(505) 983–6565

Native Son's Adventures
P.O. Box 6144
Taos, NM 87571
(800) 753–7559
(505) 758–9342

New Wave Rafting Company
Route 5 Box 302A
Santa Fe, NM 87501
(505) 984–1444

Rio Grande Rapid Transit
Box A, Pilar Route
Pilar, NM 87531
(800) 222–7238
(505) 758–9700

Rio Grande River Tours
Box 1D Pilar Route
Embudo, NM 87531
(800) 525–4966
(505) 758–0762

Santa Fe Rafting Company
P.O. Box 23525
Santa Fe, NM 87502–3525
(800) 467–7238
(505) 988–4914

Southwest Wilderness Adventures
P.O. Box 9380
Santa Fe, NM 87504
(800) 869–7238
(505) 983–7262

RIO GRANDE (BIG BEND), TEXAS

Sections: Colorado Canyon; Canyons of Big Bend National Park
Location: Presidio and Brewster counties, Big Bend National Park, southwest Texas, United States–Mexico border
Driving Time: El Paso—5 hours; Midland—4.5 hours
Difficulty: Class I–II (Colorado Canyon); I–IV (Big Bend canyons)
Trip Length: Colorado Canyon—9–13 miles (13–21 km); Big Bend canyons—105 miles (168 km)
Trip Options: Paddle raft, oar raft; half-day, one day (Colorado Canyon); one to seven days (Big Bend canyons)
Season: Year-round
Cost: $85–$90 one day (Colorado Canyon); $100 one day (Santa Elena Canyon); $700–$1,000 multiday (Big Bend canyons)

For nearly 300 miles (480 km), from Redford in west Texas through Big Bend National Park to Langtry near the Amistad National Recreation Area, river rafting provides the easiest way to experience the Rio Grande's legendary canyons. Waters for rafting in these southwest Texas sections of the Rio Grande are not the result of snowmelt in the river's Colorado high-mountain origins, but rather contributions from the equally large watershed of the Rio Conchos tributary that drains Chihuahua State in northern Mexico.

While the isolation of the Rio Grande's spectacular canyons requires at least two days for most adventures, one of the river's most popular trips is a one-day excursion near the western entrance to Big Bend National Park. Upstream from Lajitas, Colorado Canyon in the BB Ranch State Natural Area has relatively easy Class I–II whitewater that is ideal for families as well as other park visitors. Oarguided raft trips leave ample time to enjoy the canyon's beauty.

Big Bend National Park's three best-known river canyons—Santa Elena, Mariscal, and Boquillas—may be rafted individually during two- and three-day trips or as a continuous seven-day trip. Outfitters normally shuttle rafters between Lajitas and the put-in and take-out points for each river trip.

Santa Elena, the park's first and most popular canyon, is known for its picturesque waterfalls, outstanding flora and fauna, and Rock Slide Rapid—a long, technical maze created by numerous large boulders. Hikes into Santa Elena's side canyons afford a close-up look at petroglyphs, fossils, bat caves, and desert wildflowers. Its towering walls are home to numerous bird species, including eagles and the endangered peregrine falcon. During high water, some outfitters may run the 20-mile (32-km) Santa Elena Canyon as a one-day trip.

In southernmost Big Bend, Mariscal Canyon, 10 miles (16 km) long, is the park's most colorful and remote chasm. Its walls tower nearly 1,600 feet above

Rafters in Santa Elena Canyon at Big Bend National Park can hike up side canyons to view petroglyphs and fossils. Photo by Hank Mosakowski, Lizard Tail Photos.

Tight Squeeze, a 10-foot-wide rapids, and Rockpile, a technical swirling maze. Two other remote park canyons, San Vicente and Hot Springs, are usually run with the Mariscal trip.

Boquillas Canyon, the longest and most tranquil of Big Bend's canyons, carves a picturesque route through the Sierra del Carmen Mountains on the eastern edge of the park. Sheer walls over 4,000 feet high, numerous side canyons with striking rock formations, and secluded caves add to the intrigue of the Boquillas adventure. Because of the very easy Class I–II rapids, outfitters will normally take families with children as young as five on the Boquillas section.

Section:	Lower canyons
Location:	Brewster and Terrell counties, southwest Texas, United States–Mexico border
Driving Time:	El Paso—6 hours; Midland—4.5 hours
Difficulty:	Class I–IV
Trip Length:	84 miles (134 km)
Trip Options:	Oar raft, inflatable kayak; seven to ten days
Season:	Year-round
Cost:	$700

From La Linda, just north of Big Bend, to Dryden, some 84 miles (134 km) downriver, the Rio Grande provides a solitary journey through some of the most remote canyons in the Southwest. On the second day, rafters enter a section of almost 60 miles (96 km) of continuous canyon. Promoted by outfitters as the Lower Canyons of the Rio Grande trip, its entire length is protected by Wild and Scenic Rivers legislation and consists principally of one deep canyon after another. Because of the trip's remoteness, difficult access, and seven- to ten-day length, it should be attempted only by physically fit and adventurous campers. Oar-guided raft trips, often accompanied by canoes and kayaks, provide an abundance of time to hike side canyons or relax in the shade or warm springs.

Rio Grande (Big Bend) Outfitters

Big Bend River Tours
P.O. Box 317
Lajitas, TX 79852
(800) 545–4240
(915) 424–3219

Outback Expeditions
P.O. Box 229
Terlingua, TX 79852
(800) 343–1640
(915) 371–2490

Far Flung Adventures
P.O. Box 377
Terlingua, TX 79852
(800) 359–4138
(915) 371–2489

CHAPTER 13

■ ■ ■

Alaska

Alaska, America's last frontier, offers adventure-spirited rafters more miles of wilderness waterways and more varied environs than any other state or province. From the gently flowing wilderness rivers of the Brooks Range in the tundra regions north of the Arctic Circle to the gentle—and sometimes not-so-gentle—waters beneath towering mountains in south-central and southeast Alaska, there are dozens of river trips from which to choose. Outfitters provide one-hour, half-day, one-day, multiday, and even multiweek river adventures.

Portions of twenty-five Alaska rivers are protected from development by the National Wild and Scenic Rivers system. In addition, many of the state's more frequently rafted rivers are either all or partially included within the boundaries of national parks or wildlife reserves, such as Glacier Bay, Wrangell-St. Elias, Kenai, Denali, Gates of the Arctic, Kobuk Valley, Noatak, and Arctic.

Continuous daylight during the short summer rafting season provides limitless opportunities to photograph the breathtaking scenery of the Alaskan wilderness and wildlife that includes caribou, moose, bears, deer, waterfowl, and birds of prey.

The professional outfitters of Alaska offer several half-day and one-day rafting trips for residents and visitors wanting a brief introduction to whitewater:

- The Mendenhall River raft trip near Juneau, with unique close-up viewing of the spectacular Mendenhall Glacier and towering mountain peaks, is Alaska's most popular.
- The Chilkat River provides a marvelous scenic float trip through the Bald Eagle Preserve near Haines.
- The Lowe River, just east of Valdez, has popular one-hour raft trips through Keystone Canyon.
- The Tonsina, a beautiful glacial river flowing from the Chugach Mountains, offers exciting Class III–IV whitewater near Glennallen.
- The Kenai River features Class I–II+ rapids through the Kenai National Wildlife Refuge just two hours south of Anchorage.
- The Eagle River, the state's closest one-day rafting adventure to Anchorage, offers Class II–III whitewater ending on Fort Richardson.
- The Matanuska River, northeast of Anchorage, offers both scenic float trips and the challenging Class III–IV+ Lionshead rafting adventure.
- The Nenana River provides half-day, one-day, and multiday rafting opportunities near Denali National Park.

Alaska
River Comparison

	Difficulty	Min. Age	H	D	M	Season	Raft Type P	O
Mendenhall	/	*	✗			May–Sep	✗	✗
Chilkat	/	10	✗			Jun–Oct	✗	✗
Lowe	/	5	✗			May–Sep	✗	✗
Tonsina	/ /	12		✗		May–Sep	✗	✗
Kenai	/	None		✗		May–Sep	✗	✗
Eagle	/ /	5		✗		May–Sep	✗	✗
Matanuska								
Matanuska Valley	/	5		✗		Jun–Sep	✗	✗
Lionshead	/ /	12		✗		Jun–Sep	✗	✗
Nenana	/ /	8	✗	✗	✗	May–Sep	✗	✗
Alsek and Tatshenshini	/ /	12			✗	Jun–Sep	✗	✗
Chitina and Copper	/ /	10			✗	Jun–Sep	✗	✗
Talkeetna	/ /	14			✗	Jun–Sep	✗	✗
Brooks Range								
East	/	10			✗	Jun–Aug		✗
Central	/	10			✗	Jul–Aug	✗	✗
West	/	10			✗	Jun–Sep	✗	✗

* No minimum age; minimum weight is forty pounds.

/ Beginner—Easy whitewater. Fun for everyone.
/ / Intermediate—Moderate whitewater.
No previous rafting experience is necessary.
/ / / Advanced—Difficult whitewater.
Previous Class IV paddle rafting experience is recommended or required.

H—Half-Day Trip, D—Day Trip, M—Multiday Trip
P—Paddle Raft, O—Oar Raft

The Alsek and Tatshenshini rivers in northwest British Columbia and southeastern Alaska provide some of North America's most primitive and spectacular wilderness scenery. Photo by Ric Careless, Tatshenshini Wild.

Alaska also boasts many multiday wilderness trips:

- The whitewater and spectacular scenery of the Alsek and Tatshenshini rivers in southeast Alaska and northwest Canada provide two of the best wilderness rafting trips available anywhere.
- The Chitina and Copper rivers in the Wrangell-St. Elias Mountains rank a close second to the Alsek-Tatshenshini for mountain and wilderness beauty.
- The Talkeetna River, from the Talkeetna Glacier to the mighty Susitna, provides Class III–IV+ whitewater, placid waters, and outstanding mountain scenery northeast of Anchorage.
- Northern Alaska's Brooks Range, source of hundreds of rivers and streams, offers more than a dozen fine rafting opportunities in remote national parks and wildlife reserves north of the Arctic Circle.

Access to many of Alaska's multiday river trips is so remote that small aircraft transport rafters and equipment to and from put-in or take-out points. Rafters planning to participate in any of Alaska's wilderness river trips should be properly prepared for the Far North. Glacier-fed rivers are always cold, and wet suits are almost always required. Despite any discomforts during the long wilderness trip, almost everyone calls their Alaska river adventure one of life's greatest experiences.

MENDENHALL RIVER, ALASKA

Section:	Mendenhall River Valley
Location:	North of Juneau, southeast Alaska
Driving Time:	Juneau—.5 hour
Difficulty:	Class II–III
Trip Length:	6 miles (9 km)
Trip Options:	Paddle raft, oar raft; half-day
Season:	May–September
Cost:	$50–$80

The Mendenhall raft trip, which begins on Mendenhall Lake just below renowned Mendenhall Glacier, is an exciting yet mild whitewater adventure that is enjoyed by visitors of all ages. From the lake, just prior to the downriver journey, rafters will enjoy awesome views of 12-mile-long Mendenhall Glacier, whose face rises 150 feet above the water, its medial and terminal moraines, and nearby towering peaks. Rafters can photograph icebergs floating in the lake.

Only about 1 mile (1.6 km) of the 6-mile (9-km) Mendenhall River raft trip contains whitewater. In this stretch are several exciting Class II–III rapids, including Scott's Rocks, Iatola Hola, Tourist Trap, and Pin Ball Alley. Rafters spend the remainder of the trip relaxing and enjoying the spectacular mountains that tower nearly 7,000 feet above the river. Take-out for the Mendenhall is in tidal waters near Juneau International Airport.

Midway on the trip, guests are treated to an Alaska-style shoreline snack featuring smoked salmon, reindeer sausage, cheese, and beverages. Mendenhall's outfitter also provides rainsuits, life jackets, and rubber boots.

Mendenhall River Outfitter

Alaska Travel Adventures
9085 Glacier Hwy.
Suite 204
Juneau, AK 99801
(907) 789–0052

CHILKAT RIVER, ALASKA

Section:	Alaska Chilkat Bald Eagle Preserve
Location:	Haines Borough near Haines, southeast Alaska
Driving Time:	Haines—1 hour; Haines Junction—3.5 hours
Difficulty:	Class I
Trip Length:	5 miles (8 km)
Trip Options:	Paddle raft, oar raft; half-day
Season:	June–October
Cost:	$30–$70

The Chilkat River, which flows through the Chilkat Valley near Haines in southeast Alaska, boasts the world's largest concentration of bald eagles. Every fall thousands of these majestic birds migrate to the Chilkat, where they spend the winter feeding on salmon in the unfrozen sections of the river. During the summer months a large number of these eagles remain in the valley. Summer raft float trips allow guests to see and photograph scores of eagles, many perched in trees and stumps along the shore. Grizzly bears, black bears, moose, and wolves are also sometimes on the riverbanks. The magnificent snow-covered peaks of the Chilkat Mountains provide a spectacular backdrop.

Although the Chilkat's waters move swiftly, there is no whitewater. Anyone over seven years of age can enjoy the trip. The raft trip, including the shuttle from Haines, takes four hours.

Chilkat River Outfitter

Chilkat Guides
P.O. Box 170
Haines, AK 99827
(907) 766–2491

LOWE RIVER, ALASKA

Section:	Keystone Canyon
Location:	Northeast of Valdez, south-central Alaska
Driving Time:	Anchorage—6 hours; Valdez—.5 hour
Difficulty:	Class II–III
Trip Length:	4 miles (6.5 km)
Trip Options:	Paddle raft, oar raft; one hour
Season:	May–September
Cost:	$20–$35

The Lowe River through Keystone Canyon gives rafters a brief yet very enjoyable introduction to whitewater less than 20 miles (32 km) northeast of Valdez. While the rafting trip takes only an hour, the canyon doesn't lack either spectacular scenery or exciting whitewater. Its nonintimidating Class II–III rapids can be enjoyed by anyone above the age of five.

The raft trip, which starts about 1 mile (1.6 km) above Keystone Canyon, includes a midtrip stop at Bridal Veil Falls, where waters cascade 900 feet down rock walls to the riverbank.

Keystone's outfitter provides rainsuits, life jackets, and rubber boots.

Lowe River Outfitter

Keystone Raft & Kayak Adventures
P.O. Box 1486
Valdez, AK 99686
(800) 328–8460
(907) 835–2606

TONSINA RIVER, ALASKA

Section:	Lower
Location:	Near Chitina, east of Valdez, south-central Alaska
Driving Time:	Anchorage—4.5 hours
Difficulty:	Class III–IV
Trip Length:	22 miles (35 km)
Trip Options:	Paddle raft, oar raft; one day
Season:	Mid-May through mid-September
Cost:	$70–$80

The Tonsina, a pretty blue-green glacial river, flows eastward out of the Chugach Mountains before turning south and creating a portion of the western border of Wrangell–St. Elias National Park.

The most popular one-day rafting trip begins at Mile 79 on the Richardson Highway and continues for 22 miles (35 km) south to the Copper River near Chitina. The trip offers plenty of exciting Class III–IV whitewater, majestic mountain scenery, and abundant wildlife.

Tonsina River Outfitters

Alaska Whitewater
P.O. Box 142294
Anchorage, AK 99514
(907) 337–7238

Keystone Raft & Kayak Adventures
P.O. Box 1486
Valdez, AK 99686
(800) 328–8460
(907) 835–2606

KENAI RIVER, ALASKA

Section:	Kenai Canyon
Location:	Kenai Peninsula near Cooper Landing, south-central Alaska
Driving Time:	Anchorage—2 hours
Difficulty:	Class I–II+
Trip Length:	11 and 17 miles (17.5 and 27 km)
Trip Options:	Paddle raft, oar raft; one day
Season:	May–September
Cost:	$20–$40 half-day; $45–$85 one day

The emerald-green upper Kenai River, which originates at Kenai Lake on the Kenai Peninsula, offers one of Alaska's premier one-day river trips for persons wanting easy whitewater. While Kenai's Class I–II+ whitewaters are not considered difficult, they do have some exhilarating stretches that can be enjoyed by all ages. The Kenai River, one of the state's most productive for salmon and trout fishing, has abundant wildlife including brown bears.

Kenai's outfitters provide necessary rain gear and boots. Rafters may choose between two trips, both which begin near Kenai Lake and travel through Kenai National Wildlife Refuge. The easier 11-mile (17.5-km) float trip takes out at Jim Landing, whereas the longer 17-mile (27-km) trip continues to Skilak Lake downstream from Cooper Landing.

Kenai River Outfitters

Alaska Rivers Company
P.O. Box 827
Cooper Landing, AK 99572
(907) 595–1226

Alaska Wildland Adventures
HC 64 Box 26
Cooper Landing, AK 99572
(800) 334–8730
(907) 595–1279

EAGLE RIVER, ALASKA

Section: Lower
Location: Near Eagle River, northeast of Anchorage, south-central Alaska
Driving Time: Anchorage—20 minutes
Difficulty: Class II–III
Trip Length: 9 miles (14 km)
Trip Options: Paddle raft, oar raft; one day
Season: May–September
Cost: $70–$80

The Eagle River, a glacial-melt river that flows west from the Chugach Mountains to the Knik Arm of Cook Inlet, is the closest rafting adventure to Anchorage. Yet while less than a half-hour drive from downtown Anchorage, the Eagle River rafting trip offers typical Alaska wilderness scenery, including mountain vistas. The coordinated efforts of all passengers are required to maneuver paddle rafts through the river's numerous Class II–III rapids.

Put-in for the daily raft trip is at Chugach State Park near the town of Eagle River. Take-out is at Bravo Bridge in Fort Richardson.

Each evening, Eagle River's only outfitter also offers a dinner float trip beginning near the north fork of the Eagle, several miles upriver.

Eagle River Outfitter

Eagle River Raft Trips
P.O. Box 140141
Anchorage, AK 99614
(907) 333–3001

MATANUSKA RIVER, ALASKA

Sections:	Matanuska River Valley and Lionshead
Location:	Below Matanuska Glacier, east of Anchorage, south-central Alaska
Driving Time:	Anchorage—1.5 hours
Difficulty:	Class II–III (valley); III–IV (Lionshead)
Trip Length:	Valley—12 mile (19 km); Lionshead—14 miles (22 km)
Trip Options:	Paddle raft, oar raft; one day
Season:	June–September
Cost:	$25–$50 (valley); $70 (Lionshead)

The Matanuska River raft trip through the Matanuska Valley provides an easy introduction to whitewater. Its relatively simple Class II–III rapids and mellow waters make it a great way to relax and enjoy the beautiful Chugach and Talkeetna mountains. Daily raft trips are available for anyone above the age of five years.

The upper reaches of the Matanuska, known as the Lionshead, contain Class III–IV+ whitewater evocative of its name. Rafters on the Lionshead trip are able to start with a 2-mile warm-up stretch on the Class II–III Chickaloon River. Shortly after the Chickaloon meets the Matanuska and its Lionshead, a rock wall where the river converges with the Matanuska Glacier, the real whitewater begins. Several miles of fairly continuous and thrilling Class III–IV whitewater follow.

Guests are treated to a lunch stop on a glacial moraine, frequent sightings of Dall sheep, and excellent views of the 27-mile-long (43-km) Matanuska Glacier.

Matanuska River Outfitter

NOVA Riverrunners
P.O. Box 1129
Chickaloon, AK 99674
(907) 745-5753

NENANA RIVER, ALASKA

Section:	Canyon
Location:	Denali National Park near Healy, south-central Alaska
Driving Time:	Anchorage—5 hours; Fairbanks—2.5 hours
Difficulty:	Class III–IV
Trip Length:	10–15 miles (16-24 km)
Trip Options:	Paddle raft, oar raft; two hours, half-day, one to three days
Season:	May–September
Cost:	$35–$45; $325–$525 multiday

The Nenana River, on the eastern boundary of Alaska's magnificent Denali National Park, is fed from the Yannert and Nenana glaciers of the park's 20,320-foot Mount McKinley. The Nenana's proximity to Anchorage and Fairbanks, its beautiful scenery, and its exciting whitewater make it Alaska's favorite rafting trip.

The most popular stretch of the Nenana is the canyon section near George Parks Highway between Anchorage and Fairbanks. Anyone age eight and above can enjoy the exciting waves and holes of the river's numerous rapids. Outfitters offer frequent two-hour and four-hour trips and all-day trips ranging from 10 to 15 miles (16 to 24 km).

Denali National Park is known for its abundant wildlife. Dall sheep, moose, caribou, grizzly bears, wolves, and eagles are sometimes seen during half- and one-day raft trips and are frequently seen on multiday trips.

Nenana River Outfitters

Denali Raft Adventures
Drawer 190
Denali National Park, AK 99755
(907) 683–2234

Osprey Expeditions
P.O. Box 209
Denali National Park, AK 99755
(907) 683–2734

McKinley Raft Tours
P.O. Box 138
Denali National Park, AK 99755
(907) 683–2392

Owl Rafting
P.O. Box 612
Denali National Park, AK 99755
(907) 683–2215

ALSEK AND TATSHENSHINI RIVERS, YUKON/BRITISH COLUMBIA/ALASKA

Sections: Haines Junction, Yukon, to Dry Bay, Alaska (Alsek); Dalton Post, Yukon, to Dry Bay, Alaska (Tatshenshini-Alsek)
Location: Southwest Yukon, northwest British Columbia, southeast Alaska
Driving Time: Whitehorse—3 hours
Difficulty: Class III–IV (Alsek); II–III (Tatshenshini)
Trip Length: Alsek—140 miles (224 km); Tatshenshini-Alsek—184 miles (294 km)
Trip Options: Oar raft, paddle/oar raft; nine to twelve days
Season: June–September
Cost: $1,600–$2,600 (depending on air charters)

The Alsek and Tatshenshini rivers provide two of the most incredible outdoor adventures imaginable. For as many as twelve days, it is possible to get away from virtually all traces of civilization and enjoy the remote northern wilderness environment of the Yukon, British Columbia, and Alaska. In 1993, British Columbia announced creation of Tatshenshini-Alsek Provincial Park, twice the size of the Grand Canyon. Canadian and U.S. officials are now discussing proposals for an international park that would link the new park with Alaska's adjoining Glacier Bay and Wrangell-St. Elias national parks and the Yukon's Kluane Park. The four parks would become the world's largest international wilderness reserve.

Rafters may run the Alsek River from Haines Junction, Yukon, to Dry Bay, Alaska, or the Tatshenshini River from Dalton Post, Yukon, to its confluence with the Alsek in British Columbia and then down the Alsek to Dry Bay. Until recently, most outfitters offered only the Tatshenshini-Alsek river trip. Outfitters now also run the entire Alsek, which has somewhat more challenging whitewater and more varied and grander scenery. One section of the Alsek, the 4-mile (6.5-km) Class VI Turnback Canyon, must be portaged by helicopter. The lower Alsek

Massive icebergs are located on Alaska's Tatshenshini River.
Photo courtesy of Mountain Travel•Sobek.

travels between the towering glaciers and icebergs of Alaska's Glacier Bay National Park.

Both river trips offer an unforgettable primitive wilderness experience. Rafters will long remember massive glaciers and large icebergs, pristine waterfalls, majestic mountains, grizzlies, moose, mountain goats, hawks, eagles, rare wildflowers, and whitewater.

Alsek and Tatshenshini River Outfitters

Alaska Discovery
P.O. Box 20669
Juneau, AK 99802
(907) 586–1911

Chilkat Guides
P.O. Box 170
Haines, AK 99827
(907) 766–2491

Canadian River Expeditions
3524 West 16th Ave.
Vancouver, BC
Canada V64 3C1
(604) 738–4449

Mountain Travel•Sobek
6420 Fairmont Ave.
El Cerrito, CA 94530
(800) 227–2384
(510) 527–8100

CHITINA AND COPPER RIVERS, ALASKA

Sections: Kennecott, Nizina, and Chitina rivers to Chitina (Chitina River); Chitina to Flagg Point east of Cordova (Copper River)

Location: Wrangell–St. Elias National Park, east of Valdez, southeast Alaska

Driving Time:	Anchorage—6 hours
Difficulty:	Class I–III
Trip Length:	Chitina River—70 miles (112 km); Copper River—110 miles (176 km)
Trip Options:	Paddle raft, oar raft; six to twelve days
Season:	June–September
Cost:	$1,250–$2,100

Alaska's most extensive and rugged glaciated wilderness is in the Wrangell–St. Elias National Park. It is here in the massive icefields of the St. Elias Range that the Chitina River gets its start. This huge river bisects the Wrangell Mountains as it flows west toward the mighty Copper River. Most raft trips begin at McCarthy on the Kennecott River, which then flows into the Nizina, Chitina, and Copper. This seemingly circuitous route allows rafters time to visit the interesting ghost town of McCarthy and the abandoned Kennecott copper mine before the multiday wilderness river journey to the Copper River at the small town of Chitina.

The Copper River, below Chitina, flows swiftly through the beautiful Copper River Valley adjacent to Wrangell–St. Elias National Park until it reaches the park's coastal Chugach Mountains. The Childs and Miles glaciers enter the Copper River, creating Miles Lake. During summer, rafters frequently observe ice calving: large chunks of ice breaking away from the glacier.

Chitina and Copper River Outfitters

Alaska Whitewater
P.O. Box 142294
Anchorage, AK 99514
(907) 337–7238

Copper Oar
P.O. Box MXY McCarthy
Glennallen, AK 99588
(907) 522–1670

Equinox Wilderness Expeditions
618 W. 14th Ave.
Anchorage, AK 99501
(907) 274–9087

Keystone Raft & Kayak Adventures
P.O. Box 1486
Valdez, AK 99686
(800) 328–8460
(907) 835–2606

Nichols River Expeditions
497 N. Main St.
Moab, UT 84532
(800) 635–1792
(801) 259–7882

Osprey Expeditions
P.O. Box 209
Denali National Park, AK 99755
(907) 683–2734

St. Elias Alpine Guides
P.O. Box 111241
Anchorage, AK 99511
(907) 277–6867

TALKEETNA RIVER, ALASKA
| **Section:** | Yellowjacket Creek to Talkeetna |
| **Location:** | East of Talkeetna, south-central Alaska |

Driving Time: Anchorage—2.5 hours
Difficulty: Class III–IV+
Trip Length: 60 miles (96 miles)
Trip Options: Paddle raft, oar raft; four to five days
Season: June–September
Cost: $700–$1,100

The Talkeetna River, a tributary of the Sustina River north of Anchorage, flows out of the Talkeetna Mountains in south central Alaska. Its headwaters, below Sovereign Mountain's Talkeetna Glacier, can be reached only by aircraft.

While the Class I–II waters of the upper Talkeetna raft trip allow plenty of time to enjoy pristine mountain wilderness beauty and wildlife, the river does not remain easy. The granite walls of Devil's Canyon, usually reached on the third day of the trip, dramatically change the river's profile. Here, thrill-seeking rafters will enjoy some of the state's finest wilderness whitewater. During a 14-mile (22-km) stretch of the canyon, a number of difficult Class III–IV+ rapids like Toilet Bowl and Sluice Box are almost nonstop.

Talkeetna's mountain environs are home to caribou, grizzly and black bears, and bald eagles.

Talkeetna River Outfitters

Keystone Raft & Kayak Adventures
P.O. Box 1486
Valdez, AK 99686
(800) 328–8460
(907) 835–2606

Osprey Expeditions
P.O. Box 209
Denali National Park, AK 99755
(907) 683–2734

NOVA Riverrunners
P.O. Box 1129
Chickaloon, AK 99674
(907) 745–5753

BROOKS RANGE RIVERS, ALASKA

Section: Eastern Brooks Range—Canning, Hulahula, and Kongakut rivers
Location: Arctic National Wildlife Refuge, northeast Alaska
Driving Time: Call or write to outfitter for transportation arrangements.
Difficulty: Class I–II
Trip Length: 100–150 miles (160–240 km)
Trip Options: Oar raft; five to twelve days
Season: June–August
Cost: $2,200–$2,900

The Brooks Range, which spans northern Alaska from the Canadian border to the Chukchi Sea, offers a wide selection of wilderness rafting adventures in three fairly distinctive environments: the Arctic National Wildlife Refuge, Gates of the Arctic National Park, and the Noatuk and Kobuk Valley national parks.

The Arctic National Wildlife Refuge, adjacent to the Canadian border in northeast Alaska, is one of the world's largest nature preserves. Nowhere else in North America is the transition of biotic communities from the Arctic slopes to the adjacent mountains so abrupt. Flowing northward out of the valleys of the eastern Brooks Range across the tundra to the Arctic Ocean are three rivers, the Canning, Hulahula, and Kongakut. They provide rare opportunities to see undisturbed plant and animal communities.

During late-summer trips on any of the Arctic National Wildlife Refuge rivers, it is not uncommon to see thousands of animals including migrating caribou, moose, musk ox, Dall sheep, wolves, grizzly bears, and waterfowl. Polar bears may also be seen near the Arctic Ocean.

Section:	Central Brooks Range—Koyukuk (North Fork), Alatna, Jago, Killik, John, and Wild rivers
Location:	Gates of the Arctic National Park, north-central Alaska
Driving Time:	Call or write to outfitter for transportation arrangements.
Difficulty:	Class I–II
Trip Length:	100–140 miles (160–224 km)
Trip Options:	Paddle raft, oar raft; seven to fourteen days
Season:	July–August
Cost:	$1,450–$2,000

Gates of the Arctic National Park is the source of dozens of wild rivers enjoyed by hikers and rafters each summer. Several Class I–II wild rivers, such as the North Fork of the Koyukuk, and the Alatna, Jago, Killik, John, and Wild, offer a relaxing way to enjoy the Brooks wilderness. Many outfitters plan short day hikes into the scenic mountains and side valleys.

The Gates of the Arctic is a photographer's paradise. In addition to the wilderness scenery, Dall sheep, moose, grizzly bears, and wolves are frequently seen.

The small village of Bettles, located just north of the Arctic Circle near the John and Wild rivers' confluence with the Koyukuk River, is the outfitting and travel center for Central Brooks Range river expeditions.

Section:	Western Brooks Range—Noatak and Kobuk rivers
Location:	Gates of the Arctic National Park, Noatak National Park, and Kobuk Valley National Park, northwest Alaska
Driving Time:	Call or write to outfitter for transportation arrangements.
Difficulty:	Class I–II
Trip Length:	Noatak—350 miles (560 km); Kobuk—300 miles (480 km)
Trip Options:	Paddle raft, oar raft; ten to fifteen days
Season:	June–September
Cost:	$2,000–$2,300

The Noatak and Kobuk rivers, which begin in the Arrigetch Peaks in the Gates of the Arctic National Park, flow westward for more than 300 miles (480 km) to Kotzebue Sound in the Chukchi Sea. The Noatak, the northernmost of the two rivers, which are separated by the Baird Mountains of the western Brooks Range, flows for more than 200 miles (320 km) through Noatak National Park with no signs of civilization. The Kobuk River trip, which begins at Walker Lake, south of the Arrigetch Peaks, parallels the southern slopes of the Baird Mountains. The river passes a few Eskimo villages and runs through the southern edge of Kobuk Valley National Park.

Neither of the rivers is difficult. Their mellow Class I–II waters are even more popular with canoeists and kayakers. Fishing for both salmon and trout is excellent. There is also ample time to observe and photograph the caribou, wolves, foxes, goats, sheep, and abundant summer birdlife.

Brooks Range River Outfitters

ABEC's Alaska Adventures
1550 Alpine Vista Ct.
Fairbanks, AK 99712
(907) 457–8907

Sourdough Outfitters
P.O. Box 90
Bettles, AK 99726
(907) 692–5252

Alaska Discovery
P.O. Box 20669
Juneau, AK 99802
(907) 586–1911

Wilderness Alaska
P.O. Box 83044
Fairbanks, AK 99708
(907) 345–3567

Arctic Treks
P.O. Box 73452
Fairbanks, AK 99707
(907) 455–6502

Wilderness: Alaska-Mexico
1231 Sundance Loop
Fairbanks, AK 99709
(907) 479–8203

Equinox Wilderness Expeditions
618 W. 14th Ave.
Anchorage, AK 99501
(907) 274–9087

PART III
■ ■ ■

Eastern United States

Nineteenth-century factory and mill ruins provide a historic backdrop to the Black River Canyon trip in Watertown, New York.

CHAPTER 14

■ ■ ■

Northeast States

The most popular whitewater rafting trips in the northeastern United States are within two well-known resort areas: the Moosehead Lake–Baxter State Park region of north-central Maine and the Adirondack Mountains in northern New York.

In Maine, whitewater rafting was introduced on the Kennebec, Penobscot, and Dead rivers almost immediately after log drives were ended by the paper companies in the mid-1970s. In the ensuing years, these rivers experienced a tremendous increase in popularity as adventure-seeking rafters discovered the unique blend of primitive northern forest wilderness beauty and warm, big whitewater, all summer long. While Maine's rivers have traditionally been popular with adventurous rafters, families can now enjoy the milder waters of the Kennebec below its Class III–IV+ gorge.

New York's rivers offer whitewater trips for families, adventurers, and thrill-seekers. Tops in popularity are the spring and fall season Hudson River Gorge trip and the family-oriented Sacandaga River trip near Lake George and Lake Saratoga in the eastern Adirondacks. Near Lake Ontario, the Black River raft trip, cascading down a steep-walled canyon through the industrial city of Watertown, offers a unique blend of history and challenging whitewater rapids. The Moose, one of the northeast's most challenging commercially run rivers, can only be rafted during April.

In western New York, the relatively easy Genesee River raft trip through Letchworth State Park, just west of the Finger Lakes, can be enjoyed by almost anyone above the age of eight.

New commercial raft trips on two sections of the Deerfield River in northwest Massachusetts offer both beginning and intermediate whitewater. Southern Vermont's West River, with but a brief spring and fall weekend whitewater season from special dam releases, provides a highly scenic and exciting rafting opportunity.

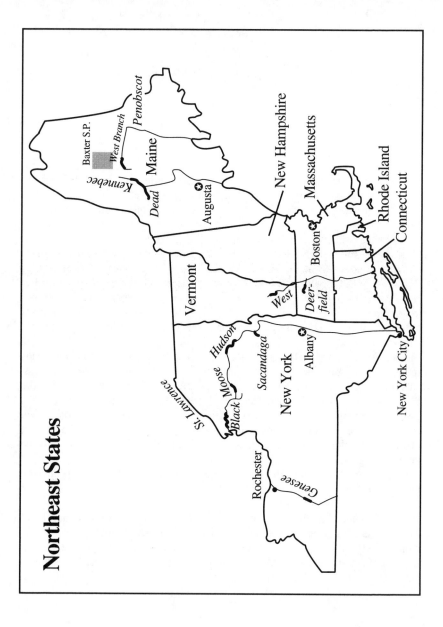

Northeast States

Northeast States
River Comparison Chart

	Difficulty	Min. Age	H	D	M	Season	Raft Type P	O	K
Maine									
Kennebec									
Gorge	/ /	12	✗	✗	✗	May–Sep	✗	✗	✗
Carry Brook	/	5	✗			Jun–Aug	✗		
Penobscot (West Branch)									
Ripogenus Gorge	/ /	16	✗			May–Oct	✗		
Big Eddy	/ /	12	✗	✗	✗	May–Oct	✗		
Dead	/ /	14		✗		May–Oct	✗		✗
New York									
Hudson	/ /	12	✗			Spring/Fall	✗		
Moose	/ / /	16	✗			April	✗		
Sacandaga	/	5	✗			May–Sep	✗		
Black	/ /	14		✗		May–Sep	✗		
Genesee	/	8	✗			May–Sep	✗		
Massachusetts									
Deerfield									
Fife Brook	/	7	✗			Apr–Oct	✗		
Dryway	/ /	14	✗			Apr–Oct	✗		
Vermont									
West	/ /	12	✗			Spring/Fall	✗		

/   Beginner—Easy whitewater. Fun for everyone.

/ /   Intermediate—Moderate whitewater.
No previous rafting experience is necessary.

/ / /   Advanced—Difficult whitewater.
Previous Class IV paddle rafting experience is recommended or required.

H—Half-Day Trip, D—Day Trip, M—Multiday Trip
P—Paddle Raft, O—Oar Raft, K—Inflatable Kayak

KENNEBEC RIVER, MAINE

Section: Kennebec Gorge, Harris Station to West Forks
Location: Somerset County, near West Forks, north-central Maine
Driving Time: Portland—3 hours; Quebec City—2.5 hours
Difficulty: Class III–IV+ (Gorge); I–III (Carry Brook)
Trip Length: 12 miles (19 km); shorter trips available
Trip Options: Paddle raft, oar raft, inflatable kayak; half-day, one day, and multiday
Season: May–September
Cost: $75–$95

Kennebec River Gorge rafting begins at the Harris Station Dam below Indian Pond and continues for 12 miles (21 km) through nearly unspoiled forest wilderness to West Forks, where the Dead River joins the Kennebec.

Demanding Class III–IV+ rapids start in the upper Gorge, almost immediately below the dam, and remain quite intense for nearly the first 5 miles. Notable rapids include the breathtaking Three Sisters, Alley Way, and Magic Falls, the largest drop on the river. During the summer, hiking and swimming at Dead Stream Falls and the 90-foot Moxie Falls add a special memory to the trip.

Rafting on the Kennebec River is the result of controlled water releases at the Harris Station Dam by the Central Maine Power Company. Normally seven days a week during the rafting season, these releases provide Kennebec Gorge paddlers with some of the best continuous whitewater and large waves in the East. The Kennebec's rolling waves and surprisingly warm summer waters are also ideal for individual paddling in inflatable kayaks.

Section: Carry Brook
Location: Somerset County, near West Forks, north-central Maine
Driving Time: Portland—3 hours; Quebec City—2.5 hours
Difficulty: Class I–III
Trip Length: 6 miles (9 km)
Trip Options: Paddle raft; half-day
Season: June–August
Cost: $40–$50 for children

Many Maine rafting outfitters offer half-day family whitewater rafting on the more gentle Kennebec waters called the Carry Brook section, immediately below the Gorge. By special arrangement with outfitters, children usually five years and older, after watching their parents begin the Class III–IV+ whitewater trip below Harris Dam, may travel with drivers to rejoin their parents halfway down the river at Carry Brook. The 6-mile (9.5-km) Class I–III Carry Brook section, having much of the same wilderness scenery as the more demanding Gorge, offers time for swimming easy rapids and gentle waves on warm summer days. Inflatable kayaks are an enjoyable option for family trips.

Outfitters listed on pages 160–161.

PENOBSCOT RIVER (WEST BRANCH), MAINE

Sections: Ripogenus Gorge and Big Eddy
Location: Piscataquis County, near Baxter State Park, north-central Maine
Driving Time: Portland—3.5 hours; Quebec City—4 hours
Difficulty: Class III–V (Rip Gorge); III–IV (Big Eddy)
Trip Length: 10–14 miles (16–22 km); Ripogenous Gorge—2 miles (3 km); Big Eddy—8–12 miles (13–19 km)
Trip Options: Paddle raft; half-day, one day, and multiday
Season: May–early October
Cost: $75–$95

Ripogenus Gorge is one of the most scenic whitewater stretches in all of eastern America. Incredibly beautiful and primitive, it is located at the beginning of the west branch of the Penobscot River rafting trip. During the first two miles of the steep-walled granite gorge, the Penobscot has several drops, including the intense Class V Exterminator and Cribworks and the exciting Class IV Staircase and Big Heater rapids. Cribworks, which received its name from an area where early log drivers constructed lattice-like log walls along the banks to keep floating logs in the main channel, is the most difficult rapids on the river.

Below Rip Gorge is less-strenuous whitewater and alternating flatwater called the Big Eddy section. This 12-mile (19-km) stretch abounds with interesting Indian names, such as Class IV Big Amberjackmockamus Falls and Nesowadnehunk Falls. Here, rafters parallel Baxter State Park and enjoy spectacular views of mile-high Mount Katahdin. Along these calmer stretches of the river, the chances of seeing moose, bald eagles, and ospreys are excellent. Some outfitters begin their rafting trip on the Big Eddy to Big Pockwacamus Falls section and after lunch shuttle back to run the more difficult Ripogenus Gorge. Anyone wishing to avoid the Class V Rip Gorge can raft only the calmer Big Eddy.

Outfitters listed on pages 160–161.

DEAD RIVER, MAINE

Section: Spencer Stream to West Forks (lower)
Location: Somerset County, near West Forks, north-central Maine
Driving Time: Portland—3 hours; Quebec City—2.5 hours
Difficulty: Class III–IV during spring and fall water releases; II–III+ during late spring and summer
Trip Length: 15 miles (24 km)
Trip Options: Paddle raft, inflatable kayak; one day
Season: May–October
Cost: $75–$100

The lower Dead River offers 15 miles (24 km) of almost continuous whitewater through some of Maine's most remote wilderness forest. Following the Grand Falls put-in, the Class III–IV rapids maintain intensity along the entire stretch and are highlighted by exciting Poplar Falls, with deep holes and large waves just before the Dead joins the Kennebec River at West Forks.

The Kennebec's Alley Way Rapids is typical of the Northeast's many excellent Class IV–V rapids. Photo courtesy of Northern Outdoors.

Rafting on the Dead River is made possible by scheduled water releases from the Kennebec Water Power Company's Flagstaff Dam. High-water releases are normally on at least six weekends during May, June, September, and October, with one very high release during May. In the late-spring and summer seasons, low-water releases are ideal for guided Class II–III+ inflatable kayak trips. Rafters interested in the high-water spring trips should make reservations very early in the year.

Kennebec River, Penobscot River (West Branch), and Dead River Outfitters

Crab Apple Whitewater
HC63 Box 25
West Forks, ME 04985
(800) 553–7238
(207) 663–4491

Maine Whitewater
P.O. Box 633
Bingham, ME 04920
(800) 345–6246
(207) 672–4814

Downeast Whitewater Rafting
P.O. Box 119
Center Conway, NH 03813
(800) 677–7238
(603) 447–3002

New England Whitewater Center
P.O. Box 21
Caratunk, ME 04925
(800) 766–7238
(207) 672–5506

Eastern River Expeditions
P.O. Box 1173
Greenville, ME 04441
(800) 634–7238
(207) 695–2411

North Country Rivers
P.O. Box 47
E. Vassalboro, ME 04935
(800) 348–8871
(207) 923–3492

Northern Outdoors
P.O. Box 100
West Forks, ME 04985
(800) 765–7238
(207) 663–4466

Voyagers Whitewater
Route 201
West Forks, ME 04985
(800) 289–6307
(207) 663–4423

Professional River Runners of Maine
P.O. Box 92
West Forks, ME 04985
(800) 325–3911
(207) 663–2229

Wilderness Expeditions
P.O. Box 41
Rockwood, ME 04478
(800) 825–9453
(207) 534–7305

Unicorn Rafting Expeditions
P.O. Box T
Brunswick, ME 04011
(800) 864–2676
(207) 725–2255

HUDSON RIVER, NEW YORK

Sections:	Indian River and Hudson River Gorge
Location:	Hamilton, Essex, and Warren counties, near North Creek, eastern New York
Driving Time:	Albany—2 hours; Syracuse—3.5 hours
Difficulty:	Class III–IV+
Trip Length:	16 miles (26 km)
Trip Options:	Paddle raft; one day
Season:	April–June; September–October (weekends and holidays)
Cost:	$70–$90

The Hudson River Gorge raft trip in the southeastern region of New York's Adirondack Mountains, one of the northeast's most popular, offers an excellent blend of magnificent wilderness scenery and challenging whitewater action.

Put-in for the Hudson River Gorge trip is on the Indian River, below the Abanakee Dam near the town of Indian Lake. For two hours each morning, Indian Lake releases water for rafters to "ride the bubble" for 3.5 miles (5.5 km) of exciting, nearly continuous Class III whitewater to the Indian's confluence with the Hudson. During the next 13 miles (21 km) to North Creek, the trip passes through the remote and spectacular Hudson River Gorge, where high cliffs and canyon walls tower above the narrow river, creating continuous and demanding Class III–IV+ whitewater. Of the dozen major rapids in the gorge, the following are rated Class III–IV: Blue Ledge, Blue Ledge Narrows, Osprey Nest, Beaver Dam or Mile Long, Kettle Mountain, and Harris Rift.

The Hudson's biggest whitewater action occurs during April and May when Adirondack snowmelt and spring rains push several rapids well into the Class IV+ range. Water temperatures in the forties and fifties, and air temperatures often not much higher, make wet suits, gloves, and extra wool clothing mandatory.

The Indian River water releases combined with the natural flow of the Hudson stabilize late-spring water flows. Again in the fall, as Indian Lake is drawn down in preparation for winter runoff, commercial outfitters offer weekend rafting trips between Labor Day and Columbus Day.

Outfitters listed on pages 162–163.

MOOSE RIVER, NEW YORK

Section:	McKeever to Fowlerville Bridge (middle)
Location:	Lewis County, near Old Forge, western Adirondack Mountains, north-central New York
Driving Time:	Syracuse—2 hours; Albany—3 hours
Difficulty:	Class IV–V; Class IV paddle rafting experience is highly recommended
Trip Length:	12 miles (18 km)
Trip Options:	Paddle raft; one day
Season:	April
Cost:	$90–$100

Each spring, New York's Moose River becomes a raging stretch of river reserved for experienced and physically fit whitewater enthusiasts. Magnificent geology featuring large boulders and wide ledges produce numerous Class IV complex rapids; flipping rafts is common, so be ready to swim. Class V Tannery and Mixmaster are two of the most difficult rapids in the East.

Rafting on the Moose River is not for everyone. In addition to being adventurous and hardy, rafters must be willing to undertake a certain degree of risk. Outfitters caution potential rafters that the Moose is difficult, and previous rafting experience is highly recommended. The Moose River is rafted only during April, when the water is extremely cold. Wet suits are required and extra wool clothing is usually needed.

Hudson River and Moose River Outfitters

Adirondack River Outfitters
P.O. Box 649
Old Forge, NY 13420
(800) 525–7238
(315) 369–3536

Adirondack Wildwaters
P.O. Box 801
Corinth, NY 12822
(518) 696–2953

Adventure Sports Rafting Company
P.O. Box 775
Indian Lake, NY 12842–0775
(800) 441–7238
(518) 648–5812

Hudson River Rafting Company
North Creek, NY 12853
(800) 888–7238
(518) 251–3215

Unicorn Rafting Expeditions
P.O. Box T
Brunswick, ME 04011
(800) 864–2676
(207) 725–2255

Whitewater Challengers
P.O. Box 8
White Haven, PA 18661
(800) 443–8554
(717) 443–9532

Whitewater World
Route 903
Jim Thorpe, PA 18229
(800) 944–8392
(717) 325–3656

W.I.L.D./W.A.T.E.R.S.
Outdoor Center
HCR01 Box 197A
Warrensburg, NY 12885
(518) 696–4604

SACANDAGA RIVER, NEW YORK

Section:	The Great Sacandaga
Location:	Saratoga County, near Hadley, Lake George, and Saratoga regions, southern Adirondack Mountains
Driving Time:	Albany—1 hour
Difficulty:	Class II–III
Trip Length:	3.5 miles (5.5 km)
Trip Options:	Paddle raft; two hours
Season:	Memorial Day–Columbus Day
Cost:	$10–$15

The Sacandaga River, in the scenic Lake George and Saratoga regions of the southern Adirondack Mountains, offers an inexpensive introduction to whitewater rafting for the whole family. Class II–III rapids alternating with fast-moving flatwater provide the perfect environment to learn basic paddling techniques. The river's wild and secluded corridor normally provides ample opportunity for swimming and splashing on warm summer days.

The Sacandaga rafting adventure is a two-hour trip covering about 3.5 miles (5.5 km) between Stewart's Dam in the town of Hadley and the Sacandaga's confluence with the Hudson River. Controlled water releases by Niagara-Mohawk provide sufficient water levels for daily rafting from Memorial Day until Columbus Day.

Sacandaga's professional outfitters offer hourly trips each day during the summer and can almost always accommodate walk-in customers. Fall trips are run on weekends or by reservation.

Sacandaga River Outfitters

Adirondack River Outfitters
P.O. Box 649
Old Forge, NY 13420
(800) 525–7238
(315) 369–3536

Adirondack Wildwaters
P.O. Box 801
Corinth, NY 12822
(518) 696–2953

Hudson River Rafting Company
North Creek, NY 12853
(800) 888–7238
(518) 251–3215

W.I.L.D./W.A.T.E.R.S.
Outdoor Center
HCR01 Box 197A
Warrensburg, NY 12885
(518) 696–4604

BLACK RIVER, NEW YORK

Section: Watertown to Brownville
Location: Jefferson County, Thousand Islands Region, near Watertown, northern New York
Driving Time: Albany—3 hours; Syracuse—1.25 hours
Difficulty: Class III–IV+
Trip Length: 7 miles (11 km)
Trip Options: Paddle raft; one day
Season: May–September
Cost: $50–$70

The Black River Canyon in the industrial city of Watertown offers one of the more interesting and exciting urban whitewater rafting opportunities in the eastern United States. Between Watertown and Brownville near the Thousand Islands Region, the Black cuts through a dramatic 140-foot-deep limestone and shale canyon featuring old dam sites, nineteenth-century factory and mill ruins, spectacular natural scenery, and challenging whitewater.

After several Class II rapids and fast-moving flatwater, rafters must skillfully navigate Class IV+ Knife's Edge, the Black's most technically difficult rapids. Big waves and three ledge-type drops with hydraulics demand the coordinated paddling support of every rafter. Below Knife's Edge, a Class II rapids and nearly a mile of fast-moving water precede a short carry around Glen Park Falls. Immediately below the falls, the canyon's cliffside beauty and whitewater action excel. During the river's final descent to Lake Ontario, Class III–IV rapids—Three Rocks, Zig Zag, Panic Rock, Cruncher, Rocket Ride, Ontario Pitch, Square Rock, Shave-and-a-Haircut, and Swimming Rapids—follow in quick succession.

Scheduled releases from a network of Niagara-Mohawk water-control dams permit daily rafting from May through Columbus Day. This predictable and relatively warm summer water flow, and the Black's proximity to northeastern United States and Canadian summer vacation resorts, are important reasons for the Black's rafting popularity.

Black River Outfitters

Adirondack River Outfitters
P.O. Box 649
Old Forge, NY 13420
(800) 525–7238
(315) 369–3536

Hudson River Rafting Company
North Creek, NY 12853
(800) 888–7238
(518) 251–3215

GENESEE RIVER, NEW YORK

Section: Letchworth State Park
Location: Wyoming and Livingston counties, west of the Finger Lakes Region
Driving Time: Buffalo—1.5 hours; Syracuse—2.5 hours
Difficulty: Class I–II
Trip Length: 6 miles (9.5 km)

Trip Options:	Paddle raft; half-day
Season:	May–September; weekends and holidays; weekdays in July and August
Cost:	$20–$25

For decades, visitors to Letchworth State Park have been wondering what it is like at the bottom of the 600-foot-gorge. Now they can find out as they raft through the deepest part of this immense shale and sandstone gorge. Traveling by raft one can see geologic history and appreciate the gorge from a new and dramatic perspective.

The 6-mile (9.5-km) raft trip, with mostly easy Class I–II rapids, is perfect for families and first-time rafters. If you are lucky enough to catch the river at high water, you will ride over exciting 6-foot waves during the first part of the trip. During normal summer water levels, rafters will visit the picturesque Wolf Creek Falls, which cannot be seen from park overlooks.

Genesee River Outfitter

Adventure Calls Rafting
20 Ellicott Ave.
Batavia, NY 14020
(716) 343–4710

DEERFIELD RIVER, MASSACHUSETTS

Section:	Fife Brook (Zoar Gap)
Location:	Franklin County, near Charlemont, northwest Massachusetts
Driving Time:	Boston—2 hours; New York City—3.5 hours
Difficulty:	Class II–III
Trip Length:	10 miles (16 km)
Trip Options:	Paddle raft; one day
Season:	April–October
Cost:	$45–$60

The Deerfield River, in the Berkshire Mountains of northwest Massachusetts, offers an exciting new rafting opportunity in the eastern United States. Beginning in 1989, outfitters scheduled a limited number of trips through the Fife Brook section of the Deerfield River. As word of this new whitewater gem spread, the popularity of rafting on the Deerfield soared.

Today, almost anyone above age seven can enjoy paddle rafting through the picturesque Zoar Gap on the Deerfield. With more than 10 miles (16 km) of fast-flowing yet not intimidating Class II–III rapids, the river can be rafted from mid-April until mid-October. During the early fall, a raft trip on the Deerfield in Mohawk Trail State Forest is a unique way to enjoy the famed southern New England foliage.

Section:	Dryway (Monroe Bridge)
Location:	Franklin County, near Charlemont, northwest Massachusetts
Driving Time:	Boston—2 hours; New York City—3.5 hours

Difficulty:	Class III–IV
Trip Distance:	4.5 miles (7 km)
Trip Options:	Paddle raft; one day
Season:	April–October
Cost:	$45–$60

Deerfield rafters seeking more demanding whitewater than Zoar Gap should ask outfitters about the Monroe Bridge, or Dryway, section. The Dryway, considerably more difficult than either Deerfield's Zoar Gap or southern Vermont's West River, requires coordinated paddler participation throughout most of the trip. Rafters must carefully navigate around rocks and over Class III–IV ledges and holes.

The popularity of the Dryway rafting section has dramatically increased with new scheduled water-release dates by New England Power Company.

Outfitters listed below.

WEST RIVER, VERMONT

Section:	Jamaica Gorge
Location:	Windham County, near Jamaica, southwest Vermont
Driving Time:	Albany—1.5 hours; Boston—3 hours
Difficulty:	Class II–IV
Trip Length:	10 miles (16 km)
Trip Options:	Paddle raft; one day
Season:	Selected weekends in spring and fall
Cost:	$75–$80

Challenging Class III–IV rapids, such as The Dumplings and Corkscrew, combine with beautiful Green Mountains scenery to make this West River section, between Ball Mountain Dam and Townshend Reservoir, Vermont's outstanding whitewater run. As the river winds its way through granite Jamaica Gorge, past forests and picturesque farmlands, it flows alongside the quaint villages of Jamaica and Townshend. This exciting section has often been the site of regional and national whitewater kayaking championships.

Rafting on the West River is made possible by water releases from Ball Mountain Dam near Jamaica, currently limited to just two weekends a year—one in the spring and one in the fall. One of the more memorable ways to enjoy New England fall colors is to raft at the time of the October water release, which is scheduled to coincide with peak foliage.

Deerfield River and West River Outfitters

Crab Apple Whitewater	Zoar Outdoors
HC63 Box 25	P.O. Box 245
The Forks, ME 04985	Charlemont, MA 01339
(800) 553–7238	(800) 532–7483
(207) 663–4491	(413) 339–8596

CHAPTER 15

■ ■ ■

Mid-Atlantic States

Few regions of the United States or Canada can claim more whitewater diversity than the Appalachian Mountains and Piedmont slopes of Pennsylvania, Maryland, West Virginia, and Virginia. Many of the mid-Atlantic region's popular whitewater stretches are situated at the crossroads between the metropolitan centers of the Great Lakes and the eastern seaboard, only a few hours' drive from large urban populations. Its five most frequently rafted rivers—the Lehigh, Youghiogheny, Cheat, New, and Gauley—account for nearly one-third of all rafting in the eastern United States.

Pennsylvania's Lehigh and Youghiogheny rivers, two of the most frequently rafted rivers anywhere, maintain their popularity with exciting whitewater and scenery worthy of their acclaim. Both rivers offer easy summertime raft trips for families with children as young as five.

Western Maryland's upper section of the Youghiogheny River, rated by whitewater experts as one of the most technical commercially rafted stretches of whitewater in the world, continues to challenge all physically fit thrill-seekers.

West Virginia's dynamic New and Gauley rivers attract large numbers of rafters. This popularity will undoubtedly continue as professional outfitters expand their trip selections. On the upper New River, outfitters now offer introductory whitewater raft and inflatable kayak trips for first-time guests, seniors, the disabled, and families with children as young as five years. Many of these same outfitters, using small rafts and inflatable kayaks, have transformed the middle and lower sections of the traditionally "fall only" Gauley River into an intermediate-level whitewater playground during the spring and summer.

Other whitewater stretches in West Virginia include the Cheat River, always a springtime favorite, and the Shenandoah River, a picturesque and easy family-type raft trip adjacent to Harper's Ferry of Civil War fame.

In Virginia, rafters on the James River enjoy striking views of the new Richmond skyline and old factories, and a run down a dynamic series of rapids commonly known as the fall line between the eastern edge of the Appalachian Piedmont and the sedimentary rocks of the Atlantic Coastal Plain.

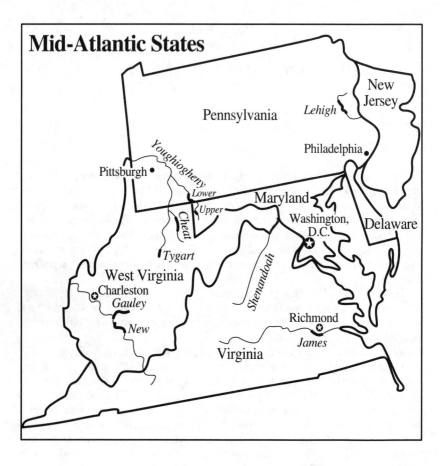

Mid-Atlantic States

Pennsylvania

New Jersey

Lehigh

Philadelphia

Youghiogheny

Pittsburgh

Lower

Upper

Maryland

Cheat

Washington, D.C.

Delaware

Tygart

West Virginia

Charleston

Gauley

Shenandoah

Richmond

New

James

Virginia

Mid-Atlantic States
River Comparison

	Difficulty	Min. Age	H	D	M	Season	P	O	K
Pennsylvania									
Lehigh									
Upper (I)	/ /	10	✗			Apr–Jun	✗		✗
Lower (II)	/ /	10	✗			Apr–Jun	✗		✗
Summer (III)	/	5	✗	✗		Jun–Sep	✗		✗
Youghiogheny									
Lower	/ /	12	✗			Apr–Oct	✗		
Middle	/	6	✗			Jun–Sep	✗		
Maryland									
Youghiogheny (Upper)	/ / /	16	✗			Apr–Oct	✗		
West Virginia									
Cheat	/ /	14	✗			Apr–Jun	✗		
New									
Lower	/ /	12	✗	✗		Apr–Oct	✗	✗	
Upper	/	6	✗	✗		Jun–Sep	✗	✗	✗
Gauley									
Upper	/ / /	16	✗	✗		Sep–Oct	✗	✗	
Lower	/ /	14	✗	✗		Sep–Oct	✗	✗	
Middle	/ /	12	✗			Apr–Sep	✗	✗	✗
Tygart	/ /	12	✗			Apr–Oct	✗		✗
West Virginia/Virginia									
Shenandoah	/	8	✗			Apr–Oct	✗		
Virginia									
James	/ /	12	✗			Apr–Oct	✗	✗	

/   Beginner—Easy whitewater. Fun for everyone.

/ /   Intermediate—Moderate whitewater.
No previous rafting experience is necessary.

/ / /   Advanced—Difficult whitewater.
Previous Class IV paddle rafting experience is recommended or required.

H—Half-Day Trip, D—Day Trip, M—Multiday Trip
P—Paddle Raft, O—Oar Raft, K—Inflatable Kayak

The Lehigh River Gorge in the Pocono Mountains offers the closest whitewater rafting to the metropolitan centers of New York, New Jersey, and Pennsylvania.

LEHIGH RIVER, PENNSYLVANIA

Sections:	Upper Gorge (I) and Lower Gorge (II)
Location:	Carbon County, Pocono Mountains between White Haven and Jim Thorpe, northeastern Pennsylvania
Driving Time:	Philadelphia—2 hours; New York City—2.5 hours
Difficulty:	Class I–III
Trip Length:	Upper Gorge (I)—8 miles (13 km); Lower Gorge (II)—12 miles (19 km)
Trip Options:	Paddle raft, inflatable kayak; one day
Season:	April–early June, and special water releases from dam during the summer
Cost:	$40–$50 for each gorge or section

The Lehigh River offers more than 20 miles (32 km) of fast-moving whitewater through Lehigh River Gorge State Park in northeastern Pennsylvania's world-renowned Pocono Mountains.

The 8-mile (13-km) Upper Gorge, or Section I, trip features numerous Class II–III rapids such as Triple Drop, Z, No Way, Tannery Falls, Popcorn, Second Chance, Wilhoyt's, and Scott's Hole. Depending upon water levels, this is an excellent trip for first-time as well as experienced rafters.

The longer and slightly more demanding Lower Gorge, or Section II, trip gives rafters plenty of whitewater thrills. This very popular 12-mile (19-km) whitewater run from Rockport to Jim Thorpe features many continuous Class III rapids such as Pinball, Needle's Eye, and Mile-Long.

Rafters will find the best whitewater on the Lehigh during April and May. Spring rafting, which begins with the late-March runoff, provides adventurous wet-suit rafters excellent Class III+ whitewater.

During June and again in the fall, there are several scheduled moderate-level weekend water releases from Francis E. Walter Dam. Rafters should call the outfitters for the dates of these releases and make reservations well in advance.

Residents of the Northeast can readily enjoy the convenience of the Lehigh because the river is two hours from Philadelphia and less than three hours from New York City.

Section:	Summer (III)
Location:	Carbon County, near Jim Thorpe, northeastern Pennsylvania
Driving Time:	Philadelphia—2 hours
Difficulty:	Class I–II
Trip Length:	8 miles (13 km)
Trip Options:	Paddle raft, inflatable kayak; half-day and one day
Season:	June–September
Cost:	$15–$30

During the summer months when water levels are too low for rafting on Sections I and II of the Lehigh River, outfitters offer slow-paced introductory raft trips for families and seniors on the mild waters of Lehigh's Section III, beginning at the town of Jim Thorpe. This 8-mile (13-km) trip, with beautiful mountain scenery and easy Class I–II rapids, provides time for swimming, splashing, and relaxing. Outfitters normally allow families with children as young as five years to raft this section.

Lehigh River Outfitters

Jim Thorpe River Adventures
1 Adventure Lane
Jim Thorpe, PA 18229
(800) 424–7238
(717) 325–2570

Whitewater Challengers
P.O. Box 8
White Haven, PA 18661
(800) 443–8554
(717) 443–9532

Pocono Whitewater Rafting Center
Route 903
Jim Thorpe, PA 18229
(800) 944–8392
(717) 325–3656

Whitewater Rafting Adventures
P.O. Box 88
Albrightsville, PA 18210
(800) 876–0285
(717) 722–0285

YOUGHIOGHENY RIVER, PENNSYLVANIA

Section: Ohiopyle to Bruner Run (lower)
Location: Fayette County, Ohiopyle State Park near Ohiopyle, southwestern Pennsylvania
Driving Time: Pittsburgh—1.5 hours; Washington, D.C.—3.5 hours
Difficulty: Class II–IV
Trip Length: 7.5 miles (12 km)
Trip Options: Paddle raft; one day
Season: April–October
Cost: $35–$65

The lower Youghiogheny, or "Yough," in 1964 became the first river to be commercially rafted in the eastern United States, and it continues to be one of the most popular. Each season more than one hundred thousand rafters enjoy the whitewater excitement of the 7.5-mile (12-km) trip from Ohiopyle Falls through the Laurel Mountains in Ohiopyle State Park to Bruner Run. Controlled releases from Youghiogheny Dam by the U.S. Army Corps of Engineers generally allow favorable water flows throughout the rafting season.

Numerous challenging Class III–IV rapids—which include Entrance, Cucumber, Railroad, Dimple, Swimmers, Double Hydraulics, and Rivers End—are separated by calm pools, providing alternating moments of excitement and relaxation. Perhaps the most technical and exciting rapid on the lower Yough is the Class III–IV Dimple, above Swimmers rapid. Encounters with Dimple Rock, as the current crashes rafts against it, are long remembered.

To reduce weekend overcrowding on the lower Yough, Pennsylvania's Bureau of State Parks administers an effective river management plan that includes assigned put-in or launch times for commercial outfitters. Anyone interested in weekend trips during the summer should contact outfitters in early spring for reservations. While weekday trips are both less crowded and less expensive, reservations are also recommended.

Section:	Middle
Location:	Fayette County, near Ohiopyle, southwestern Pennsylvania
Driving Time:	Pittsburgh—1.5 hours
Difficulty:	Class I–II
Trip Length:	8 miles (13 km)
Trip Options:	Paddle raft; one day
Season:	June–September
Cost:	$16–$28

On warm summer days, families can enjoy the Class I–II middle section of the Youghiogheny River above Ohiopyle. Here, children as young as six years can paddle if they wish. Many seniors and disabled paddlers also enjoy both the forested mountain scenery and easy whitewater. Since guided raft trips on the middle Yough are scheduled on demand, reservations are important.

Youghiogheny River (Lower and Middle) Outfitters

Laurel Highlands River Tours
P.O. Box 107
Ohiopyle, PA 15470
(800) 472–3846
(412) 329–8531

White Water Adventurers
P.O. Box 31
Ohiopyle, PA 15470
(800) 992–7238
(412) 329–8850

Mountain Streams & Trails Outfitters
P.O. Box 106
Ohiopyle, PA 15470
(800) 245–4090
(412) 329–8810

Wilderness Voyageurs
P.O. Box 97
Ohiopyle, PA 15470
(800) 272–4141
(412) 329–5517

YOUGHIOGHENY RIVER (UPPER), MARYLAND

Section:	Sang Run to Friendsville
Location:	Garrett County, near Friendsville, western Maryland
Driving Time:	Baltimore—3.5 hours; Pittsburgh—2 hours
Difficulty:	Class IV–V; Class IV paddle rafting experience is highly recommended
Trip Length:	10 miles (16 km)
Trip Options:	Paddle raft; one day
Season:	April–October; weekdays and on the first Saturday of each month
Cost:	$80–$130

The upper Youghiogheny in western Maryland is a highly technical and demanding Class IV–V stretch of river that should be attempted only by physically fit people with previous Class IV whitewater experience. Outfitters, using a guide in each raft, require each rafter to be an active paddler.

Sang Run, just north of Deep Creek Lake in western Maryland, is the put-in point for the upper Yough. After 4 miles (6.5 km) of flatwater and Class III rapids, the big-time whitewater action begins at Bastard Falls. In its middle canyon the river drops an average of 116 feet per mile through more than twenty Class IV and V rapids. (For comparison, the New River drops 12 feet per mile, the Cheat 25, and the Gauley 28.) Below Bastard Falls, powerful rapids come in quick succession: Charlie's Choice, Snaggle Tooth, Triple Drop, National Falls, Tommy's Hole, Zinger, Hinzerling, Meat Cleaver, Powerful Popper, Lost-n-Found, Cheeseburger, Wright's Hole, and Double Pencil Sharpener.

Rafting on the upper Yough is made possible by weekday water releases (and at least the first Saturday of each month for recreational boating) for electric power at Deep Creek Lake Dam in western Maryland. While these controlled releases by Pennsylvania Electric normally provide predictable water flows, excess water in early spring or following heavy rains often provide rafters with "high-water excitement" and sometimes additional weekend whitewater trips.

Youghiogheny River (Upper) Outfitters

Appalachian Wildwaters
P.O. Box 100
Rowlesburg, WV 26425
(800) 624–8060
(304) 454–2475

Precision Rafting Expeditions
P.O. Box 185
Friendsville, MD 21531
(800) 477–3723
(301) 746–5290

Laurel Highlands River Tours
P.O. Box 107
Ohiopyle, PA 15470
(800) 472–3846
(412) 329–8531

Upper Yough Whitewater Expeditions
P.O. Box 158
Friendsville, MD 21531
(800) 248–1893
(301) 746–5808

North American River Runners
P.O. Box 81
Hico, WV 25854–0081
(800) 950–2585
(304) 658–5276

White Water Adventurers
P.O. Box 31
Ohiopyle, PA 15470
(800) 992–7238
(412) 329–8850

CHEAT RIVER, WEST VIRGINIA

Section:	Cheat Canyon
Location:	Preston County, near Albright, northern West Virginia
Driving Time:	Charleston—2 hours; Pittsburgh—2 hours
Difficulty:	Class III–IV, V
Trip Length:	12 miles (19 km)
Trip Options:	Paddle raft; one day
Season:	April through mid-June
Cost:	$45–$80

The Cheat River Canyon, despite a short spring season, is host to one of the more popular whitewater trips in the mid-Atlantic region. Each spring, thousands of rafters descend on the small northern West Virginia town of Albright prepared to challenge the canyon's acclaimed whitewater. During high water, many of the Cheat's normal Class III–IV rapids—Decision, Big Nasty, Even Nastier, Tear

Drop, High Falls, Maze, and Coliseum Falls—become very demanding Class IV-V rapids.

A November 1985 flood on the Cheat River not only destroyed most of the town of Albright near the put-in, but also dramatically rearranged large rocks and boulders, creating a vastly different river. Outfitters and paddlers alike claim many of the Cheat's rapids are now bigger, better, and more exciting. Rapids such as Big Nasty and Coliseum have intensified and are more challenging than before.

On days when water levels are too high to safely run the Cheat River Canyon, outfitters bus rafters south to a put-in near Rowlesburg and run the Cheat Narrows. The Narrows section has a number of exciting Class III–IV rapids, including Cave, "S" Turn, Double Hydraulic, Calamity, Wind, and Rocking Horse.

During moderate and low-water levels of the late spring and summer, several outfitters offer guided inflatable kayak trips on both the canyon and narrows sections.

Cheat River Outfitters

Appalachian Wildwaters
P.O. Box 100
Rowlesburg, WV 26425
(800) 624–8060
(304) 454–2475

North American River Runners
P.O. Box 81
Hico, WV 25854–0081
(800) 950–2585
(304) 658–5276

Cheat River Outfitters
P.O. Box 134
Albright, WV 26519
(304) 329–2024
(410) 489–2837

Precision Rafting Expeditions
P.O. Box 185
Friendsville, MD 21531
(800) 477–3723
(301) 746–5290

Laurel Highlands River Tours
P.O. Box 107
Ohiopyle, PA 15470
(800) 472–3846
(412) 329–8531

White Water Adventurers
P.O. Box 31
Ohiopyle, PA 15470
(800) 992–7238
(412) 329–8850

Mountain Streams & Trails Outfitters
P.O. Box 106
Ohiopyle, PA 15470
(800) 245–4090
(412) 329–8810

Whitewater World
Route 903
Jim Thorpe, PA 18229
(800) 944–8392
(717) 325–3656

NEW RIVER, WEST VIRGINIA

Section: New River Gorge, Thurmond or Cunard to Fayette Station or Teays Landing (lower)
Location: Fayette County, near Beckley, south-central West Virginia
Driving Time: Charleston—1.5 hours
Difficulty: Class III–V+

Trip Length:	10-17 miles (16-27 km)
Trip Options:	Paddle raft, oar raft; one and two days
Season:	April–October
Cost:	$50–$90 one day; $140–$200 two days

Geologically considered the world's second-oldest river (next to the Nile), the New River begins in the Appalachian foothills of North Carolina and flows northwest through southwest Virginia and West Virginia before joining the Gauley to form the Kanawha River, east of Charleston.

The New River, in south-central West Virginia between the quaint old mining town of Thurmond and Fayette Station, offers an incredibly beautiful 14-mile (23-km) stretch now called the New River Gorge National River. Its unique blend of challenging whitewater, flatwater, waterfalls, and abandoned mining towns can only be fully appreciated by river runners. Here, at the bottom of a canyon 1,400-feet deep, the river drops nearly 250 feet as its large volume pours over countless ledges and boulders. The drop generates fantastic Class IV-V rapids—Surprise, The Keeneys Brothers, Double Z, Greyhound Bus Stopper, and Undercut Rock—with big waves, drops, and holes. During high water, the Keeneys become long and intense Class V+ rapids.

Near the end of the river trip is an impressive view of 876-foot New River Gorge Bridge, the highest and longest single-span steel arch bridge in the world.

Although the New River is free-flowing, dependent upon spring runoff and summer rainfall, its large volume provides ample water for rafting from early spring until late fall.

Section:	Upper
Location:	Fayette County, near Beckley, south-central West Virgina
Driving Time:	Charleston—1.5 hours
Difficulty:	Class I–II
Trip Length:	8 miles (13 km); 14-16 miles (22-26 km)
Trip Options:	Paddle raft, oar raft, inflatable kayak; one day, two days
Season:	June–September
Cost:	$30–$80 one day; $140–$200 multiday

The calmer upper sections of the New River between Hinton and Thurmond, also part of the New River Gorge National River, are well suited to families, senior citizens, the disabled, or anyone wanting a friendly introduction to whitewater rafting. Children as young as six will enjoy the scenery and the easy Class I–II+ rapids alternating with slowly moving flatwater.

On warm days, either of two popular 8-mile (13-km) rafting trips allow ample time for swimming, a short hike to a waterfall, or simple relaxation. Two-day trips, normally 14–16 miles (22–26 km), with riverside overnight camping, are also available. In addition to paddle and oar rafts, inflatable kayaks are available for those wishing to paddle their own boat.

Outfitters listed on page 179.

GAULEY RIVER, WEST VIRGINIA

Sections: Summersville Dam to Swiss (upper and lower)
Location: Nicholas and Fayette counties, near Summersville, south-central West Virginia
Driving Time: Charleston—1.5 hours; Pittsburgh—4 hours
Difficulty: Class IV–V+ (upper); paddle rafting experience highly recommended or required; III–IV+ (lower)
Trip Length: Upper—11–15 miles (18–24 km); Lower—13–17 miles (21–27 km)
Trip Options: Paddle raft, oar raft, paddle/oar raft; one and two days
Season: September–October
Cost: $70–$120 (upper); $60–$120 (lower); $120–$150 (upper and lower)

The Gauley River, one of the world's premier whitewater opportunities, is exciting, exhilarating, demanding, and highly technical. With over fifty major rapids—one hundred rapids in all—the Gauley is justly promoted by outfitters and other whitewater experts as "the best two-day whitewater rafting trip in North America."

The Gauley River is one of the world's most thrilling whitewater trips.

"Intense" accurately describes the high-water Gauley experience. Five major Class V rapids—Insignificant, Pillow Rock, Lost Paddle, Iron Ring, and Sweets Falls—challenge rafters' technical skills on the upper Gauley. The lower Gauley follows with dozens of Class III–IV+ rapids, including Koontz's Flume, Mash, Heaven Help You, and Pure Screaming Hell.

The Gauley's renowned fall rafting season is a result of the drawdown of Summersville Lake as the U.S. Army Corps of Engineers lowers the water level to prepare for winter and spring runoff. Large-volume water releases normally begin the first Friday after Labor Day and continue for five or six four-day weekends (Friday through Monday), ending with a two-day weekend release in mid-October. It is important to make reservations for the Gauley many weeks in advance; by September, very few spaces are available.

Gauley rafting customers consider a variety of trip options: one-day trips on either the upper or lower sections versus two-day trips covering both sections; tent camping versus indoor lodging on overnight trips; and trips using paddle rafts versus oar-assisted paddle rafts. The use of the latter does not lessen the need for individual paddle participation. Many outfitters use 16- to 20-foot rafts with rear-mounted oar frames to allow maximum guide maneuverability. Rafters should consider the cool West Virginia fall weather and the cold water from Summersville Lake when preparing for the Gauley trip. On other than very warm days, wet suits are usually recommended.

Section:	Middle
Location:	Fayette County, near Summersville, south-central West Virginia
Driving Time:	Charleston—1.5 hours; Pittsburgh—4 hours
Difficulty:	Class II–III+
Trip Length:	7 miles (11 km)
Trip Options:	Paddle raft, oar raft, inflatable kayak; one day
Season:	April–September
Cost:	$50–$95

Several outfitters on the Gauley River offer a variety of exciting intermediate-level rafting opportunities on the middle section, between Sweets Falls and Koontz Bend, a 7-mile (11-km) stretch with more than twenty Class II–III rapids, during the spring and summer. This recent development is the result of new state-of-the-art rafting equipment and construction of new access roads to the river.

The type of raft used is primarily dependent upon daily water levels. During lower water, rafters often paddle inflatable kayaks. These small, one-person, self-bailing kayaks provide an excellent opportunity to learn and improve paddling skills in the company of skilled guides and supportive friends. At medium water levels, outfitters commonly use 12- and 14-foot rafts. Should seasonal rains provide the Gauley with water levels comparable with the fall drawdown flows, outfitters offer regular raft trips on the upper and lower sections.

New River and Gauley River Outfitters

ACE Whitewater
P.O. Box 1168
Oak Hill, WV 25901
(800) 223-2641
(304) 469-2651

Appalachian Wildwaters
P.O. Box 100
Rowlesburg, WV 26425
(800) 624-8060
(304) 454-2475

Class VI River Runners
P.O. Box 78
Lansing, WV 25862-0078
(800) 252-7784
(304) 574-0704

Drift-a-Bit
P.O. Box 885
Fayetteville, WV 25840
(800) 633-7238
(304) 574-3282

Mountain River Tours
P.O. Box 88
Hico, WV 25854
(800) 822-1386
(304) 658-5266

Mountain Streams & Trails Outfitters
(Gauley only)
P.O. Box 106
Ohiopyle, PA 15470
(800) 245-4090
(412) 329-8810

New and Gauley River Adventures
P.O. Box 44
Lansing, WV 25862
(800) 759-7238
(304) 574-3008

New River Scenic Whitewater Tours
P.O. Box 637
Hinton, WV 25951
(800) 292-0880
(304) 466-2288

North American River Runners
P.O. Box 81
Hico, WV 25854-0081
(800) 950-2585
(304) 658-5276

Passages to Adventure
P.O. Box 71
Fayetteville, WV 25840
(800) 634-3785
(304) 574-1037

Precision Rafting Expeditions
(Gauley only)
P.O. Box 185
Friendsville, MD 21531
(800) 477-3723
(301) 746-5290

Rivers
P.O. Drawer 39
Lansing, WV 25862
(800) 879-7483
(304) 574-3954

Songer Whitewater
P.O. Box 300
Fayetteville, WV 25840-0300
(800) 356-7238
(304) 658-9926

The Riverman
P.O. Box 360
Fayetteville, WV 25840
(800) 545-7238
(304) 574-0515

Whitewater Information
P.O. Box 243
Glen Jean, WV 25846
(800) 782-7238
(304) 465-0855

Wildwater Expeditions Unlimited
P.O. Box 155
Lansing, WV 25862
(800) 982-7238
(304) 658-4007

TYGART RIVER, WEST VIRGINIA

Section: Arden to Cove Run (Arden)
Location: Barbour County, near Tygart Lake State Park, northern West Virginia
Driving Time: Charleston—2.5 hours; Pittsburgh—2.5 hours
Difficulty: Class III–IV, V
Trip Length: 8 miles (13 km)
Trip Options: Paddle raft, inflatable kayak; one day
Season: April–October
Cost: $45–$70

Whitewater enthusiasts seeking an alternative to some of the well-known mid-Atlantic rivers should find the Tygart an exciting surprise.

Whitewater thrills on the Arden section, the Tygart's most popular commercial raft trip, begin almost immediately below the Arden Bridge put-in. For nearly 8 miles (13 km), the river drops quickly through some twenty-five major rapids on its journey to Tygart Lake.

Many of the Tygart's Class III-V rapids are 4- to 5-foot drops. The final rapid, unforgettable Wells Falls, is considered the Tygart's best. Rafters must negotiate a blind turn and crash through several large hydraulics before reaching the placid waters of Tygart Lake. Not all of Tygart's rapids are runnable; 18-foot "Class VII" Moats Falls must be portaged.

Although the river's Arden section above Tygart Lake is not dam controlled, adequate water levels for rafting are usually available for the entire season. At lower water levels, outfitters use inflatable kayaks or switch raft trips to the Valley Falls section below Grafton Dam. During the early spring or when water levels are too high to run the Arden section, outfitters run trips on the Class IV–V Tygart Gorge. Contact outfitters for information about either of these alternative trips.

Tygart River Outfitters

Appalachian Wildwaters
P.O. Box 100
Rowlesburg, WV 26425
(800) 624–8060
(304) 454–2475

Mountain Streams & Trails Outfitters
P.O. Box 106
Ohiopyle, PA 15470
(800) 245–4090
(412) 329–8810

SHENANDOAH RIVER, WEST VIRGINIA/VIRGINIA

Section: Shenandoah Staircase to Potomac
Location: Jefferson County, near Harpers Ferry National Historical Park, eastern West Virginia
Driving Time: Baltimore—1 hour; Washington, D.C.—1 hour
Difficulty: Class I–II, III
Trip Length: 5–6 miles (8–9 km)
Trip Options: Paddle raft; half-day
Season: April–October
Cost: $35–$45

The Shenandoah River offers an enjoyable family-type rafting experience through the beautiful Blue Ridge Mountains above its confluence with the Potomac River at the historic town of Harpers Ferry.

Class III Bull Falls, the Shenandoah River's largest rapid, comes after a relaxing start that includes about 2 miles (3 km) of flatwater and small waves. Below the falls, the river drops over a series of Class II (III in high water) rapids and wide rock ledges called the Staircase.

Downstream from the U.S. 340 bridge, as the Shenandoah passes Harpers Ferry National Historic Park and joins the Potomac, there are impressive views of old stone bridges, railroad trestles, and rustic buildings. The final 2 miles (3 km) on the Potomac before the Sandy Hook take-out include the Class II–III White Horse Rapids.

Either a morning or afternoon rafting trip on the Shenandoah still leaves time for a leisurely stroll in charming Harpers Ferry where, prior to the Civil War, falling water powered one of the nation's most important rifle factories. This factory and the nearby federal armory were objects of the famous John Brown raid in 1859.

Shenandoah River Outfitters

Blue Ridge Outfitters
P.O. Box 750
Harpers Ferry, WV 25425
(304) 725–3444

Historical River Tours
RR-3 Box 1258
Harpers Ferry, WV 25425
(304) 535–6649
(410) 489–2837

River and Trail Outfitters
604 Valley Rd.
Knoxville, MD 21758
(301) 834–9950
(301) 695–5177

JAMES RIVER, VIRGINIA

Section:	The Falls of the James
Location:	City of Richmond
Driving Time:	Washington, D.C.—2 hours
Difficulty:	Class II–IV
Trip Length:	4–8 miles (6.5–13 km)
Trip Options:	Paddle raft; one day
Season:	March–November
Cost:	$25–$45

Richmond's James River offers an unusual rafting opportunity in the heart of a metropolitan area. Historic sites and natural beauty complement the exciting whitewater. The trip, which begins northwest of the Richmond suburbs, passes through the city's 500-acre James River Park nature refuge, where an abundance of birds and other wildlife can be observed. It concludes with impressive views of the modern downtown Richmond skyline, numerous bridges, and old factories.

Challenging Class III–IV rapids—First Break, Hollywood, Vepco Levee, Second Break, Pipeline, and Southside—through Richmond are created by the changing elevations between the Appalachian piedmont and the Atlantic coastal plain, commonly referred to as the fall zone. The falls comprise large waves, ledge drops, broken-down dams, and swift chutes and holes. During high water, the wide James has one of the largest whitewater volumes of any river in the United States.

James River Outfitter

Richmond Raft Company
4400 E. Main St.
Richmond, VA 23231
(804) 222–7238

CHAPTER 16

■ ■ ■

Southeast States

Accessible mountains, deep canyons, rock-filled rivers and streams, numerous dams and reservoirs, and plentiful rainfall provide the necessary ingredients for a wide range of whitewater rafting opportunities in the southeastern United States. Nine popular intermediate and advanced whitewater trips are located within the Appalachian Mountain regions of northern Georgia, western North and South Carolina, eastern Tennessee, and eastern Kentucky.

Eight beginner and family-oriented rafting trips welcome children from seven to ten years old. Many of these fine trips are located near one of the most-visited national parks in the United States, Great Smoky Mountains National Park.

The famed Chattooga River, a National Wild and Scenic River along the Georgia–South Carolina border, has both beginning and advanced all-season whitewater stretches through beautiful and largely inaccessible canyons.

North Carolina's most popular raft trip, the Nantahala River, which flows through ancient Cherokee tribal lands, is also the southeast's favorite for beginners and families. Nearby, the milder Tuckaseigee provides family rafting for even younger children. Northwest of Asheville, the scenic French Broad River has a variety of family rafting choices including inflatable kayaks. Farther north in western North Carolina, Wilson Creek and the Watauga Gorge provide some of the state's best technical whitewater.

The Nolichucky River, which creates Tennessee's and North Carolina's deepest canyon, has both challenging and easy whitewaters. After exciting springtime water levels become too low for adventure rafting, outfitters offer summertime introductory raft and kayak trips for families. Similarly, on the Watauga River near Elizabethton in northeastern Tennessee, there are daily family raft trips.

Tennessee's Ocoee River, the southeast region's favorite technical whitewater because of its continuous rapids, was chosen as whitewater course for the 1996 Summer Olympic Games. Just north of Great Smoky Mountains National Park, visitors may enjoy a scenic and exciting raft trip on the Big Pigeon River. Elsewhere in Tennessee, the Cumberland River, in the Big South Fork National River and Recreation Area, has trips for adventurous rafters in the spring and for families in the early summer.

Eastern Kentucky's North Fork of the Cumberland, below spectacular Cumberland Falls, provides a scenic and enjoyable trip for first-time rafters. Above Lake Cumberland, the Rockcastle River provides intense whitewater each spring.

Finally, the Russell Fork of the Levisa River, between southwestern Virginia and eastern Kentucky, is often touted as eastern America's most technically difficult commercial whitewater trip.

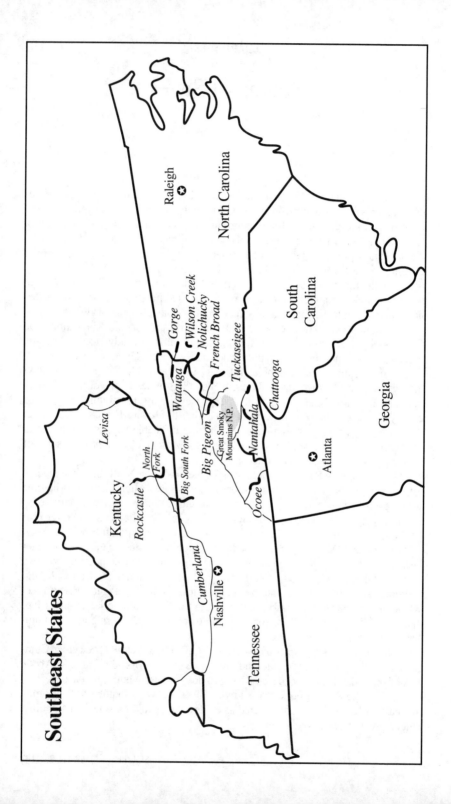

Southeast States

Southeast States
River Comparison

	Difficulty	Min. Age	H	D	M	Season	P	O	K
Georgia/South Carolina									
Chattooga									
Section III	/ /	10	✗			Mar–Nov	✗		
Section IV	/ / /	13	✗			Mar–Nov	✗		
North Carolina									
Nantahala	/	7	✗			Mar–Nov	✗		
Tuckaseigee	/	4	✗			May–Sep	✗	✗	
French Broad	/	8	✗	✗		Mar–Nov	✗	✗	
Wilson Creek	/ /	12	✗			Mar–Jun			✗
North Carolina/Tennessee									
Watauga (Gorge)	/ / /	16	✗			Mar–Apr	✗		
Watauga (Section V)	/	3	✗	✗		Apr–Oct	✗		✗
Nolichucky									
Gorge	/ /	12	✗	✗		Mar–Jun	✗	✗	✗
Family Gorge	/	5	✗	✗		Jun–Sep	✗	✗	
Tennessee									
Big Pigeon	/	10	✗			Apr–Sep	✗		
Ocoee	/ /	12	✗			Apr–Oct	✗		
Cumberland (Big South Fork)									
Gorge	/ /	13	✗			Mar–Apr	✗	✗	
Canyon	/	7	✗			May	✗	✗	
Kentucky									
Cumberland (North Fork)	/	8	✗	✗		May–Oct	✗		
Rockcastle	/ /	12	✗			Spring/Fall	✗		
Virginia/Kentucky									
Levisa	/ / /	18	✗			October	✗		

/ Beginner—Easy whitewater. Fun for everyone.
/ / Intermediate—Moderate whitewater.
No previous rafting experience is necessary.
/ / / Advanced—Difficult whitewater.
Previous Class IV paddle rafting experience is recommended or required.

H—Half-Day Trip, D—Day Trip, M—Multiday Trip
P—Paddle Raft, O—Oar Raft, K—Inflatable Kayak

The Five Falls on the Chattooga River provide the best all-season Class IV–V whitewater in the Southeast.

CHATTOOGA RIVER, GEORGIA/SOUTH CAROLINA

Section: III
Location: Rabun County, near Clayton, northeastern Georgia; Oconee
                    County, near Long Creek, western South Carolina
Driving Time: Atlanta—2 hours; Knoxville—3 hours
Difficulty: Class II–III, IV
Trip Length: 5–14 miles (8–22.5 km)
Trip Options: Paddle raft; one day
Season: March–early November
Cost: $35–$75

The Chattooga, one of the eastern United States' first rivers to be protected under the National Wild and Scenic Rivers Act, offers 20 miles (32 km) of splendid rafting through the beautiful Sumter and Chattahoochee national forests along the Georgia–South Carolina border.

Rafters have their choice between an introductory trip on the longer and less demanding Section III and the challenging and quite technical Section IV. It was on the remote Chattooga that most of the whitewater scenes in the movie *Deliverance* were filmed.

Section III whitewater action includes numerous Class I–II rapids, some slowly flowing flatwater, and Class III rapids: the Narrows, Keyhole, and Eye of the Needle. Bull Sluice, the only Class IV rapid, can either be rafted or walked around. Section III is recommended for large groups, first-timers, and less-experienced rafters.

The Chattooga, like most free-flowing rivers in the eastern United States, is subject to low water levels in late summer and fall. At low water levels, trips are sometimes shortened, and outfitters use smaller rafts. Even this more leisurely pace provides rafters the opportunity to enjoy the incredible natural beauty of the canyons with little or no visual contact with other rafting groups.

Section: IV
Location: Rabun County, near Clayton, northeastern Georgia; Oconee
                    County, near Long Creek, western South Carolina
Driving Time: Atlanta—2 hours; Knoxville—3 hours
Difficulty: Class III–V; paddle rafting experience is recommended
Trip Length: 6–8 miles (9.5–13 km)
Trip Options: Paddle raft; one day
Season: March–early November
Cost: $55–$80

Section IV from the U.S. 76 bridge to Lake Tugaloo has challenging whitewater in some of the wildest and most inaccessible canyons in the southeast. The river drops nearly 50 feet per mile over numerous ledges and falls as it cascades between towering cliffs, spectacular rock formations, and beautiful waterfalls. Riverside scouting and utmost caution are the norm.

The first half of Section IV consists of a number of "warm-up" rapids: Surfing, Screaming Left Turn, and Rock Jumble. After Woodall Shoals and the thrilling Seven Foot Falls, the Five Falls run challenges rafters with five technical Class IV-V rapids—First Falls, Corkscrew, Crack in the Rock, Jawbone, and Sock-Em-Dog—in quick succession. Below the Five Falls, only Class III Shoulder Bone rapids remains before the calm of Lake Tugaloo.

Rafters considering Section IV should be in good physical shape, able to swim well, and have previously rafted Class IV whitewater.

Chattooga River Outfitters

Nantahala Outdoor Center
13077 Hwy. 19 West
Bryson City, NC 28713–9114
(800) 232–7238
(704) 488–6900

Wildwater Ltd.
P.O. Box 100
Long Creek, SC 29658
(800) 451–9972
(803) 647–9587

Southeastern Expeditions
2936-H N. Druid Hills Rd.
Atlanta, GA 30329
(800) 868–7238
(404) 329–0433

NANTAHALA RIVER, NORTH CAROLINA

Section:	Nantahala Gorge
Location:	Macon and Swain counties, southwest of Bryson City, western North Carolina
Driving Time:	Asheville—1 hour; Atlanta—2.5 hours
Difficulty:	Class II–III
Trip Length:	8 miles (13 km)
Trip Options:	Paddle raft; half-day
Season:	March–November
Cost:	$20–$30

Near the Great Smoky Mountains National Park in western North Carolina, the Nantahala Gorge offers an ideal introduction to whitewater rafting. With a guide-escorted trip, families as well as the most inexperienced paddler can enjoy this beautiful, mostly Class II mountain stream. Just prior to the take-out, newly acquired paddling skills may be tested on Nantahala Falls, an exciting Class III rapid.

The Nantahala, a dam-controlled river, is raftable all season, and the water remains cool throughout the summer heat as it comes from the bottom of Nantahala Lake. Trips on the Nantahala take about three hours and are scheduled both mornings and afternoons. Reservations are recommended as the Nantahala is one of the four most popular whitewater rivers in the eastern United States. Each year more than one hundred fifty thousand people experience the thrills of whitewater rafting on the Nantahala.

The Indian word Nantahala means "land of the noonday sun," and aptly describes the steep-sided Nantahala Gorge, perfect habitat for lush groves of rhododendron, mountain laurel, and the unusual princess tree.

Nantahala River Outfitters

Great Smokies Rafting Company
13077 Hwy. 19 West
Bryson City, NC 28713–9114
(800) 238–6302
(704) 488–6302

Nantahala Outdoor Center
13077 Hwy. 19 West
Bryson City, NC 28713–9114
(800) 232–7238
(704) 488–6900

Nantahala Rafts
U.S. 19 West, Box 45
Bryson City, NC 28713
(800) 245–7700 (May–Oct)
(704) 488–3854 (Nov–Apr)

Rafting in the Smokies
P.O. Box 592
Gatlinburg, TN 37738
(615) 436–5008

Rolling Thunder River Company
P.O. Box 88
Almond, NC 28702
(800) 344–5838
(704) 488–2030

USA Raft
P.O. Box 277
Rowlesburg, WV 26425
(800) 872–7238
(304) 454–2475

Wildwater Ltd.
P.O. Box 100
Long Creek, SC 29658
(800) 451–9972
(803) 647–9587

TUCKASEIGEE, NORTH CAROLINA

Section:	Lower gorge
Location:	Jackson County, near Sylva, western North Carolina
Driving Time:	Asheville—1 hour; Atlanta—3 hours
Difficulty:	Class I–II
Trip Length:	5–7 miles (8–11 km)
Trip Options:	Paddle raft, inflatable kayak; half-day
Season:	May–September
Cost:	$18–$25

Western North Carolina's Tuckaseigee River offers an enjoyable alternative to some of the more crowded southeastern rivers. Its mellow waters are likewise easier and warmer than either the Nantahala or Ocoee rivers.

The Tuckaseigee's easy Class I–II whitewaters are ideal for families with children as young as four years. Together they may quickly learn new paddling skills and navigate the river's currents in either guide-supervised small rafts or inflatable kayaks.

Rafting on the Tuckaseigee is a relaxing and fun way for almost anyone to enjoy the Great Smoky Mountains' wildlife and scenery. Depending upon water levels, the Tuckaseigee River rafting trip normally takes about three to four hours.

Tuckaseigee River Outfitters

Blue Ridge Outing Company
P.O. Box 15308
Asheville, NC 28813
(800) 572–3510
(704) 687–9715

Tuckaseegee Outfitters
P.O. Box 1719
Cullowhee, NC 28723
(704) 586–5050

FRENCH BROAD RIVER, NORTH CAROLINA

Section:	Barnard to Hot Springs (Section IX)
Location:	Madison County, northwest of Asheville, western North Carolina
Driving Time:	Asheville—.5 hour; Knoxville—1.5 hours
Difficulty:	Class II–III, IV
Trip Length:	8 miles (13 km)
Trip Options:	Paddle raft, inflatable kayak; half-day and one day
Season:	March–November
Cost:	$45–$50

For much of its course through western North Carolina's Pisgah National Forest, the French Broad River offers little whitewater for rafting enthusiasts. In the 8-mile (13-km) section between Barnard and Hot Springs, however, rafters are able to enjoy an exciting trip through beautiful gorges, over ledges, and around large boulders as the river alternates between quiet pools and swift-moving rapids. The French Broad is ideal for families and first-time rafters as it is neither too demanding nor technically difficult.

Among the French Broad's seven or eight larger rapids—such as Pillow Rock, Stackhouse, Needle Rock, and Frank Bell's—none are more than Class III with the exception of Frank Bell's, however, which rates Class IV+ during high water.

Generally the French Broad maintains adequate water levels for rafting through spring and summer. During lower summer water levels, outfitters more frequently offer half-day trips from Barnard to Stackhouse Rapids as well as guided inflatable kayak trips.

French Broad River Outfitters

Carolina Wilderness
P.O. Box 488
Hot Springs, NC 28743
(800) 872–7437
(704) 622–3535

Nantahala Outdoor Center
13077 Hwy. 19 West
Bryson City, NC 28713–9114
(800) 232–7238
(704) 488–6900

French Broad Rafting Company
1 Thomas Bridge Rd.
Marshall, NC 28753
(800) 842–3189
(704) 649–3574

USA Raft
P.O. Box 277
Rowlesburg, WV 26425
(800) 872–7238
(304) 454–2475

Wahoo's Adventures
P.O. Box 1915
Boone, NC 28607
(800) 444–7238
(704) 262–5774

WILSON CREEK, NORTH CAROLINA

Section:	Lower
Location:	Caldwell County, near Lenoir, western North Carolina
Driving Time:	Knoxville—3 hours; Winston-Salem—2 hours
Difficulty:	Class III–IV, V
Trip Length:	5 miles (8 km)
Trip Options:	Inflatable kayak; one day
Season:	March–June
Cost:	$65

Wilson Creek, in western North Carolina's Pisgah National Forest, offers adventuresome rafters an excellent late-winter and early-spring alternative to some of the better-known southeastern rivers. At high water levels, the 2.5-mile (4-km) Wilson Creek Gorge is one of the most technically difficult whitewater stretches in the southeast.

Outfitters quickly prepare rafters for the dramatic Wilson Creek whitewater descent—more than 100 feet per mile in some sections—with two Class III rapids, School House and Final Exam. After the brief tune-up, cascading whitewater with large holes and ledge drops requires fast and precise maneuvering through narrow chutes and around blind turns. Class III-V rapids—Ten Foot Falls, Saniflush, Thunderball, Maytag, Three Falls, and Benner's Falls—highlight the nonstop action.

Although in most years, the free-flowing Wilson Creek is runnable from late February until late May, the best water levels for big whitewater are generally during March and April.

Wilson Creek Outfitter

Wahoo's Adventures
P.O. Box 1915
Boone, NC 28607
(800) 444–7238
(704) 262–5774

WATAUGA RIVER (GORGE), NORTH CAROLINA/TENNESSEE

Section:	Gorge (Section IV)
Location:	Avery and Watauga counties, western North Carolina; Johnson County, eastern Tennessee
Driving Time:	Knoxville—2.5 hours; Winston-Salem—2 hours
Difficulty:	Class III–V
Trip Length:	8 miles (13 km)
Trip Options:	Paddle raft; one day

Season:	March–April
Cost:	$100–$150

The Watauga Gorge, above Watauga Lake, is a spectacular whitewater run for fit, adventuresome rafters. This not-too-well-known stretch has nearly continuous Class III–IV whitewater and a lot of surprises, including a couple of dramatic Class V drops. The gorge has an average gradient of 100 feet per mile and three sections dropping over 190 feet per mile.

The 5-mile (8-km) gorge raft trip has fifteen rapids rated Class IV or greater. Immediately after the western North Carolina put-in at Guys Ford Bridge, the river's action starts with three steep ledge-type Class III–IV rapids, followed by Class V Hydro, which may be run depending on water levels. Next is a continuous Class IV stretch with Vernons, Maggies Drop, Edge of the World, Hud's Hook, and Boogie Two Shoes. After a very brief lull, constant Class IV–V action—Big Ass Plunge, Heavy Water, Knuckle, and Dougs Drop—requires quick decisions and precision maneuvering through numerous mazelike chutes.

Tennessee the Wrong Way, a 16-foot vertical Class VI+ falls, must be portaged. Ledge, a 9-foot diagonal slide, provides a long-remembered ride. Just before the eastern Tennessee take-out, the river eases up with two Class III–IV rapids, Last Hair and Rewind.

Watauga rafting is dependent on adequate late-winter and early-spring water levels. Rafters are encouraged to make early reservations and maintain close contact with their outfitter just prior to the trip.

Watauga River (Gorge) Outfitters

High Mountain Expeditions
P.O. Box 1299
Blowing Rock, NC 28605
(800) 262–9036
(704) 295–4200

Wahoo's Adventures
P.O. Box 1915
Boone, NC 28607
(800) 444–7238
(704) 262–5774

WATAUGA RIVER (SECTION V), TENNESSEE

Section:	Wilber Dam to Elizabethton (Section V)
Location:	Carter County, near Elizabethton, eastern Tennessee
Driving Time:	Knoxville—2.5 hours; Asheville—2 hours
Difficulty:	Class I–II, III
Trip Length:	4–8 miles (7–13 km)
Trip Options:	Paddle raft, inflatable kayak; half-day and one day
Season:	April–October
Cost:	$40–$55

The Watauga River below Wilber Dam is an excellent beginning-level raft trip. Its friendly Class II+ whitewater is considered small enough for families with very young children. Outfitters allow children as young as three years to enjoy the trip.

The Watauga River's scenic course, featuring numerous waves and continuous flow, is lined by limestone bluffs, old farms, homesteads, and hardwood trees.

Water releases from the Tennessee Valley Authority's Watauga Lake and Dam east of Elizabethton are normally sufficient for afternoon rafting throughout the season.

Watauga River (Section V) Outfitters

Edge of the World Outfitters
P.O. Box 1137
Banner Elk, NC 28604
(704) 898–9550

High Mountain Expeditions
P.O. Box 1299
Blowing Rock, NC 28605
(800) 262–9036
(704) 295–4200

Wahoo's Adventures
P.O. Box 1915
Boone, NC 28607
(800) 444–7238
(704) 262–5774

NOLICHUCKY RIVER, NORTH CAROLINA/TENNESSEE

Section: Poplar, North Carolina, to Erwin, Tennessee (Gorge)
Location: Mitchell County, western North Carolina; Unicoi County, near Erwin, eastern Tennessee
Driving Time: Asheville—1.5 hours; Knoxville—1.5 hours
Difficulty: Class III–IV+
Trip Length: 10 miles (16 km)
Trip Options: Paddle raft, oar raft, inflatable kayak; one and two day
Season: Late March–June
Cost: $42–$70

The Nolichucky Gorge in the Appalachian's Unaka Mountains of western North Carolina and eastern Tennessee provides a spectacular backdrop for rafting on the Nolichucky River. Throughout much of the gorge the walls rise more than 2,800 feet above the river, which originates on the slopes of Mount Mitchell—at 6,684 feet, eastern America's highest point. The Clinchfield Railroad line follows the entire river course between Poplar, North Carolina, and Erwin, Tennessee.

The first half of the 10-mile (16-km) Nolichucky trip is the most intense. Large boulders, giant waves, and a gradient dropping at a rate of 66 feet per mile create numerous long Class III–IV+ rapids such as On the Rocks, Jaws, Quarter Mile, Rooster Tail, and The Sousehole. This portion of the river requires active rafter participation, leaving little time to enjoy the passing scenery.

Section: Family Gorge
Location: Mitchell County, western North Carolina; Unicoi County, near Erwin, eastern Tennessee
Driving Time: Asheville—1.5 hours; Knoxville—1.5 hours
Difficulty: Class I–III
Trip Length: 5–10 miles (8–16 km)
Trip Options: Paddle raft, inflatable kayak; half-day, one day
Season: June–September
Cost: $42–$70

The high-water rafting season on the Nolichucky, a free-flowing river through Pisgah and Cherokee national forests, usually lasts only from early March until mid-June.

During the summer months when water levels on the Nolichucky become too low for large rafts, outfitters offer guided trips using smaller rafts and inflatable kayaks. These superior low-water runs are popular with families, seniors, the disabled, and vacationers just wanting to relax and enjoy the scenery. On typical warm summer days, outfitters allow time for swimming and hiking.

Nolichucky River Outfitters

Carolina Wilderness
P.O. Box 488
Hot Springs, NC 28743
(800) 872–7437
(704) 622–3535

Nantahala Outdoor Center
13077 Hwy. 19 West
Bryson City, NC 28713–9114
(800) 232–7238
(704) 488–6900

Cherokee Adventures
Route 1, Box 605
Erwin, TN 37650–9524
(800) 445–7238
(615) 743–7733

USA Raft
P.O. Box 277
Rowlesburg, WV 26425
(800) 872–7238
(304) 454–2475

High Mountain Expeditions
P.O. Box 1299
Blowing Rock, NC 28605
(800) 262–9036
(704) 295–4200

Wahoo's Adventures
P.O. Box 1915
Boone, NC 28607
(800) 444–7238
(704) 262–5774

BIG PIGEON RIVER, TENNESSEE

Section: Waterville to Hartford
Location: Cooke County, near Hartford, eastern Tennessee
Driving Time: Knoxville—1 hour; Asheville—1.5 hours
Trip Length: 5 miles (8 km)
Difficulty: Class III–IV
Trip Options: Paddle raft; two hours
Season: April–September
Cost: $35

The Big Pigeon River in eastern Tennessee offers a scenic rafting opportunity in Cherokee National Forest just north of Great Smoky Mountains National Park. This river, which parallels Interstate 40 and is crossed by the Appalachian Trail, is easily accessible to park visitors.

Although the Pigeon River rafting trip is short, there is no lack of whitewater action. Class III–IV Lost Guide and Double Reactionary rapids are the largest of twelve Class III+ drops during the Pigeon's course. This two-hour trip provides an excellent nontechnical introduction to whitewater.

Rafting trips are dependent on water releases from Carolina Power and

Light's Walter's power generation plant. The most consistent whitewater is in April, May, and August.

Big Pigeon River Outfitter

Rafting in the Smokies
P.O. Box 592
Gatlinburg, TN 37738
(615) 436–5008

OCOEE RIVER, TENNESSEE

Section:	Ocoee Dam 2 to its powerhouse
Location:	Polk County, east of Cleveland, eastern Tennessee
Driving Time:	Atlanta—2.5 hours; Chattanooga—1 hour
Difficulty:	Class III–IV
Trip Length:	4.5 miles (7 km)
Trip Options:	Paddle raft; half-day
Season:	April–October
Cost:	$25–$40

The Ocoee River, in eastern Tennessee, is one of the premier whitewater rivers in the southeast. It rivals North Carolina's Nantahala and Pennsylvania's Lehigh and Youghiogheny as the most popular commercial rafting trip in eastern America.

The Ocoee River has been chosen as the whitewater course for the 1996 Olympic Summer Games. Photo courtesy of Ocoee Rafting.

The 4.5-mile (7-km) Ocoee raft trip features almost continuous whitewater during its 60-foot-per-mile drop between the Ocoee Diversion Dam (Dam 2) and its powerhouse. Many Class III–IV rapids—such as Entrance, Broken Nose, Double Trouble, Tablesaw, Diamond Splitter, and Hell Hole—feature big holes and large waves.

Rafting on the Ocoee has only been possible since 1976, when an old flume built in 1912–13 was condemned as unsafe and water was returned to the original channel. Today the Ocoee's flow is regulated by the Tennessee Valley Authority to assure continuous rapids and dependable water levels. Guaranteed water flows are now available Thursday through Monday during the summer and on weekends during spring and fall.

U.S. 64, which parallels much of the river, provides several excellent views of the Ocoee's impressive rapids, chosen as the whitewater course for the 1996 Olympic Summer Games.

Ocoee River Outfitters

Cripple Creek Expeditions
P.O. Box 98
Hwy. 64
Ocoee, TN 37361
(800) 338–7238
(615) 338–8441

Eagle Adventure Company
P.O. Box 970
McCaysville, GA 30555
(800) 288–3245
(706) 492–2277

High Country
Rt. 1, Box 538
Ocee, TN 37361
(615) 338–8634

Nantahala Outdoor Center
13077 Hwy. 19 West
Bryson City, NC 28713–9114
(800) 232–7238
(704) 488–6900

Ocoee Inn Rafting
Rt. 1, Box 347
Benton, TN 37307
(800) 272–7238
(615) 338–2064

Ocoee Outdoors
P.O. Box 72
Ocoee, TN 37361
(800) 533–7767
(615) 338–2438

Ocoee Rafting
P.O. Box 461
Ducktown, TN 37326
(800) 251–4800
(615) 496–3388

Outdoor Adventure Rafting
P.O. Box 109
Ocoee, TN 37361
(800) 627–7636
(615) 338–8914

Quest Expeditions
P.O. Box 499
Benton, TN 37307
(800) 277–4537
(615) 338–2979

Rolling Thunder River Company
P.O. Box 88
Almond, NC 28702
(800) 344–5838
(704) 488–2030

Southeastern Expeditions
2936-H N. Druid Hills Rd.
Atlanta, GA 30329
(800) 868–7238
(404) 329–0433

USA Raft
P.O. Box 277
Rowlesburg, WV 26425
(800) 872–7238
(304) 454–2475

Sunburst Adventures
P.O. Box 329
Benton, TN 37307
(800) 247–8388
(615) 338–8388

Wahoo's Adventures
P.O. Box 1915
Boone, NC 28607
(800) 444–7238
(704) 262–5774

Wildwater Ltd.
P.O. Box 100
Long Creek, SC 29658
(800) 451–9972
(803) 647–9587

CUMBERLAND RIVER (BIG SOUTH FORK), TENNESSEE

Section:	Gorge
Location:	Scott County, near Oneida, north-central Tennessee
Driving Time:	Knoxville—1.5 hours
Difficulty:	Class III–IV
Trip Length:	12 miles (19 km)
Trip Options:	Paddle raft, inflatable kayak; one day
Season:	March–early May
Cost:	$65

In Tennessee, rafting on the Cumberland is located in a remote and wild rock gorge of the Big South Fork National River and Recreation Area.

Raft trips through the Big South Fork Gorge usually begin at the Burnt Mill bridge on the Clearfork, which has several significant rapids before the waterway joins Tennessee's New River to become the Cumberland River downstream. As the Big South Fork's volume increases and the drops become more frequent, Class IV rapids—Deliverance and the Big Three (Double Falls, Washing Machine, and Ell)—turn this whitewater experience into a springtime delight. The 5-mile (8-km) canyon section, beginning at Pine Creek below the Class IV rapids, includes the Narrows, Jake's Hole, and the O and W.

Big South Fork Gorge rafting trips are scheduled to coincide with maximum spring runoff conditions, which generally run from late March until early May.

Section:	Canyon
Location:	Scott County, near Oneida, north-central Tennessee
Driving Time:	Knoxville—1.5 hours
Difficulty:	Class II–III
Trip Length:	5 miles (8 km)
Trip Options:	Paddle raft, inflatable kayak; one day

Season:	May
Cost:	$40–$60

After spring water levels drop, usually by early May, outfitters use inflatable kayaks and small rafts to provide exciting low-water trips through the 5-mile (8-km) canyon section. These trips, which normally extend until the end of May, are becoming popular with first-time rafters and families. Children as young as seven are welcome.

Because of the increasing popularity of this wilderness low-water rafting experience, early reservations are recommended.

Cumberland River (Big South Fork) Outfitters

Cumberland Rapid Transit	Sheltowee Trace Outfitters
Rock Creek Route, Box 200	P.O. Box 1060
Jamestown, TN 38556	Whitley City, KY 42653
(615) 879–4818	(800) 541–7238
	(606) 376–5567

CUMBERLAND RIVER (NORTH FORK), KENTUCKY

Section:	Cumberland Falls
Location:	Whitley and McCreary counties, Cumberland Falls State Park, south-central Kentucky
Driving Time:	Knoxville—2 hours; Louisville—2 hours
Difficulty:	Class II–III
Trip Length:	5–8 miles (8–13 km)
Trip Options:	Paddle raft; half-day and one day
Season:	May–October
Cost:	$30–$40

In Kentucky, rafters may enjoy an interesting whitewater trip on the Cumberland's beautiful North Fork as it follows a very narrow course through a rocky gorge in the primitive Cumberland Falls State Park.

This relatively easy trip begins with several Class II rapids just below awesome Cumberland Falls. Downstream, several more-challenging Class II–III rapids—Center Rock, Surfing, Screaming Right Turn, Stair Steps, and Last Drop—follow in quick succession. Cumberland's North Fork whitewater is exciting but not intimidating. During the warmer months, it is enjoyed by families and first-time rafters.

Outfitter listed on page 199.

ROCKCASTLE RIVER, KENTUCKY

Section:	Lower
Location:	Pulaski and Laurel counties, between Corbin and Somerset, south-central Kentucky
Driving Time:	Knoxville—2 hours; Louisville—2 hours
Difficulty:	Class III–IV
Trip Length:	7 miles (11 km)
Trip Options:	Paddle raft; one day

Season:	March–June; September–October
Cost:	$35

The Rockcastle River through Daniel Boone National Forest to Lake Cumberland provides the opportunity to raft some of south-central Kentucky's most intense whitewater. The free-flowing, boulder-strewn, pool-drop river is quite technical, and paddler participation is a must. S-Turn, Stairsteps, Optional, Beach Narrows, and Lower Narrows are all Class III–IV rapids.

Commercial rafting on the Rockcastle River began in 1987. Although water levels on the lower section of the Rockcastle are best in the spring, fall trips are available when water levels permit.

Cumberland River (North Fork) and Rockcastle River Outfitter
Sheltowee Trace Outfitters
P.O. Box 1060
Whitley City, KY 42653
(800) 541–7238
(606) 376–5567

LEVISA RIVER, VIRGINIA/KENTUCKY

Section:	Russell Fork, The Breaks
Location:	Dickenson County, southwestern Virginia; Pike County, near Breaks Interstate Park, eastern Kentucky
Driving Time:	Knoxville—3.5 hours; Winston-Salem—3.5 hours
Difficulty:	Class IV–V; Class IV–V paddle rafting experience required
Trip Length:	10 miles (16 km)
Trip Options:	Paddle raft; one day
Season:	October
Cost:	$120–$220

Whitewater enthusiasts seeking a rare challenge above and beyond the upper Gauley or upper Yough rafting trips should take note of the Russell Fork of the Levisa River along the southwest Virginia–eastern Kentucky border. The Russell Fork, considered unrunnable just a decade ago, is rated by knowledgeable whitewater experts as the most technically difficult commercially rafted river in the eastern United States.

Put-in for the Russell Fork trip is at Bartlick Bridge just downriver from its confluence with the Pound River. Rafters must immediately begin their final tune-up for the unbelievable whitewater action of Breaks Interstate Park. Within the park the river drops about 500 feet in just 2.5 miles (4 km). Eight huge rapids consisting of high drops, powerful hydraulics, and chutes (barely wide enough for rafts) require the utmost in maneuvering and course execution. Class IV–V rapids—Twist and Shout, Tower Falls, Triple Drop, El Horrendo, and S-Turn—will provoke lifetime memories. El Horrendo, more like a waterfall, is the highest commercially run drop in the eastern United States.

Water releases on four October weekends, from Pound Reservoir above Flanagan Dam enable the Army Corps of Engineers to draw down the water level in preparation for winter and spring runoff. Because of the extreme difficulty and technical nature of the Russell Fork, professional outfitters screen prospective rafters very carefully. Most outfitters require upper Gauley or upper Youghiogheny (Class IV+) paddle rafting experience.

Levisa River Outfitters

ACE Whitewater
P.O. Box 1168
Oak Hill, WV 25901
(800) 223–2641
(304) 469–2651

Cherokee Adventures
Route 1, Box 605
Erwin, TN 37650–9524
(800) 445–7238
(615) 743–7733

Laurel Highlands River Tours
P.O. Box 107
Ohiopyle, PA 15470
(800) 472–3846
(412) 329–8531

Mountain Streams & Trails Outfitters
P.O. Box 106
Ohiopyle, PA 15470
(800) 245–4090
(412) 329–8810

Precision Rafting Expeditions
P.O. Box 185
Friendsville, MD 21531
(800) 477–3723
(301) 746–5290

Sheltowee Trace Expeditions
P.O. Box 1060
Whitley City, KY 42653
(800) 541–7238
(606) 376–5567

Upper Yough Whitewater Expeditions
P.O. Box 158
Friendsville, MD 21531
(800) 248–1893
(301) 746–5808

USA Raft
P.O. Box 277
Rowlesburg, WV 26425
(800) 872–7238
(304) 454–2475

Wahoo's Adventures
P.O. Box 1915
Boone, NC 28607
(800) 444–7238
(704) 262–5774

PART IV

■ ■ ■

Canada, Mexico,
and Costa Rica

British Columbia and Alberta's wide variety of whitewater trips attract increasing numbers of international visitors.

CHAPTER 17

Western Canada

Commercial whitewater rafting in western Canada, which began in British Columbia in the early seventies, has achieved widespread popularity. Outfitters offer excellent one- and two-hour, half-day, one-day, and multiday rafting opportunities for adventure-seekers, families, and seniors.

Spring and summer visitors to the popular Whistler Resort region north of Vancouver now have three whitewater selections. After the late-spring waters of the Birkenhead become too low for rafting, guests have their choice of either the Green or Elaho Squamish. The Elaho Squamish also offer a fine family float trip during the summer.

British Columbia's interior mountains feature excellent rafting on the Fraser and many of its scenic tributaries:

- An exciting motor and paddle raft ride travels the incredibly beautiful Thompson Valley between Spences Bridge and Lytton. In late summer, Thompson River rafters can continue onto the Fraser River through the famed Hells Gate.
- An action-packed Class III–IV run takes adventure-seekers through Acocymum Canyon on the Nahatlatch River.
- A good intermediate-level springtime run heads down the Chilliwack River an hour's drive east of Vancouver.
- The Clearwater and Adams, two exciting tributaries of the Thompson River, offer summertime raft trips through remote canyons in south-central British Columbia.

In eastern British Columbia, the Kicking Horse River between Yoho National Park and Golden is popular with visitors to the Canadian Rockies.

British Columbia also proudly claims three of North America's finest multiday wilderness river-rafting experiences:

- The six- to ten-day Chilko Chilcotin Fraser trip in central British Columbia's remote mountains southwest of Williams Lake is similar in length to the Grand Canyon trip and in beauty to Idaho's Middle Fork Salmon.
- The Babine River, nestled in the majestic Pacific Coast mountain ranges of northern British Columbia, features a superbly remote multiday adventure.
- The waters of the spectacular Alsek and Tatshenshini rivers flow from British Columbia into Alaska. (The Alsek and Tatshenshini rivers are described in the Alaska chapter.)

Alberta's whitewater rafting trips are located in the canyons of the Rocky Mountains' eastern slopes west of Calgary and Edmonton. The Upper Red Deer

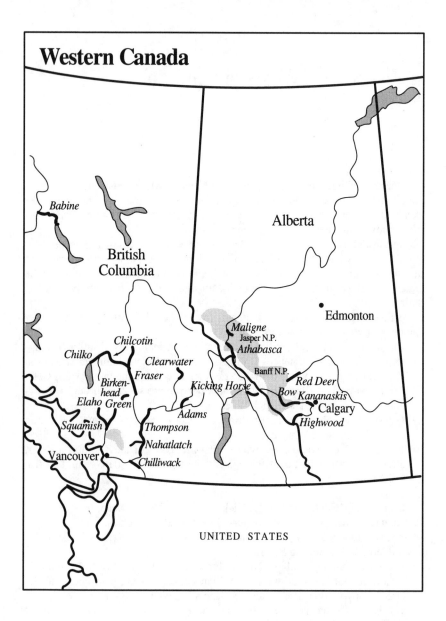

Western Canada

Babine

British
Columbia

Alberta

Chilko

Chilcotin

Clearwater

Fraser

Birken-
head

Elaho Green

Squamish

Vancouver

Adams

Thompson

Nahatlatch

Chilliwack

Maligne

Jasper N.P.

Athabasca

Banff N.P.

Kicking Horse

Edmonton

Red Deer

Bow Kananaskis

Calgary

Highwood

UNITED STATES

Western Canada
River Comparison

	Difficulty	Min. Age	H	D	M	Season	P	O	K	M
British Columbia										
Birkenhead	/ /	12	✗			May–Jun	✗			
Green	/ /	*	✗			Jun–Sep	✗			
Elaho and Squamish										
Lower Elaho and Squamish	/ /	*		✗		Jun–Aug	✗	✗		
Lower Squamish	/	None		✗		Jul–Aug	✗			
Thompson	/ /	10	✗	✗	✗	May-Sep	✗	✗		✗
Nahatlatch	/ /	**		✗		May–Jul	✗	✗		
Chilliwack	/ /	10		✗		Apr–Jun	✗	✗		
Clearwater	/ /	12	✗	✗	✗	Jun–Sep	✗	✗		
Adams	/ /	9		✗		May–Sep	✗	✗		
Kicking Horse	/ /	12	✗	✗		May–Sep	✗			
Chilko/Chilcotin/Fraser	/ / /	12			✗	Jun–Sep	✗	✗		✗
Babine	/ /	12			✗	Jun–Sep	✗	✗		
Alberta										
Red Deer	/ /	10	✗	✗		May–Sep	✗	✗		
Maligne	/ /	**		✗		Jun–Jul	✗			
Athabasca	/	**		✗		Jun–Sep	✗	✗		
Bow	/	4		✗		Jun–Sep		✗		
Kananaskis	/	8		✗		May–Sep	✗			
Highwood	/ /	14	✗	✗		May–Jun	✗			

   *   No minimum age; minimum weight is 60 lbs.
 ** No minimum age; minimum weight is 90 lbs.

   /   Beginner—Easy whitewater. Fun for everyone.
 / / Intermediate—Moderate whitewater.
     No previous rafting experience is necessary.
/ / / Advanced—Difficult whitewater.
     Previous Class IV paddle rafting experience is recommended or required.

     H—Half-Day Trip, D—Day Trip, M—Multiday Trip
     P—Paddle Raft, O—Oar Raft, K—Inflatable Kayak, M—Motorized Raft

River, the province's most popular adventure whitewater trip, offers both exciting waters and wilderness experience northwest of Calgary. Five other rafting opportunities in Alberta are either in or near its renowned Jasper and Banff national parks:

- The intermediate-level Maligne River and the mellow Athabasca River in Jasper National Park provide rafters with spectacular views of the Canadian Rockies.
- A quiet float trip on the Bow River in Banff gives visitors of all ages a relaxing look at the majestic mountain peaks of Canada's best-known national park.
- Near Canmore, site of the downhill ski events during the 1988 Winter Olympics, is the Kananaskis River, with Class I–III that is popular with families.
- About an hour south of Calgary, the Highwood River offers some of Alberta's most continuous springtime Class III–IV whitewater.

BIRKENHEAD RIVER, BRITISH COLUMBIA

Section:	Owl Creek
Location:	Whistler area, north of Mount Currie, southwest British Columbia
Driving Time:	Vancouver—2 hours
Difficulty:	Class II–III
Trip Length:	5 miles (8 km)
Trip Options:	Paddle raft; half-day
Season:	May–June
Cost:	Canadian $55

The Birkenhead River, a few miles north of Garibaldi Provincial Park and the world-famous Whistler ski resort, offers a very enjoyable half-day rafting trip.

The 5-mile (8-km) Birkenhead trip, with continuous but not-too-difficult Class II–III rapids, offers excitement for both novices and experienced rafters. Paddle trips permit maximum participation of rafters. Many guests choose to refine newly learned paddling skills by running the river twice in a day.

Outfitter listed on page 207.

GREEN RIVER, BRITISH COLUMBIA

Section:	Whistler Resort
Location:	Garibaldi Provincial Park, southwest British Columbia
Driving Time:	Vancouver—2 hours
Trip Length:	4.5 miles (7 km)
Difficulty:	Class II–III
Trip Options:	Paddle raft; two hours
Season:	June–September
Cost:	Canadian $35–$41

The Green River, in the Whistler region of southwest British Columbia, gives visitors to Garibaldi Provincial Park an opportunity to experience whitewater rafting and still have time to enjoy the park's many other attractions. The Green's easy, fun-filled rapids with its panorama of stunning snowcapped peaks make this a memorable recreational experience.

On the placid waters of Green Lake, just 5 miles (8 km) from Whistler Village, rafters have an opportunity to practice and synchronize their paddle strokes before starting the downriver voyage. The 4.5-mile (7-km) Green River trip is a favorite with Canadian as well as foreign visitors. Many of the guides are able to provide basic paddle commands in Japanese and other languages.

Outfitter listed below

ELAHO AND SQUAMISH RIVERS, BRITISH COLUMBIA

Section:	Lower Elaho and Squamish
Location:	Near Brackendale, north of Vancouver, southwest British Columbia
Driving Time:	Vancouver—2 hours
Difficulty:	Class II–III+
Trip Length:	17 miles (27 km)
Trip Options:	Paddle raft, oar raft; one day
Season:	June–August
Cost:	Canadian $99 by van shuttle, $195 by helicopter

The Elaho and Squamish rivers, about 15 miles (24 km) west of British Columbia's Garibaldi Provincial Park and the Whistler ski resort, provide first-time and experienced rafters an opportunity to see many of the province's glacier-laden coastal mountain peaks.

The two-river raft trip, which usually includes the last four miles (6.5 km) of the Elaho and more than 10 miles (16 km) on the Squamish, features the lively Class III–III+ Steamroller, White Dog, Devil's Elbow, and Cheeseball rapids.

Section:	Lower Squamish
Location:	Near Brackendale, southwest British Columbia
Driving Time:	Vancouver—2 hours
Difficulty:	Class I
Trip Length:	11 miles (18 km)
Trip Options:	Oar raft; one day
Season:	July–August
Cost:	Canadian $55–$85

During the warmer summer months, an easy Class I float trip on the lower Squamish is ideal for families with young children, providing frequent glimpses of bears, deer, and eagles. Its quiet waters are a perfect way to relax and enjoy both the wildlife and spectacular mountain scenery.

Birkenhead, Green, and Elaho and Squamish River Outfitter

Whistler River Adventures
P.O. Box 202
Whistler, British Columbia
Canada V0N 1B0
(604) 932–3532

THOMPSON RIVER, BRITISH COLUMBIA

Section: Spences Bridge to Lytton
Location: West of Kamloops, south-central British Columbia
Driving Time: Vancouver—3 hours
Difficulty: Class III–IV
Trip Length: 25 miles (40 km); 50 miles (80 km), two days
Trip Options: Paddle raft, oar raft, motorized raft; half-day, one and two days
Season: May–September
Cost: Canadian $65–$95 one day; $159–$229 two days

In 1973 the Thompson River became British Columbia's first whitewater river to be commercially rafted. As word of the exciting rapids and magnificent canyon scenery spread, the number of rafters grew. The Thompson continues to be one of the province's favorite whitewater stretches.

The Thompson's most popular rafting trip is the 25-mile (40-km) one-day trip through the lower Thompson Valley and White Canyon between Spences Bridge and Lytton. This section has the river's best whitewater and most awesome scenery. Its thirty rapids—including The Frog, Devils Kitchen, Witch's Cauldron, Washing Machine, and everyone's favorite, Jaws of Death—will excite both first-time and experienced rafters.

While the demanding whitewater of the Thompson doesn't always permit full appreciation of the spectacular landscape, there is still plenty of scenery to enjoy during the more relaxing stretches. The Trans-Canada Highway and Canadian National and CP railways closely parallel the river throughout most of the trip.

During spring and early summer, outfitters primarily use Colorado River–style motorized pontoon rafts to shoot the Thompson River's big rapids. As summer water levels lower, usually by early July, paddle raft trips become more frequent.

On weekends in August and September, two of the outfitters listed below—Fraser River Raft Expeditions and Kumsheen Raft Adventures—offer overnight trips on the Thompson and Fraser rivers, including a hair-raising ride through the famed Class V Hell's Gate rapids on the Fraser.

Thompson River Outfitters

Fraser River Raft Expeditions
P.O. Box 10
Yale, British Columbia
Canada V0K 2S0
(604) 863–2336

Hyak Wilderness Adventures
1975 Maple St.
Vancouver, British Columbia
Canada V6J 3S9
(604) 734–8622

Kumsheen Raft Adventures
P.O. Box 30
Lytton, British Columbia
Canada V0K 1Z0
(800) 663–6667 (Canada only)
(604) 455–2296

River Rogues Adventures
P.O. Box 115
Spences Bridge, British Columbia
Canada V0K 2L0
(604) 458–2252

Ryans Rapid Rafting
P.O. Box 600
Vancouver, British Columbia
Canada V6G 3B7
(604) 875–9745

NAHATLATCH RIVER, BRITISH COLUMBIA

Section:	Hannah or Frances lakes to Acocymum
Location:	North of Hope, southwest British Columbia
Driving Time:	Vancouver—2 hours
Difficulty:	III–IV
Trip Length:	12 miles (19 km)
Trip Options:	Paddle raft, oar raft; one day
Season:	May–July
Cost:	Canadian $90–$105

The Nahatlatch, in southern British Columbia, offers rafters one of the province's most challenging and exhilarating paddle adventures. Paddle rafters prepare for the Nahatlatch trip by running the half-mile or so between Hannah and Frances lakes. Shortly below Frances Lake, the exciting whitewater action of the Nahatlatch begins. Many Class III–IV rapids, like Rose Garden, Meatgrinder, and Headwall, require active rafter participation and leave little time to enjoy the passing scenery.

The 6-mile (9.5-km) canyon section of the Nahatlatch is the most intense. Large boulders, giant waves, and a gradient dropping at a rate of nearly 100 feet per mile create more than a dozen technical Class III–IV+ rapids. During high water, one Class V rapid may be portaged.

The canyon should be attempted only by experienced rafters in good physical condition who are at least eighteen years old. The best time for the canyon section is usually during the more moderate water of July and August.

Nahatlatch River Outfitters

Fraser River Raft Expeditions
P.O. Box 10
Yale, British Columbia
Canada V0K 2S0
(604) 863–2336

REO Rafting Adventures
612-1200 W. Pender St.
Vancouver, British Columbia
Canada V6E 2S9
(604) 684–4438

CHILLIWACK RIVER, BRITISH COLUMBIA

Section:	Slesse Creek to Veddar Crossing (lower)
Location:	Near Chilliwack, southern British Columbia
Driving Time:	Vancouver—1.5 hours
Difficulty:	Class III–IV
Trip Length:	12 miles (19 km)
Trip Options:	Paddle raft, paddle/oar raft; one day
Season:	April–July
Cost:	Canadian $79–$89

The Chilliwack River, British Columbia's southernmost commercial rafting trip, is an exciting springtime adventure. The scenic Chilliwack Valley is easily accessible from Washington state as well as metropolitan Vancouver and southern British Columbia.

Chilliwack's outfitters offer raft trips on the 12-mile (19-km) lower river from Slesse Creek to Veddar Crossing. Most of the early raft trip, from Slesse Creek to Rock Garden rapids, provides a relaxing warm-up for the exciting Tamihi section, the highlight of the Chilliwack. Tamihi, annual site of the Canadian junior kayak championships, is a 1-mile section with almost continuous Class III–IV rapids. The Chilliwack's rapids, exciting yet not too difficult, can be enjoyed by first-time as well as experienced rafters.

The Chilliwack flows from the North Cascade Mountains in Washington state to its confluence with the Fraser River near the city of Chilliwack, southeast of Vancouver. While Chilliwack rafting trips can be run from April into July, the best whitewater levels and weather are normally during May and June.

Chilliwack River Outfitters

Hyak Wilderness Adventures
1975 Maple St.
Vancouver, British Columbia
Canada V6J 3S9
(604) 734–8622

Ryan's Rapid Rafting
P.O. Box 600
Vancouver, British Columbia
Canada V6G 3B7
(604) 875–9745

CLEARWATER RIVER, BRITISH COLUMBIA

Section: Upper and lower
Location: North of Kamloops, eastern British Columbia
Driving Time: Kamloops—1.5 hours; Vancouver—5.5 hours
Difficulty: Class III–IV+
Trip Length: 6–25 miles (9.5–40 km)
Trip Options: Paddle/oar raft; half-day, one and two days
Season: June–September
Cost: Canadian $43 half-day; $99 one day; $210 two days

British Columbia's Clearwater Valley and Wells Gray Provincial Park, popular areas for horseback riding, canoeing, fishing, hiking, and camping, also offer some of the province's most exciting whitewater rafting. The Clearwater flows south from Wells Gray Park to its confluence with the north Thompson at the town of Clearwater.

Clearwater rafters may choose between one-day trips on the popular 15-mile (24-km) lower section or 10-mile (16-km) upper section, a two-day trip that includes both sections, or a half-day trip on a portion of the lower river. All trips contain superb wilderness scenery, abundant wildlife, and spectacular Class III–IV+ whitewater.

The one-day upper Clearwater trip includes a hike to 175-foot Spahats Falls. Two-day trips include brief hikes to the base of White Horse Bluff, an 800-foot cliff, and Moul Creek Falls, which cascades through volcanic canyons.

Outfitter listed on page 211.

ADAMS RIVER, BRITISH COLUMBIA

Section:	Adams Lake to Highway Bridge above Shuswap Lake
Location:	Near Shuswap Lake, east of Kamloops, south-central British Columbia
Driving Time:	Kamloops—1 hour; Vancouver—5 hours
Difficulty:	Class II–III
Trip Length:	6 miles (9.5 km)
Trip Options:	Paddle/oar raft; two hours
Season:	May–September
Cost:	Canadian $24–$32

The Adams River, in the scenic Shuswap country of south-central British Columbia, offers an easy introduction to whitewater rafting for the whole family. Easy Class II–III rapids alternating with fast-moving flatwater provide the perfect environment to learn the paddling and safety skills needed to help maneuver the raft.

The 6-mile (9.5-km) Adams rafting trip between Adams Lake and Shuswap Lake takes about two hours and is less than ten minutes from the Trans-Canada Highway. The Adams rafting season runs from late May through early September.

Clearwater River and Adams River Outfitter

Interior Whitewater Expeditions
P.O. Box 129
Celista, British Columbia
Canada V0E 1L0
(800) 661–7238 (Canada only)
(604) 955–2447

KICKING HORSE RIVER, BRITISH COLUMBIA

Sections:	Upper and lower
Location:	Yoho National Park to Golden, southeast British Columbia
Driving Time:	Calgary—2.5 hours
Difficulty:	Class III–IV (upper); IV+ (lower)
Trip Length:	Upper—12 miles (19 km); Lower—5 miles (8 km)
Trip Options:	Paddle raft; half-day, one day
Season:	May–September (upper); August (lower)
Cost:	Canadian $60–$80

One of the Canadian Rockies' most popular whitewater rafting trips is on the scenic Kicking Horse River, west of Alberta's Banff National Park. Rafting on the Kicking Horse, a tributary of the upper Columbia River, is primarily done through the rocky and heavily forested upper canyons. The Class III–IV rapids of the upper river are not for children or timid first-time rafters.

When water levels are just right, outfitters will also offer experienced rafters an exciting adventure on the Class IV+ lower Kicking Horse. The 5-mile (8-km) lower trip is usually preceded by a morning run of the upper Kicking Horse and includes the portage of an unrunnable Class V-VI rapid.

The half-day Green River trip offers easy, fun-filled rapids with a panorama of stunning snowcapped peaks.

Kicking Horse River Outfitters

Alpine Rafting Company
P.O. Box 1409
Golden, British Columbia
Canada V0A 1H0
(800) 663–7080
(604) 334–5016

Kootenay River Runners
P.O. Box 81
Edgewater, British Columbia
Canada V0A 1E0
(604) 347–9210

Glacier Raft Company
P.O. Box 428
Golden, British Columbia
Canada V0A 1H0
(604) 344–6521
(403) 762–4347

CHILKO, CHILCOTIN, AND FRASER RIVERS, BRITISH COLUMBIA

Section: Chilko Lake to Lillooet
Location: West and south of Williams Lake, south-central British Columbia
Driving Time: Williams Lake—5 hours
Difficulty: Class II–V
Trip Length: Chilko—40 miles (64 km); Chilcotin—75 miles (120 km); Fraser—120 miles (192 km)

Trip Options:	Oar raft, paddle/oar raft, motorized raft; six to eleven days
Season:	June–September
Cost:	Canadian $1,200–$2,200

The Chilko and Chilcotin rivers, in central British Columbia, provide one of the premier multiday rafting trips available. The Chilko's dynamic Lava Canyon and the Chilcotin Plateau's distinctive semiarid environment—which includes ridgetop forests, cacti in grass valleys, California bighorn sheep, and mule deer—combine to create a wilderness river experience similar to Idaho's famed Middle Fork of the Salmon.

Access to the isolated Chilko is normally made via small aircraft to its source, 4,000-foot Chilko Lake. Below the lake, the easy first stretch of the river provides an ideal introduction to whitewater rafting. Mellow Class I–II waters give rafters an opportunity to test their whitewater skills and experience the pristine wilderness.

The Chilko River, after 23 miles (37 km), enters spectacular Class IV-V Lava Canyon. Much of the anticipation (and anxiety) of the 17-mile (27-km) canyon comes because some of its more difficult Class V rapids cannot be scouted. Immediately below Lava Canyon, the Chilko joins the Taseko to form the Chilcotin River.

The Chilcotin also has its share of whitewater rapids, which get more difficult as the trip proceeds downriver. Its best Class III–IV rapids are found in Farewell and Big John canyons, just before the Chilcotin's confluence with the Fraser River.

Following the five or six days of rafting on the Chilko and Chilcotin rivers, outfitters frequently run for three or four additional days on the Fraser. During the southward journey of the Fraser through isolated steep canyons, the most prominent features are the breathtaking hoodoos—rock spires capped with slate—and the 2,000-foot-deep Moran Canyon, location of some of the Fraser's best whitewater. Rafters will frequently see Indians netting salmon on the Fraser.

The ten- to eleven-day Chilko/Chilcotin/Fraser trip to Lillooet is similar in time and distance (230 miles, 345 km) to the Colorado River's Grand Canyon rafting trip.

Chilko, Chilcotin, and Fraser River Outfitters

Canadian River Expeditions
3524 W. 16th Ave.
Vancouver, British Columbia
Canada V6R 3C1
(604) 738–4449

Hyak Wilderness Adventures
1975 Maple St.
Vancouver, British Columbia
Canada V6J 3S9
(604) 734–8622

BABINE RIVER, BRITISH COLUMBIA

Section:	Below Salmonoid Project Weir to Kispiox Village or Hazelton
Location:	North of Smithers, northern British Columbia
Driving Time:	Prince George—4.5 hours
Difficulty:	Class II–IV
Trip Length:	95 miles (152 km)

Trip Options: Paddle/oar raft; five and six days
Season: June–September
Cost: Canadian $1,200–$1,300

Nestled amid the majestic Pacific Coast mountains of northern British Columbia, the Babine River offers a superb five- or six-day adventure featuring hiking, camping, and river rafting in isolated wilderness. Beginning at Nilkitkwa Lake, 60 miles (95 km) of the Babine flows in view of the Babine and Atna mountain ranges.

The first four days of the Babine's multiday raft trips include several Class III rapids and numerous opportunities to photograph the unspoiled wilderness and its eagles, moose, and grizzly bears. On day five, rafters journey through a narrow, steep-walled canyon that creates the Babine's most exciting Class IV whitewater. Guests frequently see grizzlies feeding on salmon during the stretch. The final day is spent floating the larger Skeena River to the take-out at Kispiox Indian Village.

Babine River Outfitter

Suskwa Adventure Outfitters
P.O. Box 3262
Smithers, British Columbia
Canada V0J 2N0
(604) 847–2885

RED DEER RIVER, ALBERTA

Section: Upper
Location: Near Sundre, west-central Alberta
Driving Time: Calgary—1.5 hours; Edmonton—3 hours
Difficulty: Class II–III+
Trip Length: 12–15 miles (19–24 km) one day; 25–30 miles (40–48 km) two days
Trip Options: Paddle raft, oar raft; one and two days
Season: May–September
Cost: Canadian $95–$100 one day; $200 two days

The upper Red Deer River, which flows through the Rocky Mountain Forest Reserve, is Alberta's most popular adventure whitewater rafting trip. The Red Deer's attraction can be attributed to its location near Banff and Jasper national parks, its proximity to Alberta's largest cities, and its stable and exciting whitewater. The Red Deer was twice the site of the Canadian whitewater championships.

The Red Deer's exciting whitewater consists of both pool drops and continuous stair-step ledges. Many of its more technical Class II–III+ rapids—Big Rock, First Ledge, Gooseberry Ledge, Jimbo's Staircase, National's Site, Cache Hill, and Double Ledge—require precise maneuvering by paddle rafters.

The Red Deer's rafting season is from mid-May until mid-September. Its waters are always cold, and wet suits are highly recommended throughout the season. Some outfitters provide transportation to the river from Calgary, Red Deer, and Edmonton.

Red Deer River Outfitters

Chinook River Sports
341 10th Ave. SW
Calgary, Alberta
Canada T2R 0A5
(403) 263–7238

Mirage Adventure Tours
P.O. Box 2338
Canmore, Alberta
Canada T0L 0M0
(403) 591–7773

Hunter Valley Recreational Enterprises
P.O. Box 1620
Canmore, Alberta
Canada T0L 0M0
(403) 637–2777

MALIGNE RIVER, ALBERTA

Section:	Maligne Lake to Big Bend Campground
Location:	Jasper National Park, west-central Alberta
Driving Time:	Calgary—4 hours; Edmonton—4 hours
Difficulty:	Class II–III
Trip Length:	6 miles (9.5 km)
Trip Options:	Paddle raft; half-day
Season:	June–July
Cost:	Canadian $37–$45

The Maligne River offers a rousing challenge to people looking for exciting whitewater. The trip begins at Maligne Lake, a glacial lake in the Jasper National Park's eastern Maligne Mountains, and drops continuously for nearly 6 miles (9.5 km) to its take-out at Big Bend Campground, about 4 miles (7 km) upriver from Medicine Lake.

Paddle rafters must work together and make quick reactions to a number of Class III rapids. Although families are welcome, children must weigh at least ninety pounds (41 kg).

Depending upon winter snowpack in the Rockies, the Maligne is normally run from four to eight weeks during the late spring and early summer.

Outfitters listed on page 216.

ATHABASCA RIVER, ALBERTA

Section:	Falls
Location:	Jasper National Park, south of Jasper, west-central Alberta
Driving Time:	Calgary—3.5 hours; Edmonton—3.5 hours
Difficulty:	Class I–II+
Trip Length:	6–10 miles (9–16 km)
Trip Options:	Paddle raft, oar raft; half-day
Season:	June–September
Cost:	Canadian $45

The Athabasca River, which originates at the Columbia Icefield of western Alberta's Jasper National Park, provides a unique opportunity for visitors to enjoy some of the park's finest scenery.

Half-day raft trips beginning immediately below Athabasca Falls are run from 6 to 10 miles (9 to 16 km) downstream. Six to eight sets of moderate Class II+ rapids leave plenty of calm stretches for guests to view the inspiring park environment and its varied wildlife.

Athabasca's easy waters can be enjoyed by everyone. Outfitters welcome first-time rafters and families with children who weigh at least ninety pounds (41 kg) on paddle raft trips. There are no restrictions on oar-guided trips.

Maligne River and Athabasca River Outfitters

Maligne River Adventures
626 Connaught Dr.
Jasper, Alberta
Canada T0E 1E0
(403) 852–3370

Whitewater Rafting (Jasper)
P.O. Box 362
Jasper, Alberta
Canada T0E 1E0
(403) 852–7238

BOW RIVER, ALBERTA

Section:	Banff National Park
Location:	Town of Banff, within Banff National Park, southwest Alberta
Driving Time:	Calgary—1.5 hours
Difficulty:	Class I–II
Trip Length:	6 and 12 miles (9.5 and 19 km)
Trip Options:	Oar raft; one hour and three hours
Season:	June–September
Cost:	Canadian $18–$33

One of the more unusual ways for visitors to enjoy western Alberta's world-renowned Banff National Park is a quiet raft trip on the Bow River.

Scenic float trips on the Bow enable guests to relax and enjoy the panoramic views of Rundle and Tunnel mountains. One-hour raft trips leave the town of Banff four times a day. A single three-hour raft trip leaves each morning.

Bow River rafting trips are especially popular with senior citizens and families with young children.

Bow River Outfitter

Rocky Mountain Raft Tours
P.O. Box 1771
Banff, Alberta
Canada T0L 0C0
(403) 762–3632

KANANASKIS RIVER, ALBERTA

Section:	Barrier Dam to Seebe Dam
Location:	East of Canmore, southwest Alberta
Driving Time:	Calgary—1 hour
Difficulty:	Class I–III
Trip Length:	6 to 10 miles (9.5 to 16 km)
Trip Options:	Paddle raft; two and three hours

Season: May–September
Cost: Canadian $45

The Kananaskis River, in western Alberta's renowned Kananaskis region, features a popular half-day whitewater trip for first-time rafters and families. Raft trips, which begin at Lusk Creek, 1.5 miles (2.5 km) downstream of Barrier Lake, provide a good introduction to Class I–III whitewater rapids.

A highlight of the trip is navigating through the site of the 1988 Canadian Kayak Championships. This 1.5-mile (2.5-km) stretch of intense whitewater through a narrow canyon was redesigned in the early 1980s to accommodate kayaks.

Below the canyon, the raft trip continues through the eastern Rockies' scenic foothills, where guests commonly see wildlife including bald eagles, muskrat, and moose.

Kananaskis River Outfitters

Hunter Valley Recreational Enterprises
P.O. Box 1620
Canmore, Alberta
Canada T0L 0M0
(403) 637–2777

Mirage Adventure Tours
P.O. Box 2338
Canmore, Alberta
Canada T0L 0M0
(403) 591–7773

HIGHWOOD RIVER, ALBERTA

Section: Upper and lower
Location: Kananaskis Region near Longview; southwest Alberta
Driving Time: Calgary—1.5 hours
Difficulty: Class III–IV
Trip Length: 14 and 25 miles (22 and 40 km)
Trip Options: Paddle raft; one day and two days
Season: May–June
Cost: Canadian $79; $199 two days

Each spring the Highwood River, in the Rocky Mountain foothills of southwestern Alberta, offers hardy rafters some of the province's most continuous whitewater.

Highwood rafting trips are scheduled to coincide with maximum runoff conditions, normally between May and early July. Of Highwood's numerous Class III–IV rapids, the Horseshoe, Toilet Bowl, Highwood Falls, and Pin Ball are considered the best.

Rafters on the Highwood may choose between a one-day, 14-mile (22-km) run and a two-day, 25-mile (40-km) trip. Rafters are expected to be physically fit and able to swim.

Highwood River Outfitter

Chinook River Sports
341 10th Ave. SW
Calgary, Alberta
Canada T2R 0A5
(403) 263–7238

The waters of the Ottawa and other rivers in eastern Canada are surprisingly warm throughout the summer rafting season. Photo courtesy of Wilderness Tours.

CHAPTER 18

■ ■ ■

Eastern Canada

Since the days of the early North American explorers, countless rivers, lakes, and streams of eastern Canada have provided transportation routes for hunters, trappers, and fishermen using birchbark canoes. In the mid-1970s, the sport of whitewater rafting was introduced into eastern Canada. Since then, its popularity has increased dramatically, attracting large numbers of Canadians and thousands of foreign visitors. A vast water wilderness has become a popular recreational area for whitewater rafting, canoeing, and kayaking.

Two of eastern Canada's favorite whitewater rivers are located in Ontario. Along the Ontario–Quebec border, the Ottawa River was the first in eastern Canada to be used for recreational rafting. Near Barry's Bay, the dam-controlled Madawaska River provides a scenic and exciting introductory whitewater trip that is a family favorite.

Quebec's outfitters have popularized whitewater rafting on three rivers, and a motorboat trip through the powerful Lachine Rapids on the St. Lawrence River. The Rouge, Quebec's most popular river, located midway between Montreal and Ottawa, has rafting trips on two sections of the river throughout the spring and summer seasons. Near the ancient capital city of Quebec, outfitters on the Jacques Cartier and Batiscan rivers offer adventure-filled raft trips in predominantly French-speaking areas. Montreal's Lachine Rapids, a barrier to seventeenth-century navigators searching for the Northwest Passage on the St. Lawrence River, features daily motorized trips through the largest-volume rapids in North America.

While rafting has become, in just two decades, a well-established sport in eastern Canada, many professional river outfitters continue to explore the vast wilderness of Ontario and Quebec for recreational whitewater. Because of the Precambrian shield that covers most of eastern Canada, waterfalls and low drops are prevalent. As the northern frontiers become more accessible, new rafting locations will undoubtedly emerge.

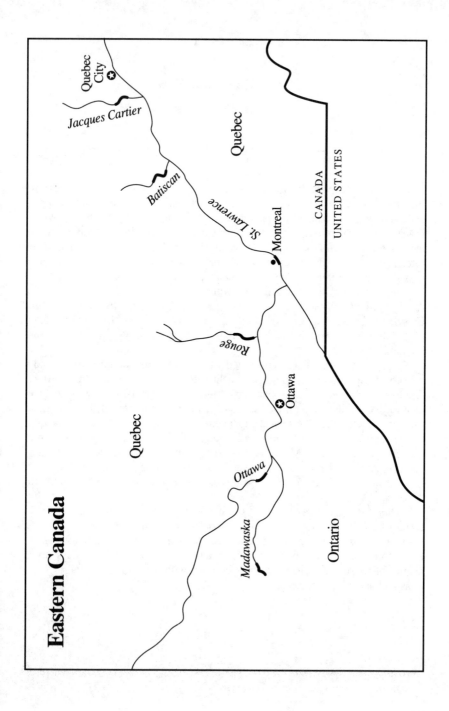

Eastern Canada
River Comparison

	Difficulty	Min. Age	H D M	Season	Raft Type P O K M
Ontario					
Ottawa					
Roche Fendu	∕ ∕	12	✗ ✗	Apr–Sep	✗ ✗
Family Float	∕	*	✗	Jun–Sep	✗
Madawaska	∕	4	✗	Jun–Sep	✗
Quebec					
Rouge					
Harrington	∕ ∕	12	✗	Apr–Oct	✗
Seven Sisters	∕ ∕	12	✗	Apr–Oct	✗
Jacques Cartier	∕ ∕	14	✗	May–Sep	✗
Batiscan	∕ ∕	12	✗	Apr–Jun	✗
St. Lawrence	∕	6	✗	May–Sep	✗

* No minimum age; minimum weight is 50 lbs.

∕ Beginner—Easy whitewater. Fun for everyone.
∕ ∕ Intermediate—Moderate whitewater.
No previous rafting experience is necessary.
∕ ∕ ∕ Advanced—Difficult whitewater.
Previous Class IV paddle rafting experience is recommended or required.

H—Half-Day Trip, D—Day Trip, M—Multiday Trip
P—Paddle Raft, O—Oar Raft, K—Inflatable Kayak, M—Motorized Raft

OTTAWA RIVER, ONTARIO

Section:	Roche Fendu
Location:	Near Forester's Falls, northeastern Ontario
Driving Time:	Montreal—3 hours; Ottawa—1.5 hours; Toronto—4.5 hours
Difficulty:	Class III–IV+
Trip Length:	5–7 miles (8–11 km)
Trip Options:	Paddle raft, paddle/oar raft; half-day and one day
Season:	April–September
Cost:	Canadian $76–$92

Spectacular wilderness scenery and large exciting rapids created by Precambrian shield rock outcrops highlight Canada's most popular commercial whitewater stretch, just 75 miles (120 km) west of Ottawa. Covering a 5-mile (8-km) stretch, the wild and isolated Roche Fendu (French for "split rock") region has more than 175 islands and many secluded inlets and beaches.

The Ottawa River's main channel, east of Beachburg, is well-known for large waves, powerful hydraulics, and breathtaking chutes. Big McCoy, Coliseum, Lorne, and Butcher's Knife rapids provide drenching Class III–IV entertainment throughout the summer season.

In the springtime, when the Ottawa's main channel is swollen by melting snow, outfitters run an alternative trip on the Class III–IV middle channel. Here, paddlers thrill to the spectacular 15-foot drop at Garvin's Chute, navigate tight channels at Little Trickle rapids, and ride large waves at No Name rapids.

Because of its large watershed, the Ottawa has surprisingly warm water and maintains good flow the entire summer.

Section:	Family Float
Location:	Near Forester's Falls, northeastern Ontario
Driving Time:	Montreal—3 hours; Ottawa—1.5 hours; Toronto—4.5 hours
Difficulty:	Class I–II
Trip Length:	3.5 miles (5.5 km)
Trip Options:	Oar raft; half-day
Season:	June–September
Cost:	Canadian $29–$39

During the summer, Owl Rafting offers a relatively easy, yet fun, family whitewater experience on the Ottawa River. With the exception of Big McCoy rapids, which is just upstream from the regular river put-in, guests in oar-guided rafts traverse "sneak" routes of all major middle-channel rapids. Described as "soft adventure" by the outfitter, children as small as fifty pounds get a safe close-up look at all Class III–IV rapids. At the conclusion of the 3.5-mile trip, rafters return to the put-in via a motorized pontoon boat.

Ottawa River Outfitters

Espirit Rafting Adventures
P.O. Box 463
Pembroke, Ontario
Canada K8A 6X7
(819) 683–3241

Owl Rafting
P.O. Box 29
Foresters Falls, Ontario
Canada K0J 1V0
(800) 461–7238 (Canada only)
(613) 238–7238

River Run
P.O. Box 179
Beachburg, Ontario
Canada K0J 1C0
(800) 267–7238 (Canada only)
(613) 646–2501

Wilderness Tours
P.O. Box 89
Beachburg, Ontario
Canada K0J 1C0
(800) 267–9166 (Canada only)
(613) 646–2291

MADAWASKA RIVER, ONTARIO

Section:	Middle
Location:	Hastings District, southwest of Barry's Bay, northern Ontario
Driving Time:	Ottawa—1.5 hours; Toronto—4 hours
Difficulty:	Class I–II
Trip Length:	3 miles (4.8 km)
Trip Options:	Paddle raft; two hours
Season:	June–September
Cost:	Canadian $15–$20

The dam-controlled waters of the Madawaska River, just east of Ontario's Algonquin Provincial Park, provide an ideal opportunity for families with small children to safely enjoy whitewater rafting. The two-hour trip, through a picturesque wilderness forest between Bark Lake and Lake Kamaniskeg, has relatively easy and friendly Class I–II rapids—Staircase, Gravelpit, Cottage, and Claudia's Roller—without steep drops.

Rafting on the Madawaska River is dependent upon Monday through Thursday water releases from Bark Lake Dam by the Ontario Hydro Authority. The surface water spills over the dam generally provide adequate warm-water supplies throughout the summer rafting season.

Madawaska River Outfitter

Madawaska Kanu Centre
P.O. Box 635
Barry's Bay, Ontario
Canada K0J 1B0
(613) 756–3620 (June–September)
(613) 594–5268 (October–May)

ROUGE RIVER, QUEBEC

Sections: Harrington Canyon (upper); Seven Sisters Canyon (lower)
Location: Mont Tremblant to Calumet, western Quebec
Driving Time: Montreal—1.25 hours; Ottawa—1 hour
Difficulty: Class III–IV
Trip Length: Harrington Canyon—8 miles (13 km); Seven Sisters Canyon—8 miles (13 km)
Trip Options: Paddle raft; one day on each section
Season: April–early October
Cost: Canadian $65–$80

The popular Rouge River provides thrilling rafting opportunities in the western Laurentian Mountains midway between Montreal and Ottawa. During its southern descent through the North Woods wilderness to the Ottawa River, the Rouge passes through several breathtaking gorges featuring impressive geologic formations and sandy beaches. Boulders and drops in these gorges produce large standing waves and fine Class III–IV rapids.

The Rouge, with nearly 16 miles (29 km) of ever-changing water flows and challenging rapids, is divided into two quite different trips. The upper, or Harrington Canyon, run—which includes Majestic Canyon and Confusion, Turbo, and Surprise rapids—provides the best springtime whitewater. Beginning in mid-June, outfitters switch most rafting operations to the lower, or Seven Sisters Canyon section, with its stimulating rapids: Steep Throat, le Seuil Elizabeth, Slice-n-Dice, Monster, Washing Machine, and the Mushroom.

The large drainage area of the Rouge generally permits warm, good water conditions throughout the summer season. Depending on water levels, outfitters offer rafters a single run through either or both canyons, runs through either one of the sections twice, or two-day combination excursions.

Rouge River Outfitters

Action Rafting
21 Chemin Rivière Rouge
R.R. 2
Calumet, Quebec
Canada J0V 1B0
(819) 242–0277 (Calumet)
(514) 942–8791 (Montreal)

Aventures en l'Eau Vive, Quebec, Ité
R.R. 2 Chemin Rivière Rouge
Calumet, Quebec
Canada J0V 1B0
(800) 567–6881 (E. Canada only)
(819) 242–6084

New World Expeditions
Nouveau Monde Expeditions
   en Rivière
100 Chemin de la Rivière Rouge
Calumet, Quebec
Canada J0V 1B0
(800) 361–5033 (Canada and
   eastern U.S. only)
(819) 242–7238

Propulsion River Expeditions
1447 Doncaster
Mont-Rolland, Quebec
Canada J0R 1G0
(800) 461–3300 (Canada only)
(514) 953–3300

JACQUES CARTIER RIVER, QUEBEC

Section: Tewkesbury
Location: Tewkesbury, west of Quebec City, central Quebec
Driving Time: Montreal—2.5 hours; Quebec City—.5 hour
Difficulty: Class III–V
Trip Length: 6 miles (11 km)
Trip Options: Paddle raft; half day
Season: May–September
Cost: Canadian $55–$75

The Jacques Cartier River, like the Batiscan to the west, is another of Quebec's recent whitewater rafting success stories. La Rivière Jacques Cartier, named after the famed seventeenth-century French explorer, features challenging rapids and breathtaking scenery less than a thirty-minute drive from the Château Frontenac in Quebec City.

The Jacques Cartier, which flows through a picturesque forested valley, consists of a series of ledge drops with steep shoots, which come in quick succession. The Class III–V rapids, fast and frequent, are interspersed with fantastic play spots and locations for swimming and body surfing. Many rafters choose to run the river twice in a single day.

Outfitter listed on page 226.

BATISCAN RIVER, QUEBEC

Section: Reserve to Portneuf
Location: Rivière-a-Pierre, near the township of Batiscan, central Quebec
Driving Time: Montreal—2.5 hours; Quebec City—1.5 hours
Difficulty: Class III–IV+
Trip Length: 15 miles (24 km)
Trip Options: Paddle raft; one day
Season: April–June
Cost: Canadian $79

One of Quebec's newest whitewater rafting trips is on the final 15 miles (24 km) of the Batiscan River, nearly midway between Montreal and the provincial capital. The Batiscan, a large-volume river, features magnificent wilderness scenery and high-water action with a seemingly endless series of giant waves. Many Class III–IV+ rapids, including Les Trois Roches and Chute Pierre Antoine, offer a challenging descent for novice and expert rafters alike.

The Batiscan flows southward out of Reserve Founique de Portneuf (Portneuf Provincial Reserve) to its confluence with the St. Lawrence River near the township of Batiscan. Access is easy, the four- to five-hour trip is exciting, and the memories are forever. While the best rafting is during May and June, outfitters are sometimes able to run trips from late April to early August.

Jacques Cartier River and Batiscan River Outfitter

New World River Expeditions
Nouveau Monde Expeditions en Rivière
100 Chemin de la Rivière Rouge
Calumet, Quebec
Canada J0V 1B0
(800) 361–5033 (Canada only)
(819) 242–7238

ST. LAWRENCE RIVER, QUEBEC

Sections:	Lachine Rapids
Location:	Near Lachine, western Quebec, Montreal (metropolitan area)
Driving Time:	0 (boat leaves from downtown Montreal)
Difficulty:	Class III–IV
Trip Length:	6 miles (9.5 km)
Trip Options:	Jet boat; 1.5 hours
Season:	May–September
Cost:	Canadian $25–$45

A Lachine Rapids jet boat ride may be the world's most unusual urban whitewater adventure. These 2.5-mile (4-km) rapids on the St. Lawrence River are exciting and constant, with ocean-size waves up to 15 feet high. Motorized craft crash through or jump waves, creating plenty of whitewater action. Guests are supplied with rain gear.

About half of the ninety-minute Lachine trip is spent in the rapids. The more leisurely portion of the trip includes sightseeing along the Montreal waterfront and a trip upriver to view the powerful waters where the Ottawa and St. Lawrence rivers meet. Riders often see oceangoing freighters on the adjacent St. Lawrence Seaway, between the Great Lakes and the Atlantic.

The departure point for the motorized trip though the Lachine Rapids is Victoria Pier at the bottom of Jacques Cartier Square in the heart of old Montreal.

St. Lawrence River Outfitter

Lachine Rapids Tours
(Saute Moutons)
105 De La Commune West
Montreal, Quebec
Canada H2Y 2C7
(514) 284–9607

CHAPTER 19

■ ■ ■

Mexico and Costa Rica

In the past decade, the whitewater enthusiasm of the United States and Canada has spilled over into Mexico and Costa Rica. Currently at least eight rivers in Mexico and Costa Rica offer a variety of whitewater rafting selections. Half-day and one-day float trips through exotic tropical jungles as well as one-day and multiday Class IV–V whitewater adventures through historical and rarely seen tropical habitats provide a variety of choices.

Southern Mexico's two rafting adventures offer virtually the only access to the avenues of early continental civilization that have only recently been rediscovered. For more than one hundred miles, the mighty Usumacinta River, which creates the border between Mexico and Guatemala, offers a classic journey past the ancient Mayan Indian ruins of Yaxchilan El Cayo and Piedras Negras. In the Chiapas Mountains, the pristine whitewaters of the Rio Jatate, flowing over travertine formations, provide a significantly more challenging Class III–V whitewater adventure through remote rain-forest jungle terrain.

Flowing eastward below Pico de Orizaba—at 18,700 feet, Mexico's highest peak—a four-day commercial rafting adventure on the Rio Antigua in Veracruz state opens a historic corridor through lands steeped in the pre-Columbian and Spanish colonial past.

Costa Rica, with some of the world's best preserved and most accessible tropical rain forests, also has some of its best whitewaters. On its many river trips, rafters are treated to unusual sights and sounds of active volcanic peaks and tropical forests with exotic jungle flora and fauna.

Costa Rica's raft trips, most with sufficient Class III–IV whitewaters for all-year rafting, are now being enjoyed by visitors from all over the world.

· The Rio Reventazon, Costa Rica's most popular whitewater river, offers one-day and multiday raft trips on four sections—Powerhouse, Tucurrique, Peralta, and Pascua. The Tucurrique, the Reventazon's favorite whitewater trip, has exciting, yet not intimidating, Class II–III waters that can usually be run all year.
· Rio Pacuare, one of North America's finest multiday whitewater adventures, offers an abundance of mostly Class III rapids through a gorgeous rain forest.
· Rio General, sometimes called the Rio Chirripo trip after a nearby mountain and a principal tributary, is Costa Rica's longest tropical river adventure. Its miles and miles of Class III–IV rapids should satisfy the most ardent of whitewater enthusiasts.

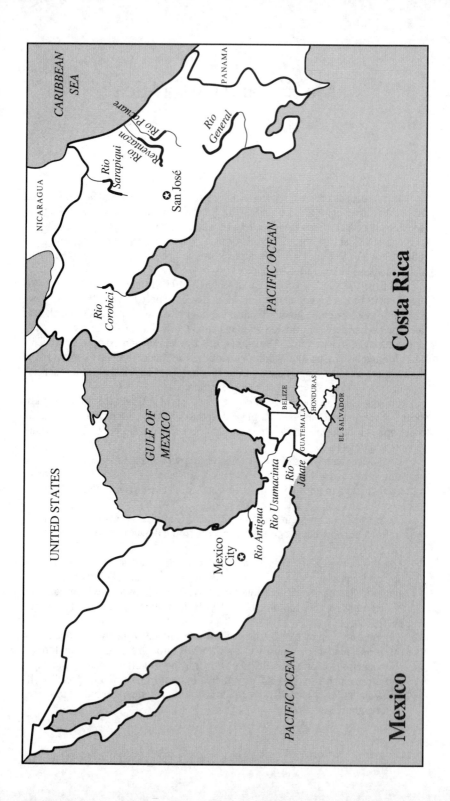

Mexico and Costa Rica
River Comparison

	Difficulty	Min. Age	H	D	M	Season	P	O	K
Mexico									
Rio Usumacinta	/	6		✗		Jan–Apr	✗	✗	
Rio Antigua	/ /	14		✗		Sep–Jan	✗	✗	
Rio Jatate	/ /	14		✗		Dec–Apr	✗	✗	✗
Costa Rica									
Rio Reventazon									
Powerhouse	/ /	14	✗	✗		Year-round	✗	✗	
Tucurrique	/ /	12		✗		Year-round	✗	✗	
Peralta	/ / /	16		✗		Year-round	✗	✗	
Pascua	/ /	16		✗		Year-round	✗		
Rio Pacuare	/ /	16		✗	✗	Year-round	✗	✗	
Rio General	/ /	14		✗		Jun–Dec	✗	✗	
Rio Corobici	/	7		✗		Year-round	✗		
Rio Sarapiqui	/	7		✗		Jun–Dec	✗	✗	

/   Beginner—Easy whitewater. Fun for everyone.

/ /   Intermediate—Moderate whitewater.
No previous rafting experience is necessary.

/ / /   Advanced—Difficult whitewater.
Previous Class IV paddle rafting experience is recommended or required.

H—Half-Day Trip, D—Day Trip, M—Multiday Trip
P—Paddle Raft, O—Oar Raft, K—Inflatable Kayak

Mexico and Costa Rica outfitters now offer more than a dozen rafting trips on eight tropical rivers including the Rio Usumacinta, pictured here. Photo courtesy of Randy Rogers, Wilderness: Alaska/Mexico.

Costa Rica's outfitters also provide two float trips for bird-watchers and nature lovers. Rio Corobici and Rio Sarapiqui in northern Costa Rica offer swift-flowing, yet moderate, Class I–II waters which provide a very long-remembered jungle perspective.

RIO USUMACINTA, MEXICO

Section:	Upper
Location:	Southeast of Villahermosa, southeast Chiapas
Driving Time:	Villahermosa—5 hours
Difficulty:	Class I–III
Trip Length:	95 miles (152 km)
Trip Options:	Paddle raft, oar raft; 10 days
Season:	January–April
Cost:	$1,000–$1,300

Mexico's Rio Usumacinta is one of the world's most exotic river adventures. Draining the Lacandon jungles adjacent to the Mexico–Guatemala border, the Usumacinta is embraced by North America's largest remaining tropical rain forest. While the Usumacinta will be enjoyed by everyone, it affords archaeology buffs, rain-forest enthusiasts, and bird-watchers an unequaled opportunity.

The Usumacinta, which translates from the Mayan language as "sacred monkey," is also known as the River of Ruins. Here, more than a thousand years ago, the Usumacinta and its tributaries saw the rise and fall of the Mayan civilization. From A.D. 200 to 900, great ceremonial centers rose in the jungle, the river serving as their highway. During the Usumacinta river trip, rafters will visit the ceremonial ruins of Yaxchilan and Piedras Negras, which are accessible only by air and water.

Rio Usumacinta, with mostly Class I–II rapids, has its best whitewater near the end of the trip. Within two narrow canyons, normally run on the last two days, several Class III rapids add the finishing touches to an unforgettable river experience.

Rio Usumacinta Outfitters

Ceiba Adventures
P.O. Box 3075
Durango, CO 81302
(303) 247–1174

Expeditiones Mexico Verde S.A.
Jose Ma. Vigil 2406
Col. Italia Providencia
44640 Guadalajara, Jalisco, Mexico
011 (523) 641–1005

Far Flung Adventures
P.O. Box 377
Terlingua, TX 79852
(800) 359–4138
(915) 371–2489

Quest Expeditions
P.O. Box 499
Benton, TN 37307
(800) 277–4537
(615) 338–2979

RIO ANTIGUA, MEXICO

Section:	Middle
Location:	West of Veracruz, east-central Veracruz
Driving Time:	Veracruz—3 hours
Difficulty:	Class III–IV
Trip Length:	45 miles (72 miles)
Trip Options:	Paddle raft, oar raft; three days
Season:	September–January
Cost:	$500–$700

Rio Antigua, which originates on the snow-covered slopes of Pico de Orizaba (18,700 feet), drains a tropical forest region of the Mexican state of Veracruz. The river passes through a wild and diverse setting—with a friendly village or two—of a land filled with reminders of its pre-Columbian and Spanish colonial past. More than four centuries ago, Cortes launched his conquest of Mexico from a point near the Antigua's mouth close to Veracruz on the Gulf of Mexico.

While the Rio Antigua's swiftly flowing current is often interrupted by exciting Class III–IV rapids such as Rock Garden, Straight Off Adolf, Rooster Tail, and Ski Jump, the overall pace of the trip is slow enough to allow guests sufficient time to explore the river's surrounding. Rafters will enjoy sampling fresh seafood, tropical fruits, and souvenirs at local markets. At one riverside campsite, guests can also relax in a large hot spring.

Rio Antigua Outfitters

Far Flung Adventures
P.O. Box 377
Terlingua, TX 79852
(915) 371–2489
(800) 359–4138

Quest Expeditions
P.O. Box 499
Benton, TN 37307
(800) 277–4537
(615) 338–2979

RIO JATATE, MEXICO

Section:	Palenque to Aqua Azul Park
Location:	Near Palenque, southeast of Villahermosa, eastern Chiapas
Driving Time:	Villahermosa—8 hours
Difficulty:	Class III–V, (VI)
Trip Length:	100 miles (160 km)
Trip Options:	Paddle raft; 11 days
Season:	December–April
Cost:	$1,400

Rio Jatate, born in the highlands of Mexico's frontier state of Chiapas, is a free-flowing adventure trip through some of the country's last remaining rain-forest wilderness. Jatate's rapids, which flow over travertine formations, are not for the fainthearted. Although most of Jatate's rapids are Class III, there are several fairly difficult Class IV and V waterfalls, chutes, and slides that are run. There are also Class VI portages.

Busidja Falls on the Usumacinta River can be seen only by raft. Photo courtesy of Expeditiones Mexico Verde, S.A.

Rio Jatate is rafted at a leisurely pace, allowing plenty of time for scouting rapids and hiking to nearby waterfalls. Extra days are allowed for visiting the famed ruins of Palenque and Agua Azul Park.

Rio Jatate Outfitters

Ceiba Adventures
P.O. Box 3075
Durango, CO 81302
(303) 247–1174

Far Flung Adventures
P.O. Box 377
Terlingua, TX 79852
(800) 359–4138
(915) 371–2489

RIO REVENTAZON, COSTA RICA

Section: Powerhouse
Location: East of San José, east-central Costa Rica
Driving Time: San José—3.5 hours
Difficulty: Class III–IV
Trip Length: 6 miles (9.5 km)
Trip Options: Paddle raft, oar raft; one day and multiday
Season: Year-round
Cost: $80

Rio Reventazon, Costa Rica's most frequently rafted river, is located east of the capital city of San José. Reventazon's tropical jungle climate and water storage reservoirs generally permit rafting throughout the year. Professional rafting outfitters commonly offer tourists and residents a choice of four one-day river trips as well as a number of multiday options.

Rafting on the Powerhouse section, the river's uppermost trip, begins at the spillway below the Cachi Dam and hydroelectric station. After a very brief period for warm-up paddling, the Reventazon's gentle waters become continuous whitewater. The second and third miles of the trip are virtually one continuous rapid. Powerhouse's best rafting is during the fall rainy season, normally September and October.

Section: Tucurrique
Location: East of San José, east-central Costa Rica
Driving Time: San José—3.5 hours
Difficulty: Class II–III
Trip Length: 12 miles (19 km)
Trip Options: Paddle raft, oar raft; one day
Season: Year-round
Cost: $65–$85

The Rio Reventazon between Tucurrique and Angostura is Costa Rica's favorite one-day whitewater trip. Tucurrique's popularity is a result of scheduled water releases from El Congo Dam, beautiful forest and farmland scenery, and proximity to San José. First-time and experienced rafters from all over the world enjoy Tucurrique's exciting, yet not difficult, Class II–III whitewater and its beautiful scenery.

Section: Peralta
Location: East of San José, east-central Costa Rica
Driving Time: San José—3.5 hours
Difficulty: Class IV–V
Trip Length: 9 miles (14.5 km)
Trip Options: Paddle raft, oar raft; one day
Season: Year-round
Cost: $80–$85

The Peralta, or Guayabo, section, is Costa Rica's most difficult whitewater stretch. Its continuous and powerful whitewaters, which include more than thirty Class IV-V rapids, require precise raft manuevering by physically fit paddle rafters. Peralta's six most respected rapids—The S's, Meatgrinder, El Horrendo, Ceja, Piedra de Fuego, and Land of 1000 Holes—and its unrunnable Class VI Jungle Run will long be cherished by those fortunate enough to experience this spectacular whitewater adventure. Outfitters, rightfully calling the Peralta section more difficult than West Virginia's upper Gauley, require guests to have had previous Class IV whitewater rafting experience.

Section: Pascua
Location: East of San José, east-central Costa Rica

Driving Time:	San José—3.5 hours
Difficulty:	Class III–IV+
Trip Length:	12–15 miles (19–24 km)
Trip Options:	Paddle raft; one day
Season:	Year-round
Cost:	$80–$85

Pascua, Reventazon's final section, can either be run with the Peralta or as a separate, less demanding one-day trip. Pascua has some dramatic Class IV rapids, such as Gran Pillow and Muerte Verde (Green Death). Class III–IV rafting experience may be required during high water.

Outfitters listed on page 237.

RIO PACUARE, COSTA RICA

Section:	San Martín to Siquirres
Location:	West of Limón, east-central Costa Rica
Driving Time:	San José—3.5 hours
Difficulty:	Class III–IV
Trip Length:	18 miles (29 km)
Trip Options:	Paddle raft, oar raft; one day and multiday
Season:	All year
Cost:	$90 one day; $250–$500 multiday

Rio Pacuare, one of Central America's premier river adventures, has a near-perfect mix of tropical forest beauty, superb whitewater, and exotic birds and animals. Within its densely vegetated canyon gorges, rafters may see jaguars, ocelots, monkeys, sloths, and a wide array of colorful birds. Pacuare's mostly Class III whitewaters, although exciting, are humane enough to allow guests sufficient time to fully enjoy the spectacular jungle adventure.

In addition to popular one-day trips on the Tres Equis section of the Rio Pacuare, outfitters offer two- and three-day trips with overnight camping in the jungle.

Outfitters listed on page 237.

RIO GENERAL, COSTA RICA

Section:	Juntas de Pacuar to Brujo
Location:	Near San Isidro, southwest Costa Rica
Driving Time:	San José—5 hours
Difficulty:	Class III–IV
Trip Length:	43 miles (69 km)
Trip Options:	Paddle raft, oar raft; multiday
Season:	June–December
Cost:	$350–$450 three and four days

Rio General—sometimes called the Rio Chirripo, after the country's highest mountain (which it drains) and one of the river's many tributaries—is Costa Rica's longest tropical river adventure. Its seemingly countless miles of exciting whitewaters, long a popular playground with foreign kayakers, will challenge the most ardent rafting enthusiast.

Few rivers match the Rio General for whitewater intensity. Dozens of exciting Class III–IV rapids with aptly descriptive names (Elephant Rock, Michael's 3 Miles, Screaming Right Turn, The Ramp, Forever Eddy, The Brew, Go Left and Die, and The Whirlpool) can be immensely enjoyed by all paddlers.

Rio General, created by the joining of the Rio Chirripo and Rio Buenvista near the small town of Rivas in southwest Costa Rica, can be run in either three or four days. While the General does not offer the same pristine tropical jungle environs as the Rio Pacuare or some sections of the Rio Reventazon, its more pastoral surrounding are nevertheless beautiful. Rafters may not even notice the riverbanks because of their intense involvement with the whitewater.

Outfitters listed on page 237.

RIO COROBICI, COSTA RICA

Section:	Canas
Location:	Near Palo Verde National Park, northwest of Puntarenas
Driving Time:	San José—3 hours
Difficulty:	Class I–II
Trip Length:	13 miles (21 km)
Trip Options:	Paddle raft; one day
Season:	All year
Cost:	$80

The Rio Corobici, in northwest Costa Rica, is aptly called a "Walt Disney style" nature float trip. Along the Corobici and in nearby Palo Verde National Park, more than three hundred species of birds have been sighted. Many species make these jungle forests their permanent habitat. Birds most commonly seen along the Coribici include ospreys, mot-mots, herons, jacanas, kingfishers, crested caracaras, and cormorants. Rafters are also commonly treated to sights of iguanas, other species of lizards, and playful howler monkeys.

While the majority of rafters on the Rio Corobici are cruise ship passengers docked at Puerto Caldera, northwest of Puntarenas, the river is often rafted by visitors from San José.

Outfitters listed on page 237.

RIO SARAPIQUI, COSTA RICA

Sections:	La Virgen to Chilamate and Chilamate to Puerto Viejo
Location:	Near Puerto Viejo, northwest of San Jose
Driving Time:	San José—2.5 hours
Difficulty:	Class II–III (La Virgen); Class I–II (Chilamate)
Trip Length:	7 miles (11 km) per section
Trip Options:	Paddle raft, oar raft; one day
Season:	June–December
Cost:	$70

Rio Sarapiqui's La Virgen to Chilamate whitewater trip is one of Costa Rica's more popular one-day rafting trips. Its 7-mile (11-km) course—which winds through tropical jungle forests, sugar cane fields, and banana, oil palm, and cacao plantations—has several exciting Class III rapids. Most memorable are Gringo's Hole, Confusion, and Pattie's Bend.

The lower Sarapiqui trip, beginning at Chilamate, is comparable in beauty to the exotic Rio Corobici. Its easy Class I–II water allows guests ample time to enjoy the forested lowland jungle habitat near the Caribbean. Rio Sarapiqui's overhanging forests have a rich variety of birdlife, including toucans, parrots, and oro pendulas.

Costa Rica Outfitters

Aventures Naturales
Apartado 10736-1000
San José, Costa Rica, C.A.
011 (506) 225–3939

Rios Tropicales
P.O. Box 472-1200 Pavas
San José, Costa Rica, C.A.
011 (506) 233–6455

Costa Rica Expeditions
Calle Central and Avenida 3
San José, Costa Rica, C.A.
011 (506) 257–0766

Accommodations

The following list of selected accommodations is for rafters who desire overnight lodging or campground facilities either prior to or following any river trip. Although most of these low- and moderate-priced accommodations have been recommended by the professional river outfitters, the inclusion or omission of any specific lodging or campground is not intended to be either an endorsement or disapproval. While the telephone numbers were in effect at the time of publication, the author and publisher cannot be responsible should any of these numbers change.

Since most of the rivers flow through or near national and state or provincial forests and parks, and other government lands, there are also countless public campgrounds available to rafting guests. Likewise, many of the river outfitters operate convenient lodging and campgrounds for their own customers. Information about these accommodations can be obtained directly from the river outfitters.

To avoid unnecessary morning driving time, rafters should check with outfitters regarding the time and location of their pre-trip meeting. While outfitters often meet guests either at their base camp or business headquarters, the diverse geography of river trips necessitates that numerous rendezvous locations be used. Finally, although outfitters usually arrange all shuttle transportation, multiday trips sometimes require that someone shuttle a rafter's automobile to or from river put-in or take-out points. In Alaska and western Canada, outfitters often arrange for pre- or post-trip flights by charter aircraft.

Hotel/Motel Toll-Free Numbers

These toll-free reservations numbers are for the hotel and motel chains that have branches located near many of the rivers in this book:

Best Western International
(800) 528–1234 USA and Canada
(525) 208–7284 Mexico

Choice Hotels International
Comfort, Clarion, Quality Inn, and
  Sleep
(800) 221–2222 USA and Canada
9 1 800 90 000 Mexico

Choice Hotels International
Econo Lodge, Friendship,
  and Rodeway
(800) 424–4777 USA and Canada
9 1 800 90 000 Mexico

Days Inn
(800) 325–2525 USA and Canada
(525) 207–1322 Mexico

Holiday Inn
(800) 465–4329 Worldwide

Ramada Inns
(800) 228–2828 USA and Canada

Super 8 Motels
(800) 800–8000 USA and Canada

Travelodge
(800) 578–7878

CHAPTER 8: CALIFORNIA

American River (South Fork), California

El Dorado Chamber of Commerce
542 Main St.
Placerville, CA 95667
(800) 457-6279
(916) 621-5885

Lodging
Best Western Cameron Park Inn
3361 Coach Lane
Cameron Park, CA 95682
(916) 677-2203

Best Western Placerville Inn
6850 Greenleaf Dr.
Placerville, CA 95667
(916) 622-9100

Cameron Park Super 8 Motel
3444 Coach Lane
Cameron Park, CA 95682
(916) 677-7177

Days Inn Placerville
1332 Broadway
Placerville, CA 95667
(916) 622-3124

Gold Trail Motor Lodge
1970 Broadway
Placerville, CA 95667
(916) 622-2906

Campgrounds
Camp Lotus
P.O. Box 578
Lotus, CA 95651
(916) 622-8672

Coloma Resort
P.O. Box 516
Coloma, CA 95613
(916) 621-2267

American River (Middle and North Forks), California

Placer County Visitors Center
13460 Lincoln Way, Suite A
Auburn, CA 95603
(916) 887-2111

Lodging
Auburn Inn
1875 Auburn Ravine Rd.
Auburn, CA 95603
(916) 885-1800

Best Western Golden Key Motel
13450 Lincoln Way
Auburn, CA 95603
(916) 885-8611

Foothills Motel
13431 Bowman Rd.
Auburn, CA 95603
(916) 885-8444

Super 8 Motel
140 E. Hillcrest Dr.
Auburn, CA 95603
(916) 888-8808

Campgrounds
Bear River Park
11476 C Ave.
Auburn, CA 95603
(916) 889-7198

Rollins Lake Resort
P.O. Box 60
Chicago Park, CA 95713
(916) 346-2212

Cache Creek, California

Lodging
Best Western El Grande Inn
15135 Lakeshore Dr.
Clearlake, CA 95422
(707) 994-2000

Highlands Inn
13865 Lakeshore Dr.
Clearlake, CA 95422
(707) 994–8982

Campground
Clear Lake State Park
Soda Bay Rd.
Kelseyville, CA 95451
(707) 279–4293

Yuba River (North Fork), California

Lodging
Best Western Gold Country Inn
11972 Sutton Way
Grass Valley, CA 95945
(916) 273–1393

The Holbrook Hotel
212 W. Main St.
Grass Valley, CA 95945
(916) 273–1353

Northern Queen
400 Railroad Ave.
Nevada City, CA 95959
(916) 265–5824

Red Castle Inn
109 Prospect St.
Nevada City, CA 95959
(916) 265–5135

Campgrounds
North Yuba Ranger Station
Star Route, Box 1
Camptonville, CA 95922
(916) 288–3231

Willow Creek Campground
17548 Hwy. 49
Camptonville, CA 95922
(916) 288–3456

*Stanislaus River (North Fork),
    California*

Lodging
Avery Hotel
P.O. Box 321
Avery, CA 95224
(209) 795–9935

Columbia Inn Motel
22646 Broadway St.
Columbia, CA 95310
(209) 533–0446

Dorrington Hotel
P.O. Box 4307
Dorrington, CA 95223
(209) 795–5800

Murphy's Hotel
457 Main St.
Murphys, CA 95247
(209) 728–3444

Campgrounds
Calaveras Big Trees State Park
Hwy. 4, P.O. Box 120
Arnold, CA 95223
(209) 795–2334

Golden Torch RV Resort & CG
Hwy. 4
Arnold, CA 95223
(209) 795–2820

*Stanislaus River (Goodwin Canyon
    Section), California*

Lodging
Holiday Motel
950 E. F St.
Oakdale, CA 95361
(209) 847–7023

Knights Ferry Bed & Breakfast
General Delivery
Knights Ferry, CA 95361
(209) 881–3418

Ramada Inn
825 East F St.
Oakdale, CA 95361
(209) 847–8181

Campground
Knights Ferry Resort Camp
General Delivery
Knights Ferry, CA 95361
(209) 881–3349

Tuolumne River, California

Lodging
Evergreen Lodge
Evergreen Rd.
Groveland, CA 95321
(209) 379–2606

Hotel Charlotte B&B
Hwy. 120
Groveland, CA 95321
(209) 962–6455

Groveland Motel
Hwy. 120
Groveland, CA 95321
(209) 962–7865

Sugar Pine Motel
Hwy. 120
Groveland, CA 95321
(209) 962–7823

Campground
Moccasin Point Campground
c/o Don Pedro Recreation Agency
P.O. Box 160
La Grange, CA 95329
(209) 852–2396

Merced River, California

Lodging
Best Western Yosemite Way Station
Hwy. 140 and S. Hwy. 49
Mariposa, CA 95338
(209) 966–7545

Cedar Lodge Motel
Hwy. 140
El Portal, CA 95318
(209) 379–2612

Mariposa Lodge
5052 Hwy. 40
Mariposa, CA 95338
(209) 966–3607

Campgrounds
Indian Flat RV Park & Campground
P.O. Box 356
El Portal, CA 95318
(209) 379–2339

Yosemite-Mariposa KOA
Hwy. 140
Midpines, CA 95345
(209) 966–2201

Kings River, California

Lodging
Best Western Holiday Lodge
40105 Sierra Dr.
Three Rivers, CA 93271
(209) 561–4119

Best Western Visalia Inn Motel
623 W. Main St.
Visalia, CA 93277
(209) 732–4561

Economy Inn
2570 S. East St.
Fresno, CA 93706
(209) 486–1188

Ramada Inn
324 E. Shaw
Fresno, CA 93710
(209) 224–4040

Campgrounds
Hume Lake Campground
Sequoia National Forest
Hume Lake, CA 93628
(209) 338–2251

Sierra Campground & RV Park
Mountain Rd. 453
Badger, CA 93603
(209) 337–2520

Kern River, California

Lodging
Kern Lodge Motel
67 Valley View Dr.
Kernville, CA 93238
(619) 376–2223

Kernville Inn
11042 Kernville Rd.
Kernville, CA 93238
(619) 376–2206

Lazy River Lodge
15727 Sierra Way
Kernville, CA 93238
(619) 376–2242

River View Lodge
2 Sirrettu St.
Kernville, CA 93238
(619) 376–6019

Sequoia Motor Lodge
1623 Sierra Way
Kernville, CA 93238
(619) 376–2535

Campground
Lake Isabella & Upper Kern
  Campgrounds
P.O. Box 3810
Lake Isabella, CA 93240
(619) 379–5646

Sacramento River (Upper), California

Dunsmuir Chamber of Commerce
P.O. Box 17
Dunsmuir, CA 96025
(916) 235–2177

Lodging
Best Western Tree House Motor Inn
P.O. Box 236
Mt. Shasta, CA 96067
(916) 926–3101

Strawberry Valley Inn
1142 S. Mt. Shasta Blvd.
Mt. Shasta, CA 96067
(916) 926–2052

Swiss Holiday Lodge
P.O. Box 335
Mt. Shasta, CA 96067
(916) 926–3446

Campground
Castle Crags State Park
Castella, CA 96017
(916) 235–2684

Salmon River, California

Lodging
Klamath River Lodge
P.O. Box 145
Orleans, CA 95556
(707) 443–7021

Orleans Hotel
P.O. Box 160
Orleans, CA 95556
(707) 627–3311

Young's Ranch Resort
92520 Hwy. 96
Somes Bar, CA 95568
(800) 552–6284
(916) 469–3322

Campgrounds
Mountain View Ranch
P.O. Box 389
Orleans, CA 95556
(916) 627–3354

Oak Bottom Campground
Klamath National Forest
Somes Bar, CA 95568
(916) 469–3331

Trinity River, California

Lodging

Madrone Lane Bed & Breakfast
HCR #34
Burnt Ranch, CA 95527
(916) 629–3642

Peach Tree Inn Bed & Breakfast
P.O. Box 295
Willow Creek, CA 95573
(916) 629–2969

Riverview Motel
P.O. Box 1219
Willow Creek, CA 95573
(916) 629–2536

Trinity Canyon Lodge
P.O. Box 51
Helena, CA 96048
(916) 623–6318

The Willow Creek Motel
P.O. Box 508
Willow Creek, CA 95573
(916) 629–2922

Campgrounds
Big Foot Campground
P.O. Box 98
Junction City, CA 96048
(916) 623–6088

Lazy Double B Campground
P.O. Box 527
Salyer, CA 95563
(916) 629–2156

Klamath River (Upper), Oregon/ California

Ashland Chamber of Commerce
110 E. Main St.
Ashland, OR 97520
(503) 482–3486

Klamath Falls Chamber of Commerce
507 Main St., Suite 2
Klamath Falls, OR 97601
(503) 884–5193

Lodging
Best Western Miner's Inn
122 E. Miner St.
Yreka, CA 96097
(916) 842–4355

Comfort Inn
2500 S. Sixth St.
Klamath Falls, OR 97601
(503) 884–9999

Klamath Motor Lodge
1111 S. Main St.
Yreka, CA 96097
(916) 842–2751

Campground
N. Klamath River Area Campgrounds
91 Dennis Lane
Hornbrook, CA 96044
(916) 475–3360

Klamath River (Lower), California

Lodging
Anglers Motel
Hwy. 96, P.O. Box 483
Happy Camp, CA 96039
(916) 493–2735

Forest Lodge Motel
Hwy. 96
Happy Camp, CA 96039
(916) 493–5424

Klamath Inn
Hwy. 96, 110 Nugget St.
Happy Camp, CA 96039
(916) 493–2860

Rustic Inn Motel
Hwy. 96, P.O. Box 925
Happy Camp, CA 96039
(916) 493–2658

Young's Ranch Resort
92520 Hwy. 96
Somes Bar, CA 95568
(800) 552–6284
(916) 469–3322

Campgrounds
Elk Creek Campground
921 Elk Creek Rd.
Happy Camp, CA 96039
(916) 493–2208

Klamath National Forest Camp-
    grounds
Happy Camp Ranger District
Happy Camp, CA 96039
(916) 627–3291

CHAPTER 9:
PACIFIC NORTHWEST STATES

Wenatchee River, Washington

Wenatchee Area Visitors Center
P.O. Box 850
Wenatchee, WA 98807
(800) 572–7753
(509) 662–4774

Lodging
Alpen Inn
405 W. Hwy. 2
Leavenworth, WA 98826
(509) 548–4326

Village Inn Motel
229 Cottage Ave
Cashmere, WA 98815
(509) 782–3522

Campgrounds
Leavenworth KOA
11401 River Bend Dr.
Leavenworth, WA 98826
(509) 548–7709

Wenatchee River County Park
Hwy. 2
Wenatchee, WA 98801
(509) 662–2525

Methow River, Washington

Lodging
Country Town Motel
Hwy. 153
Carlton, WA 98814
(509) 997–3432

Ide-a-While Motel
Hwy. 20
Twisp, WA 98856
(509) 997–3222

Lake Pateros Motor Inn
Hwys. 97 & 153
Pateros, WA 98846
(509) 923–2203

Campground
Alta Lake State Park
U.S. Hwy. 97
Pateros, WA 98846
(509) 923–2473

Tieton River, Washington

Lodging
Game Ridge Motel
27350 Hwy. 12
Rimrock, WA 98937
(509) 672–2212

Tatoosh Motel
12880 Hwy. 12
Packwood, WA 98361
(206) 494–5321

Trout Lodge
27090 Hwy. 12
Naches, WA 98937
(509) 672–2211

Campground
House Creek and Windy Point Camp-
grounds
Hwy. 12, Wenatchee National Forest
Rimrock, WA 98937

White Salmon River, Washington

Lodging
Inn of the White Salmon
P.O. Box 1549
White Salmon, WA 98672
(509) 493–2335

Llama Ranch B&B
1980 Hwy. 141
White Salmon, WA 98672
(509) 395–2786

Mio Amore Pensione
53 Little Mountain Rd.
Trout Lake, WA 98650
(509) 395–2264

Campground
Elk Meadows RV Park and Campground
78 Trout Lake Creek Rd.
Trout Lake, WA 98650
(509) 395–2843

Klickitat River, Washington

Lodging
Far Vue Motel
808 E. Simcoe Dr.
Goldendale, WA 98620
(800) 358–5881
(509) 773–5882

Flying L Ranch B&B
Mt. Adams Hwy.
Glenwood, WA 98619
(509) 364–3488

Campground
Maryhill State Park
Goldendale, WA 98620
(509) 773–5007

Nooksack River, Washington

Bellingham Chamber of Commerce
1801 Roeder Ave.
Bellingham, WA 98225
(206) 734–1330

Campground
Douglas Fir and Silver Fir Campgrounds
Mt. Baker–Snoqualmie National Forest
Hwy. 542
Glacier, WA 98244

Suiattle and Sauk Rivers, Washington

Lodging
Bradley's B&B
716 Sauk Ave.
Darrington, WA 98241
(206) 436–0120

Hemlock Hills B&B
612 Stillaguamish
Darrington, WA 98241
(206) 436–1274

Sauk River Farm B&B
32629 State Rt. 530 NE
Darrington, WA 98241
(206) 436–1794

Stagecoach Inn
P.O. Box 400 (100 Seaman St.)
Darrington, WA 98241
(206) 436–1776

Campgrounds
Clear Creek and White Chuck Campgrounds
Darrington Ranger Station
Darrington, WA 98241
(206) 436–1155

Downey Creek and Buck Campgrounds
Darrington Ranger Station
Darrington, WA 98241
(206) 436–1155

Squire Creek Campground
State Rt. 530
Darrington, WA 98241
(206) 436–1283

Skagit River, Washington

Lodging
Clark's Cabins & RV Park
5675 Hwy. 20
Rockport, WA 98283
(206) 873-2250

Eagles Nest
200 E. Hwy. 20
Concrete, WA 98237
(206) 853-8662

North Cascades Inn
4284 Hwy. 20
Concrete, WA 98237
(206) 853-8870

Campground
Colonial Creek and Newhalem Camp-
grounds
North Cascades National Park
Sedro Wooley, WA 98284
(206) 855-1331

Skykomish River, Washington

Lodging
Dutch Cup Motel
P.O. Box 336
Sultan, WA 98294
(206) 793-2215

The Fairgrounds Inn
18950 U.S. Hwy. 2
Monroe, WA 98272
(206) 794-5401

Campground
Wallace Falls State Park
U.S. Hwy. 2
Gold Bar, WA 98251
(206) 793-0420

Elwha River, Washington

N. Olympic Peninsula Visitors Bureau
338 W. First
Port Angeles, WA 98362
(206) 452-8552

Lodging
Best Western Olympic Lodge
140 Del Guzzi Dr.
Port Angeles, WA 98362
(206) 452-2993

Super 8 Motel
2104 E. 1st St.
Port Angeles, WA 98362
(206) 452-8401

Uptown Motel
101 E. 2nd St.
Port Angeles, WA 98362
(206) 457-9434

Campgrounds
Altaire Campground
Olympic National Park
Port Angeles, WA 98362
(206) 956-2300

Indian River RV Camp
7460 Hwy. 101 West
Port Angeles, WA 98362
(206) 457-4009

Hoh River, Washington

Lodging
Forks Motel
P.O. Box 510
Forks, WA 98331
(206) 374-6243

Olympic Inn
616 W. Heron St.
Aberdeen, WA 98520
(206) 533–4200

Campground
Rain Forest Resort Campground
Rt. 1, Box 40
Quinault, WA 98575
(206) 288–2535

Rogue and Illinois Rivers, Oregon

Lodging
Best Western Grants Pass Inn
111 NE Agness Ave.
Grants Pass, OR 97526
(503) 476–1117

Morrison's Rogue River Lodge
8500 Galice Rd.
Merlin, OR 97532
(800) 826–1963
(503) 476–3825

Paradise Ranch Inn
7000 Monument Dr.
Grants Pass, OR 97526
(503) 479–4333

Redwood Motel
815 NE 6th St.
Grants Pass, OR 97526
(503) 476–0878

Riverside Inn
971 SE 6th St.
Grants Pass, OR 97526
(503) 476–6873

Campgrounds
Indian Mary Park Campground
7100 Galice Rd.
Merlin, OR 97532
(503) 474–5285

Valley of the Rogue State Park
I–5 (Exit 45–B)
Gold Hill, OR 97525
(503) 582–3128

North Umpqua River, Oregon

Lodging
Idleyld Park Lodge
23834 N. Umpqua Hwy.
Idleyld Park, OR 97447
(503) 496–0132

Steamboat Inn
Steamboat, OR 97447–9703
(503) 498–2411

Steelhead Run B&B
23049 N. Umpqua Hwy.
Glide, OR 97443
(503) 496–0563

Windmill Inn of America
1450 NW Mulholland
Roseburg, OR 97470
(503) 673–0901

Campground
Bogus Creek and Eagle Rock Campgrounds
Umpqua NF, N. Umpqua District
18782 N. Umpqua Rd.
Glide, OR 97443
(503) 496–3532

McKenzie River, Oregon

Lodging
Horse Creek Lodge
56228 Delta Dr.
McKenzie Bridge, OR 97413
(503) 822–3243

Log Cabin Inn
56483 McKenzie Hwy.
McKenzie Bridge, OR 97413
(503) 822-3432

Wayfarer Resort
46725 Goodpasture Rd.
Vida, OR 97488
(503) 896-3613

Campground
Camp Yale
58980 Old McKenzie Hwy.
McKenzie Bridge, OR 97413
(503) 822-3961

Deschutes River (Upper), Oregon

Lodging
Comfort Inn
61200 S. Hwy. 97
Bend, OR 97702
(503) 388-2227

Shiloh Inn
3105 O.B. Riley Rd.
Bend, OR 97701
(503) 389-9600

The River House
3075 N. Hwy. 97
Bend, OR 97701
(503) 389-3111

Campground
Deschutes NF, Bend Ranger Dist.
1230 NE Third St.
Suite A-262
Bend, OR 97701
(503) 388-5664

Deschutes River (Lower), Oregon

The Dalles Convention & Visitors Bureau
901 E. 2nd St.
The Dalles, OR 97058
(800) 255-3385

Lodging
Best Western Tapadera Inn
2nd & Liberty
The Dalles, OR 97058
(503) 296-9107

Deschutes Motel
Rt. 1, Box 10, Hwy. 197
Maupin, OR 97037
(503) 395-2626

Shiloh Inn
3223 Bret Clodfelter Way
The Dalles, OR 97058
(503) 298-5502

Campgrounds
Maupin City Park
Bakeoven Rd.
Maupin, OR 97037
(503) 395-2252

Wasco County Fairgrounds
Tygh Valley Rd.
Tygh Valley, OR 97063
(503) 483-2288

Grande Ronde River, Oregon

Lodging
Best Western Pony Soldier Motor Inn
2612 Island Ave.
La Grande, OR 97850
(503) 963-7195

Minam Motel
P.O. Box 696
Elgin, OR 97827
(503) 437-4475

Mingo Motel
P.O. Box 462
Wallowa, OR 97885
(503) 886-2021

Shilo Lodge–Troy
HCR 62, Box 85
Enterprise, OR 97828
(503) 828–7741

Campground
Minam State Recreation Area
Oregon Hwy. 82
Elgin, OR 97827
(503) 432–4185

CHAPTER 10: NORTHERN ROCKY MOUNTAIN STATES

Salmon River (Middle Fork and Upper Main), Idaho

Lodging
Best Western Christiana
651 Sun Valley Rd.
Ketchum, ID 83340
(208) 726–3351

Creekside Lodge
P.O. Box 110
Stanley, ID 83278
(800) 523–0733

Heidelberg Inn
P.O. Box 304
Ketchum, ID 83340
(208) 726–5361

Mountain Village Lodge
P.O. Box 150
Stanley, ID 83278
(208) 774–3661

Redfish Lake Lodge
P.O. Box 9
Stanley, ID 83278
(208) 774–3536

Redwood Motel
P.O. Box 55
Stanley, ID 83278
(208) 774–3531

Campground
Red Top Meadows RV Park &
  Campground
P.O. Box 386
Ketchum, ID 83340
(208) 726–5445

Salmon River (Main), Idaho

Lodging
Wagons West Motel
P.O. Box 574
Salmon, ID 83467
(208) 756–4281

Motel Deluxe
P.O. Box 1044
Salmon, ID 83467
(208) 756–2231

Stagecoach Inn Motel
201 Hwy. 93N
Salmon, ID 83467
(208) 756–4251

Suncrest Motel
705 Challis St.
Salmon, ID 83467
(208) 756–2294

Campground
Salmon Meadows Campground
P.O. Box 705
Salmon, ID 83467
(208) 756–2640

Salmon River (Lower) and Snake River (Hells Canyon), Idaho

Lodging
Frontier Motel
P.O. Box 178
Cambridge, ID 83610
(208) 257–3851

Monty's Motel
700 W. Main St.
Grangeville, ID 83530
(208) 983–2500

Pony Soldier Motor Inn
1716 Main St.
Lewiston, ID 83501
(208) 743–9526

Ramada Inn
621 21st St.
Lewiston, ID 83501
(800) 228–2828
(208) 799–1000

Riggins Motel
P.O. Box 1157
Riggins, ID 83549
(208) 628–3456

Sacajawea Motor Inn
1824 Main St.
Lewiston, ID 83501
(208) 746–1393

Salmon River Motel
1203 S. U.S. Hwy. 95
Riggins, ID 83549
(208) 628–3231

Campground
Hells Gate State Park
Snake River Ave.
Lewiston, ID 83501
(208) 743–2363

Lochsa and Selway Rivers, Idaho

Lodging
Ida-Lee Motel
P.O. Box 16
Kooskia, ID 83539
(208) 926–0166

Snooky's Carriage Inn
U.S. Hwy. 12
Kamiah, ID 83536
(208) 935–2531

Campground
Three Rivers Resort & Campground
HC75, Box 61
Kooskia, ID 83539
(208) 926–4708

Payette River, Idaho

Lodging
Best Western Safari Motor Inn
1070 Grove St.
Boise, ID 83702
(208) 344–6556

Craig Creek Cottages
HC 76, Box 2976
Garden Valley, ID 83622
(208) 462–3033

Landmark Inn
2155 N. Garden
Boise, ID 83704
(208) 344–4030

Rodeway Inn
1115 N. Curtis Rd.
Boise, ID 83706
(208) 376–2700

Campgrounds
Americana Overnight Kampground
3600 American Terrace
Boise, ID 83706
(208) 342–9691

Silver Creek Plunge
HC 76, Box 2666
Garden Valley, ID 83622
(208) 344–8688

Flathead River (Middle and North Forks), Montana

Lodging
Glacier Highland Motel
P.O. Box 397
West Glacier, MT 59936
(406) 888–5427

River Bend Motel
P.O. Box 398
West Glacier, MT 59936
(406) 888–5662

Village Inn
P.O. Box 115
West Glacier, MT 59936
(406) 888–5632

Campgrounds
Glacier Campground
P.O. Box 447
West Glacier, MT 59936
(406) 387–5689

KOA West Glacier
P.O. Box 215
West Glacier, MT 59936
(406) 387–5341

Flathead River (Lower), Montana

Lodging
Diamond Lil's Inn
1680 U.S. 93 S.
Kalispell, MT 59901
(406) 752–3467

Outlaw Inn
1701 Hwy. 93 S.
Kalispell, MT 59901
(406) 755–6100

Red Lion Motel
1330 U.S. Hwy. 2 W.
Kalispell, MT 59901
(406) 755–6700

Super 8 Motel
1341 1st Ave. E.
Polson, MT 59860
(406) 883–6251

Campground
Spruce Park Campground
1985 Hwy. 35
Kalispell, MT 59901
(406) 752–6321

Clark Fork and Blackfoot Rivers, Montana

Missoula Chamber of Commerce
Van Buren & Front
Missoula, MT 59802
(406) 543–6623

Lodging
Best Western Executive Motor Inn
201 E. Main
Missoula, MT 59801
(406) 543–7221

Days Inn Westgate
Hwy. 93 and I–90
Missoula, MT 59802
(406) 721–9776

Super 8 Motel
3901 S. Brooks St.
Missoula, MT 59801
(406) 251–2255

Travelodge
420 W. Broadway
Missoula, MT 59802
(406) 728–4500

Campground
KOA El Mar–Missoula
3695 Tina Ave.
Missoula, MT 59802
(406) 549–0881

Gallatin River, Montana

Lodging
Best Western Buck's T–4 Lodge
P.O. Box 160279
Big Sky, MT 59716
(406) 995–4111

Golden Eagle Lodge
P.O. Box 160008
Big Sky, MT 59716
(406) 995–4800

Rainbow Ranch Lodge
42590 Gallatin Rd.
Gallatin Gateway, MT 59730
(406) 995–4132

Campground
KOA West Yellowstone
P.O. Box 327
West Yellowstone, MT 59758
(406) 646–7607

Madison River, Montana

Lodging
Rainbow Valley Motel
P.O. Box 26
Ennis, MT 59729
(406) 682–7600

Riverside Motel
346 Main St.
Ennis, MT 59729
(406) 682–4240

Sportsman Lodge
310 U.S. 287 N.
Ennis, MT 59729
(406) 682–4242

Campground
Bear Trap Hot Spring
P.O. Box 2944
Norris, MT 59745
(406) 685–3303

Yellowstone River, Montana

Lodging
Best Western Mammoth Hot Springs
U.S. 89
Gardiner, MT 59030
(406) 848–7311

Super 8 Motel
U.S. 89 S.
Gardiner, MT 59030
(406) 848–7401

Wilson's Yellowstone River Motel
P.O. Box 223
Gardiner, MT 59030
(406) 848–7303

Yellowstone Village North Motel
U.S. 89 N.
Gardiner, MT 59030
(406) 848–7414

Campground
Rocky Mountain Campground
Jardine Rt., Box 10
Gardiner, MT 59030
(406) 848–7251

Stillwater River, Montana

Red Lodge Chamber of Commerce
P.O. Box 988
Red Lodge, MT 59068
(406) 446–1718

Lodging
Best Western Lupine Inn
702 S. Hauser
Red Lodge, MT 59068
(406) 446–1321

Stillwater Lodge
28 Main St.
Absarokee, MT 59001
(406) 328–4899

Super 8 Motel
602 8th Ave. N
Columbus, MT 59019
(406) 322–4101

Yodeler Motel
601 S. Broadway
Red Lodge, MT 59068
(406) 446–1435

Campground
Cooney Fish & Wildlife Park
Absarokee, MT 59001
(406) 252–4654

Shoshone River, Wyoming

Lodging
Best Western Sunset Motor Inn
1601 8th St.
Cody, WY 82414
(307) 587–4265

Buffalo Bill Village
1701 Sheridan Ave.
Cody, WY 82414
(307) 587–5544

Comfort Inn
1601 Sheridan Ave.
Cody, WY 82414
(307) 587–5556

Holiday Inn Convention Center
1701 Sheridan Ave.
Cody, WY 82414
(307) 587–5555

Super 8 Motel
730 Yellowstone Hwy.
Cody, WY 82414
(307) 527–6214

Campgrounds
Cody KOA
5561 Greybull Hwy.
Cody, WY 82414
(307) 587–2369

Ponderosa Campground
P.O. Box 1477
Cody, WY 82414
(307) 587–9203

Snake River (Grand Teton and Upper), Wyoming

Lodging
Best Western Executive Inn
325 W. Pearl St.
Jackson, WY 83001
(307) 733–4340

Best Western Parkway Inn
125 N. Jackson St.
Jackson, WY 83001
(307) 733–3143

Days Inn
Hwys. 22 and 89
Jackson, WY 83001
(307) 739–9010

Forty-Niner Inn
330 W. Pearl St.
Jackson, WY 83001
(307) 733–7550

Rusty Parrot Lodge
175 N. Jackson St.
Jackson, WY 83001
(307) 733–2000

Snow King Resort
400 E. Snow King Ave.
Jackson, WY 83001
(307) 733–5200

Super 8 Motel
750 S. Hwy. 89
Jackson, WY 83001
(307) 733–6833

Trapper Motel
235 N. Cache St.
Jackson, WY 83001
(307) 733–2648

Campgrounds
A–1 Campground
125 Virginia Lane S.
Jackson, WY 83001
(307) 733–2697

Jackson Hole Campground
P.O. Box 2802
Jackson, WY 83001
(307) 733–2927

Virginia Lodge RV Park
P.O. Box 1052
Jackson, WY 83001
(307) 733–7189

CHAPTER 11: COLORADO

Arkansas River, Colorado

Heart of the Rockies
Chamber of Commerce
406 W. Rainbow Blvd.
Salida, CO 81201
(303) 539–2068

Lodging
Aspen Leaf Lodge
7350 U.S. Hwy. 50
Salida, CO 81201
(719) 539–6733

Best Western Colorado Lodge
352 W. Rainbow Blvd.
Salida, CO 81201
(719) 539–2514

Best Western Royal Gorge Motel
1925 Fremont Dr.
Canon City, CO 81212
(719) 275–3377

Budget Lodge
1146 U.S. Hwy. 50
Salida, CO 81201
(719) 539–6695

Coronado Motel
517 Hwy. 24 N.
Buena Vista, CO 81211
(719) 395–2251

Great Western Sumac Lodge
428 Hwy. 24 S.
Buena Vista, CO 81211
(719) 395–8111

Red Wood Lodge
7310 U.S. Hwy. 50
Salida, CO 81201
(719) 539–2528

Campgrounds
Arkansas River Campground
3745 E. Hwy. 50
Salida, CO 81201
(719) 539–2381

Brown's Campground
11430 County Rd. 197
Nathrop, CO 81236
(719) 395–8301

Buena Vista Family Campground
27700 County Rd. 303
Buena Vista, CO 81211
(719) 395–8318

Cotopaxi KOA Kampground
21435 U.S. Hwy. 50
Cotopaxi, CO 81223
(719) 275–9308

Cache la Poudre River, Colorado

Fort Collins Visitors Bureau
420 S. Howes, Suite 101
Fort Collins, CO 80524
(303) 482–5821

Lodging
Comfort Inn
1638 E. Mulberry
Fort Collins, CO 80524
(303) 484–2444

Days Inn
3625 E. Mulberry
Fort Collins, CO 80524
(303) 221–5490

Mulberry Inn Econolodge
4333 E. Mulberry
Fort Collins, CO 80524
(303) 493–9000

University Park Holiday Inn
425 W. Prospect Rd.
Fort Collins, CO 80524
(303) 482–2626

Campground
Fort Collins KOA
6670 Hwy. 287 N., Box 600
La Porte, CO 80535
(303) 493–9758

North Platte River, Colorado

North Park Chamber of Commerce
P.O. Box 227
Walden, CO 80480
(303) 723–4600

Lodging
Chedsey Motel
537 Main St.
Walden, CO 80480
(303) 723–8201

North Park Motel
625 Main St.
Walden, CO 80480
(303) 723–4271

The Hoover Roundup
361 Main St.
Walden, CO 80480
(303) 723–4680

The Village Inn
409 Main St.
Walden, CO 80480
(303) 723–4378

Campground
Colorado State Forest
Star Rt., Box 91
Walden, CO 80480

Blue River and Colorado River (Upper), Colorado

Lodging

Columbine Rentals
P.O. Box 259
Dillon, CO 80435
(303) 468–0611

Frisco Lodge
321 Main St.
Frisco, CO 80443
(303) 668–0195

Green Mountain Inn
Blue River Rt., Box 82A
Dillon, CO 80435
(303) 724–9748

Hampton Inn
560 Silverthorne Lane
Silverthorne, CO 80498
(303) 468–6200

Wildernest
P.O. Box 1069
Silverthorne, CO 80498
(303) 468–6291

Campground
Kremmling RV Park & Campground
P.O. Box 532
Kremmling, CO 80459
(303) 724–9593

Eagle River, Colorado

Eagle Valley Chamber of Commerce
P.O. Box 964
Eagle, CO 81631
(303) 328–5220

Lodging

Best Western Eagle Lodge
200 Loren Lane
Eagle, CO 81631
(303) 328–6316

Christy Lodge
Avon, CO 81620
(303) 949–7700

Comfort Inn
0161 W. Beaver Creek Blvd.
Avon, CO 81620
(303) 949–5511

West Vail Lodge Inn
2211 N. Frontage Rd.
Vail, CO 81657
(303) 476–3890

Lodging and Campground

Best Western Eagle RV Park
200 Loren Lane
Eagle, CO 81631
(303) 328–6316

Roaring Fork River and Colorado River (Glenwood), Colorado

Aspen Resort Assn.
303 E. Main St.
Aspen, CO 81611
(303) 925–1940

Glenwood Springs Chamber of Commerce
1102 Grand Ave.
Glenwood Springs, CO 81601
(303) 945–6589

Lodging

Best Western Aspenalt Lodge
160 Hwy. 82
Basalt, CO 81621
(303) 927–3191

Best Western Caravan Inn
1826 Grand Ave.
Glenwood Springs, CO 81601
(303) 945–7451

Budget Host
51429 U.S. Hwy. 6 & 24
Glenwood Springs, CO 81601
(303) 945–5682

Frontier Lodge
2834 Glen Ave.
Glenwood Springs, CO 81601
(303) 945–8545

Holiday Inn
51359 U.S. Hwy. 6 & 24
Glenwood Springs, CO 81601
(303) 945–3551

Hot Springs Lodge
401 E. 6th St.
Glenwood Springs, CO 81601
(303) 945–6571

Campgrounds

Aspen Basalt KOA
P.O. Box 880
Basalt, CO 81621
(303) 927–3532

Rock Gardens Campground
1308 County Rd. 129
Glenwood Springs, CO 81601
(303) 945–6737

Taylor River and Gunnison River (Upper and Lake Fork), Colorado

Gunnison County Chamber of Commerce
P.O. Box 36
Gunnison, CO 81230
(303) 641–1501

Lodging

Bennett's Western Motel
403 E. Tomichi Ave.
Gunnison, CO 81230
(303) 641–1722

Best Western Tomichi Village Inn
P.O. Box 763
Gunnison, CO 81230
(303) 641–1131

Dos Rios Motor Hotel
P.O. Box 1521
Gunnison, CO 81230
(303) 641–1000

Super 8 Motel
411 E. Tomichi Ave.
Gunnison, CO 81230
(303) 641–3068

Swiss Inn Motel
312 E. Tomichi Ave
Gunnison, CO 81230
(303) 641–9962

Campgrounds

Shady Island RV Park & Campground
2776 Hwy. 135 N.
Gunnison, CO 81230
(303) 641–0416

Tall Texan Campground
2460 Hwy. 135 N.
Gunnison, CO 81230
(303) 641–2927

Gunnison River (Gorge), Colorado

Montrose Chamber of Commerce
550 N. Townsend
Montrose, CO 81401
(303) 249–5515

Lodging

Best Western Red Arrow Motor Inn
1702 E. Main St.
Montrose, CO 81401
(303) 249–9641

Black Canyon Motel
1605 E. Main St.
Montrose, CO 81401
(303) 249–3495

Trapper Motel
1225 E. Main
Montrose, CO 81401
(303) 249–3426

Campgrounds

Hanging Tree RV Park & Campground
17250 Hwy. 550 S.
Montrose, CO 81401
(303) 249–9966

Montrose KOA
200 N. Cedar
Montrose, CO 81401
(303) 249–9177

San Juan River (Upper) and Piedra River, Colorado

Lodging

Best Western Oak Ridge Motor Inn
158 Hot Springs Blvd.
Pagosa Springs, CO 81147
(303) 264–4173

Pagosa Lodge at Fairfield Resort
3555 W. Hwy. 160
Pagosa Springs, CO 81147
(800) 523–7704
(303) 731–4141

San Juan Motel
191 E. Pagosa St.
Pagosa Springs, CO 81147
(303) 264–2262

Super 8 Motel
Hwy. 160 & Piedra Rd.
Pagosa Springs, CO 81147
(303) 731–4005

Campground
Pagosa Riverside Campground
P.O. Box 268
Pagosa Springs, CO 81147
(303) 264–5874

*Animas River (Upper and Lower),
Colorado*

Durango Chamber Resort Assn.
P.O. Box 2587
Durango, CO 81302
(303) 247–0312

Lodging
Best Western Durango Inn
21382 Hwy. 160 W.
Durango, CO 81302
(303) 247–3251

Best Western Rio Grande Inn
400 E. 2nd Ave.
Durango, CO 81301
(303) 385–4980

Caboose Motel
3363 Main Ave.
Durango, CO 81301
(303) 247–1191

Comfort Inn
2930 N. Main Ave.
Durango, CO 81301
(303) 259–5373

Days Inn Durango
1700 Animas View Dr.
Durango, CO 81301
(303) 259–1430

Holiday Inn
800 Camino del Rio
Durango, CO 81301
(303) 247–5393

Campgrounds
Durango N. Ponderosa KOA
13391 CR 250
Durango, CO 81301
(303) 247–4499

Lightner Creek Campground
1567 CR 207
Durango, CO 81301
(303) 247–5406

Molas Lake Park & Campground
P.O. Box 776
Silverton, CO 81433
(303) 387–5410

San Miguel River, Colorado

Telluride Chamber Resort Assn.
P.O. Box 653
Telluride, CO 81435
(303) 728–3041

Lodging
Johnstone Inn
P.O. Box 546
Telluride, CO 81435
(303) 728–3316

Tomboy Inn
619 W. Columbia St.
Telluride, CO 81435
(303) 728–6621

Campground
Switzerland of America–Ouray KOA
P.O. Box J
Ouray, CO 81427
(303) 325–4736

Dolores River, Colorado

Cortez Chamber of Commerce
P.O. Box 968
Cortez, CO 81321
(303) 565–3414

Lodging
Anasazi Motor Inn
640 S. Broadway
Cortez, CO 81321
(303) 565–3773

Best Western Sands Motel
1120 E. Main St.
Cortez, CO 81321
(303) 565–3761

Best Western Turquoise Motor Inn
535 E. Main St.
Cortez, CO 81321
(303) 565–3778

Holiday Inn Express
2121 E. Main St.
Cortez, CO 81321
(303) 565–6000

Campground
Dolores River RV Park and Camping
18680 Hwy. 145
Dolores, CO 81323
(303) 882–7761

Yampa and Green Rivers, Colorado

Vernal Chamber of Commerce
134 W. Main St.
Vernal, UT 84078
(801) 789–1352

Lodging
Antlers Best Western Motel
423 W. Main St.
Vernal, UT 84078
(801) 789–1202

Best Western Dinosaur Inn
251 E. Main St.
Vernal, UT 84078
(801) 789–2660

EconoLodge
311 E. Main St.
Vernal, UT 84078
(801) 789–2000

Split Mountain Motel
1015 E. Hwy. 40
Vernal, UT 84078
(801) 789–9020

Campground
Campground Dina
930 N. Vernal Ave.
Vernal, UT 84078
(801) 789–2148

**CHAPTER 12:
SOUTHWEST STATES**

Green River, Utah

Lodging
Bankurz Hatt Bed & Breakfast
214 Farrer St.
Green River, UT 84532
(801) 564–3382

Best Western River Terrace
880 E. Main St.
Green River, UT 84525
(801) 564–3401

Bookcliff Lodge
395 E. Main St.
Green River, UT 84525
(801) 564–3406

Robbers Roost Motel
125 W. Main St.
Green River, UT 84525
(801) 564–3452

West Winds Rodeway Inn
525 E. I–70 Business Loop
Green River, UT 84525
(801) 564–3421

Campgrounds
Green River KOA
550 S. Green River Blvd.
Green River, UT 84525
(801) 564–3651

United Campground
910 E. Main St.
Green River, UT 84525
(801) 564–8195

Colorado River, Utah

Grand County Travel Council
Main & Center
Moab, UT 84532
(800) 635–6622
(801) 259–8825

Lodging
Best Western Canyonlands Inn
16 S. Main St.
Moab, UT 84532
(801) 259–2300

Comfort Suites
800 S. Main St.
Moab, UT 84532
(801) 259–5252

Moab Travellodge
550 S. Main St.
Moab, UT 84532
(801) 259–6171

Moab Valley Inn
711 S. Main St.
Moab, UT 84532
(800) 831–6622
(801) 259–4419

Rustic Inn
120 East 100 S.
Moab, UT 84532
(800) 243–8184
(801) 259–6177

Campgrounds
Canyonlands Campark
555 S. Main St.
Moab, UT 84532
(801) 259–6848

Slickrock Campground
N. Hwy. 191
Moab, UT 84532
(801) 259–7660

San Juan River, Utah

Lodging
Canyonlands Motel
P.O. Box 310011
Mexican Hat, UT 84531
(801) 683–2230

Mexican Hat Lodge
P.O. Box 310175
Mexican Hat, UT 84531
(801) 683–2222

Recapture Lodge
P.O. Box 3098
Bluff, UT 84512
(801) 672–2281

San Juan Inn
P.O. Box 310535
Mexican Hat, UT 84531
(801) 683–2220

Valley of the Gods Inn
P.O. Box 310337
Mexican Hat, UT 84531
(801) 683–2221

Campground
Valley of the Gods Campground
P.O. Box 310337
Mexican Hat, UT 84531
(801) 683–2221

Colorado River (Grand Canyon), Arizona

Flagstaff Chamber of Commerce
101 W. Santa Fe Ave.
Flagstaff, AZ 86001
(602) 774–4505

Lodging
Cliff Dwellers Lodge
U.S. Hwy. 89A
Marble Canyon, AZ 86036
(602) 355–2228

Comfort Inn
914 S. Milton St.
Flagstaff, AZ 86001
(602) 774–7326

Days Inn
1000 W. Business Loop 40
Flagstaff, AZ 86001
(602) 774–5221

Kaibab Lodge
HC 64, Box 30
Fredonia, AZ 86022
(602) 638–2389

Marble Canyon Lodge
Lee's Ferry
Marble Canyon, AZ 86036
(800) 726–1789
(602) 355–2225

Quality Inn Kingman
1400 E. Andy Devine Ave.
Kingman, AZ 86401
(602) 753–4747

Weston's Lamplighter
207 N. Lake Powell Blvd.
Page, AZ 86040
(602) 645–2451

Campground
Lee's Ferry Campground
Glen Canyon National Recreation
  Area
Marble Canyon, AZ 86036
(602) 645–2471

Salt River, Arizona

Lodging
Best Western Copper Hills
U.S. Hwy. 60
Miami, AZ 85539
(602) 425–7151

Verde River, Arizona

Lodging
Best Western Cottonwood Inn
993 S. Main St.
Cottonwood, AZ 86326
(602) 634–5575

Campground
KOA Black Canyon
P.O. Box 569
Black Canyon City, AZ 85324
(602) 374–5318

Rio Chama, New Mexico

Lodging
Abiquiu Inn
P.O. Box A
Abiquiu, NM 85710
(505) 685–4378

Chamisa Inn
920 N. Riverside Dr.
Espanola, NM 87532
(505) 753–7291

El Vado Ranch
P.O. Box 129
Tierra Amarilla, NM 87575
(505) 588–7354

Campgrounds
Abiquiu Dam Campground
U.S. Army Corps of Engineers
Abiquiu, NM 87510
(505) 685–4371

El Vado Ranch
P.O. Box 129
Tierra Amarilla, NM 87575
(505) 588–7354

Rio Grande, New Mexico

Lodging
Best Western Kachina Lodge
413 Pueblo Norte
Taos, NM 87571
(505) 758–2275

Comfort Inn Espanola
810 Riverside Dr.
Espanola, NM 87532
(505) 753–5374

Quality Inn Taos
Hwy. 68, P.O. Box 2319
Taos, NM 87571
(505) 578–2200

Sagebrush Inn
Hwy. 68, P.O. Box 557
Taos, NM 87571
(800) 428–3626
(505) 758–2254

Super 8 Motel
Hwy. 68
Taos, NM 87571
(505) 758–1088

Campground
Bureau of Land Management
Rio Verde Recreation Area
Pilar, NM 87531
(505) 758–8851

Rio Grande, Texas

Lodging
Badlands Hotel
Rt. 70, Box 400
Lajitas, TX 79852
(915) 424–3471

Big Bend Motor Inn
Hyws. 118 & 170
Terlingua, TX 79852
(915) 371–2218

Chisos Mining Motel
P.O. Box 228
Terlingua, TX 79852
(915) 371–2254

Campgrounds
Big Bend Travel Park
P.O. Box 146
Terlingua, TX 79852
(915) 371–2250

Lajitas Rio Grande Campground
Star Rt. 70, Box 400
Lajitas, TX 79852
(915) 424–3471

CHAPTER 13: ALASKA

Mendenhall River, Alaska

Juneau Visitors Center
134 Third Street
Juneau, AK 99801
(907) 586–2201

Lodging
Best Western Country Lane Inn
9300 Glacier Hwy.
Juneau, AK 99801
(907) 789–5005

Breakwater Inn
1711 Glacier Ave.
Juneau, AK 99801
(800) 544–2250
(907) 586–6303

Driftwood Lodge
435 Willoughby Ave.
Juneau, AK 99801
(800) 544–2239
(907) 586–2280

Prospector Hotel
375 Whittier St.
Juneau, AK 99801
(907) 586–3737

Super 8 Motel Juneau
2295 Trout St.
Juneau, AK 99801
(907) 789–4858

Campground
Mendenhall Lake Campground
Juneau Ranger District
8465 Old Dairy Rd.
Juneau, AK 99801
(907) 586–8800

Chilkat River, Alaska

Haines Chamber of Commerce
P.O. Box 518
Haines, AK 99827
(907) 766–2234

Lodging
Eagle's Nest Motel
Haines Hwy., P.O. Box 250
Haines, AK 99827
(907) 766–2352

Halsingland Hotel
P.O. Box 1589
Haines, AK 99827
(800) 766–3198
(907) 766–2000

Mountain View Motel
P.O. Box 62
Haines, AK 99827
(907) 766–2900

Thunderbird Motel
P.O. Box 589
Haines, AK 99827
(907) 766–2131

Lowe River, Alaska

Valdez Visitors Bureau
P.O. Box 1603
Valdez, AK 99686
(800) 478–5954
(907) 835–2984

Lodging
Valdez Village Inn
P.O. Box 365
Valdez, AK 99686
(907) 835–4445

Westmark Inn Valdez
P.O. Box 468
Valdez, AK 99686
(907) 835–4391

Campground
Bearpaw Camper Park
P.O. Box 93
Valdez, AK 99686
(907) 835–4558

Tonsina River, Alaska

Greater Copper Basin Chamber of
  Commerce
P.O. Box 469
Glennallen, AK 99588
(907) 822–5555

Lodging
New Caribou Hotel
P.O. Box 329
Glennallen, AK 99588
(907) 822–3302

Campground
KROA-Kamping Resorts of Alaska
Mile 152 Glenn Hwy.
Glennallen, AK 99588
(907) 822–3346

Kenai River, Alaska

Kenai Visitors & Convention Bureau
P.O. Box 1991
Kenai, AK 99611-6935
(907) 283–2230

Lodging
Best Western Hotel Seward
221 5th Ave.
Seward, AK 99664
(907) 224–2378

Gwin's Lodge
Mile 52 Sterling Hwy.
Cooper Landing, AK 99572
(907) 595–1266

Kenai Merit Inn
260 S. Willow St.
Kenai, AK 99611
(907) 283–6131

Sunrise Inn
Mile 45 Sterling Hwy.
Cooper Landing, AK 99572
(907) 595–1222

Eagle River, Alaska

Anchorage Convention and Visitors
  Center
201 E. Third Ave.
Anchorage, AK 99501
(907) 276–4111

Lodging
Andy's Eagle Park B&B
9907 Wren Lane
Eagle River, AK 99577
(907) 694–2833

The Lodge at Eagle River
P.O. Box 90154
Anchorage, AK 99509
(907) 278–7575

Mountain Air Bed & Breakfast
HC 83, Box 1652
Eagle River, AK 99577
(907) 696–3116

Matanuska River, Alaska

Lodging
Fairview Motel
P.O. Box 745
Palmer, AK 99645
(907) 745–1505

Golden Eagle Motel
918 Colony Way
Palmer, AK 99645
(907) 745–6771

Valley Hotel
606 S. Alaska St.
Palmer, AK 99645
(907) 745–3330

Nenana River, Alaska

Denali Visitor Information Center
P.O. Box 7
Cantwell, AK 99729
(907) 768–2420

Lodging
Alaska's Mt. McKinley Motor Lodge
P.O. Box 77
Denali National Park, AK 99755
(907) 683–2567

Denali Riverview Inn
P.O. Box 49
Denali National Park, AK 99755
(907) 683–2663

Sourdough Cabins
P.O. Box 118
Denali National Park, AK 99755
(907) 683–2773

Campgrounds
Denali Grizzly Bear Campground
P.O. Box 7
Denali National Park, AK 99755
(907) 683–2696

Lynx Creek Campground
Denali National Park, AK 99755
(907) 683–2548

Alsek and Tatshenshini Rivers, Alaska

Tourism Yukon
P.O. Box 2703
Whitehorse, Yukon
Canada Y1A 2C6
(403) 667–5340

Lodging
Best Western Gold Rush Inn
411 Main St.
Whitehorse, Yukon
Canada Y1A 2B6
(403) 668–4500

Chitina and Copper Rivers, Alaska

Greater Copper Basin Chamber of
   Commerce
P.O. Box 469
Glennallen, AK 99588
(907) 822–5555

Lodging
New Caribou Hotel
P.O. Box 329
Glennallen, AK 99588
(907) 822–3302

Campground
KROA-Kamping Resorts of Alaska
Mile 152 Glenn Hwy.
Glennallen, AK 99588
(907) 822–3346

Talkeetna River, Alaska

Talkeetna Chamber of Commerce
P.O. Box 334
Talkeetna, AK 99676
(907) 733–2330

Lodging
Fairview Inn
P.O. Box 379
Talkeetna, AK 99676
(907) 733–2423

Latitude 62° Lodge/Motel
P.O. Box 478
Talkeetna, AK 99676
(907) 733–2262

The Talkeetna Motel
Talkeetna, AK 99676
(907) 733–2323

Talkeetna Roadhouse
P.O. Box 388
Talkeetna, AK 99676
(907) 733–2341

Brooks Range Rivers, Alaska

Consult with rafting outfitters for accommodations.

CHAPTER 14:
NORTHEAST STATES

Kennebec and Dead Rivers, Maine

Lodging
Bingham Motor Inn
P.O. Box 683
Bingham, ME 04920
(207) 672–4135

Canadian Trail Cabins
Star Route
Bingham, ME 04920
(207) 672–3771

Dead River Bed & Breakfast
West Forks, ME 04985
(207) 663–4480

Mrs. G's Bed and Breakfast
Meadow Street, Box 389
Bingham, ME 04920
(207) 672–4034

Riverside Lodge
Main Street
Bingham, ME 04920
(207) 672–3215

Campgrounds
Pleasant Pond Campground
P.O. Box 19
Caratunk, ME 04925
(207) 672–4059

Webb's Dead River Campground
West Forks, ME 04985
(207) 663–4423

Penobscot River (West Branch), Maine

Lodging
Best Western Heritage Motor Inn
935 Central St.
Millinocket, ME 04462
(207) 723–9777

Greenville Inn
Greenville, ME 04441
(207) 695–2206

Greenwood Motel
Greenville, ME 04441
(800) 477–4386

Heritage Motor Inn
Rt. 157
Millinocket, ME 04462
(207) 723–9777

Indian Hill Motel
Greenville, ME 04441
(207) 695–2623

Campgrounds
Moosehead Campground
Greenville, ME 04441
(207) 695–2210

Pray's Big Eddy Campground
P.O. Box 548
Millinocket, ME 04462
(207) 723–9581

Hudson River, New York

Gore Mountain Region Chamber of
   Commerce
Main Street
North Creek, NY 12853
(518) 251–2612

Lodging
Alpine Motel
Main Street
North Creek, NY 12853
(518) 251–2451

Black Mountain Ski Lodge
Rt. 8 & Peaceful Valley Rd.
North Creek, NY 12853
(518) 251–2800

Copperfield Inn
Main Street
North Creek, NY 12853
(518) 251–2500

Garnet Hill Lodge
13th Lake Rd.
North River, NY 12856

Lone Birch Motel & Cottages
Route 28
Indian Lake, NY 12842
(518) 648–5225

Northwind Motel
Peaceful Valley Rd.
North Creek, NY 12853
(518) 251–2522

Wilderness Lodge Motel
Indian Lake, NY 12842
(518) 648–5995

Campgrounds
Daggett Lake Campground
Warrensburg, NY 12885
(518) 623–2198

Warrensburg Travel Park
P.O. Box 277
Warrensburg, NY 12885
(518) 623–9833

Moose River, New York

Old Forge Tourist Information
Old Forge, NY 13420
(315) 369–6983

Lodging
Clark's Beach Motel
Rt. 28
Old Forge, NY 13420
(315) 369–3026

Forge Motel
P.O. Box 522
Old Forge, NY 13420
(315) 369–3313

Headwaters Motor Lodge
Rt. 12
Boonville, NY 13309
(315) 942–4493

Sunset Motel
Rt. 28
Thendara, NY 13472
(315) 369–6836

Water's Edge Inn
Rt. 28
Old Forge, NY 13420
(315) 369–2484

Campgrounds
KOA Campground
P.O. Box 51
Old Forge, NY 13420
(315) 369–6011

Moose River Campground
Youngs Rd., Box 181
Port Leyden, NY 13433
(315) 348–4444

Singing Waters Campground
Old Forge, NY 13420
(315) 369–6011

Sacandaga River, New York

Lodging
Island View Motel and Cottages
2220 Lake Ave.
Lake Luzerne, NY 12846
(518) 696–3079

Lake Luzerne Motel
RD 1, Box 1
Lake Luzerne, NY 12846
(518) 696–3012

Wagon Wheel Motel
Box 3, Lake Ave.
Lake Luzerne, NY 12846
(518) 696–2311

Campgrounds
Fourth Lake Campground
Rt. 9 N.
Lake Luzerne, NY 12846
(518) 696–2031

KOA Lake George
2526 Lake Rd.
Lake Luzerne, NY 12846
(518) 696–2615

Black River, New York

Watertown Chamber of Commerce
230 Franklin St.
Watertown, NY 13601
(315) 788–4400

Lodging
Days Inn
1142 Arsenal St.
Watertown, NY 13601
(315) 782–2700

Holiday Inn Watertown
300 Washington St.
Watertown, NY 13601
(315) 782–8000

Quality Inn Watertown
1190 Arsenal St.
Watertown, NY 13601
(315) 788–6800

Ramada Inn
6300 Arsenal St.
Watertown, NY 13601
(315) 788–0700

Campgrounds
Black River Bay Campground
Dexter, NY 13634
(315) 639–3735

Wescott's Beach State Park
Sackets Harbor, NY 13685
(315) 646–2239

Genesee River, New York

Lodging
Colonial Motel
6544 Rt. 19A
Portageville, NY 14536
(716) 493–5700

Genesee Falls Inn
P.O. Box 396
Portageville, NY 14536
(716) 493–2484

Glen Iris Inn
7 Letchworth State Park
Castile, NY 14427
(716) 493–2622

Campgrounds
Four Winds Campground
7350 Tewefly Rd.
Portageville, NY 14536
(716) 493–2794

Letchworth State Park
Castile, NY 14427
(716) 439–2611

Deerfield River, Massachusetts

Lodging
Charlemont Inn
Charlemont, MA 01339
(413) 339–5796

Olde Willow Motor Inn
Charlemont, MA 01339
(413) 339–4483

Oxbow Motel
Charlemont, MA 01339
(413) 625–6011

Campgrounds
Country Aire Campground
Charlemont, MA 01339
(413) 625–2996

Mohawk Trail State Park
Charlemont, MA 01339
(413) 339–5504

West River, Vermont

Lodging
Best Western Lodge at Mt. Snow
P.O. Box 755
West Dover, VT 05356
(802) 464–5112

Days Inn
I–91, Exit 3, Putney Rd.
Brattleboro, VT 05301
(802) 254–4583

River Bend Motel
Newfane, VT 05345
(802) 365–7592

Super 8 Motel
Rt. 5, Box 137 Putney Rd.
Brattleboro, VT 05301
(802) 254–8889

Campgrounds
Jamaica State Park
Jamaica, VT 05343
(802) 874–4600

Townshend State Park
Townshend, VT 05353
(802) 365–7500

CHAPTER 15:
MID-ATLANTIC STATES

Lehigh River, Pennsylvania

Lodging
Pocono Mountain Lodge
Rt. 940, P.O. Box 1414
White Haven, PA 18661
(717) 443-8461

Pocono Ramada Inn
Rt. 940
White Haven, PA 18661
(717) 443-8471

Poconos Days Inn
Rt. 940
Lake Harmony, PA 18624
(717) 443-0391

The Inn at Jim Thorpe
24 Broadway
Jim Thorpe, PA 18229
(717) 325-2599

Campgrounds
Fern Ridge Campground
Rt. 115
Blakeslee, PA 18610
(717) 646-3380

Hickory Run State Park
Rt. 534, Box 81, RD 1
White Haven, PA 18661
(717) 443-9991

Lehigh Gorge Campground
Rt. 940
White Haven, PA 18661
(717) 443-9191

Youghiogheny River, Pennsylvania

Lodging
Blue Mountain Motel
RD 2, Box 674
Uniontown, PA 15401
(412) 439-4880

Falls Market and inn
Ohiopyle, PA 15470
(412) 329-4973

Holiday Inn Uniontown
700 West Main St.
Uniontown, PA 15401
(412) 437-2816

Mt. Summit Inn
Rt. 40, Box T
Uniontown, PA 15401
(412) 438-8594

National Trails Motel
Rt. 40
Markleysburg, PA 15459
(412) 329-5531

Ramada Inn
P.O. Box 511
Somerset, PA 15501
(814) 443-4646

Campgrounds
Benners Meadow Run Campground
RD, Box 483
Farmington, PA 15437
(412) 329-4097

Ohiopyle State Park Campground
Ohiopyle, PA 15470
(412) 329-8591

Youghiogheny River (Upper), Maryland

Lodging
Holiday Inn Grantsville
I–68 and 219 (Exit 22)
Grantsville, MD 21536
(301) 895–5993

Royal Oaks Inn
Rt. 219
McHenry, MD 21541
(301) 387–4200

Yough Valley Motel
138 Walnut St.
Friendsville, MD 21531
(301) 746–5836

Campgrounds
Deep Creek Lake State Park
Rt. 2, Box 70
Swanton, MD 21561
(301) 387–5563

Swallow Falls State Park
Rt. 5, Box 2180
Oakland, MD 21550
(301) 334–9180

Cheat River, West Virginia

Lodging
Heldreth Motel and Restaurant
Rt. 26
Kingwood, WV 26537
(304) 329–1145

Holiday Inn Grantsville
I–68 and 219 (Exit 22)
Grantsville, MD 21536
(301) 895–5993

Preston County Inn
Main Street
Kingwood, WV 26537
(304) 329–2220

Ramada Inn
I–68 and Rt. 119
Morgantown, WV 26505
(304) 296–3431

The Wisp Resort
Marsh Hill Rd.
Deep Creek Lake, MD 21541
(301) 387–5581

Campgrounds
Chestnut Ridge Campground
Rt. 1, Box 267
Bruceton Mills, WV 26525
(304) 594–1773

Coopers Rock State Forest Campground
RR 1, Box 270
Bruceton Mills, WV 26525
(304) 594–1561

Pinehill Campground
RD 3, Box 233A
Bruceton Mills, WV 26525
(304) 379–4612

Sand Springs Campground
P.O. Box 697
Morgantown, WV 26507
(304) 594–2415

New and Gauley Rivers, West Virginia

Beckley Chamber of Commerce
P.O. Box 1798
Beckley, WV 25802
(304) 252–7328

Lodging
Beckley Hotel
1940 Harper Rd.
Beckley, WV 25801
(800) 274–6010
(304) 252–8661

Best Western Motel
1203 Broad St.
Summersville, WV 26651
(304) 872–6900

Comfort Inn Beckley
1909 Harper Rd.
Beckley, WV 25801
(304) 255–2161

Comfort Inn Fayetteville
U.S. 19 and Laurel Creek Rd.
Fayetteville, WV 25840
(304) 574–3443

Comfort Inn Summersville
U.S. 19
Summersville, WV 26651
(304) 872–6500

Hawk's Nest State Park Lodge
Rt. 60, P.O. Box 417
Ansted, WV 25812
(800) 225–5982
(304) 658–5212

Holiday Inn-Oak Hill
U.S. 19 and Oyler Rd.
Oak Hill, WV 25901
(304) 465–0571

Campgrounds
Babcock State Park Campground
Rt. 1, Box 150
Clifftop, WV 25831
(304) 438–6205

Mountain Laurel RV Park
Rt. 2, Box 68, Laurel Creek Rd.
Fayetteville, WV 25840
(304) 574–0188

Mountain Lake Campground
P.O. Box 486
Summersville, WV 26651
(304) 872–4220

Tygart River, West Virginia

Lodging
Crislip Motor Lodge
300 Moritz Ave.
Grafton, WV 26354
(304) 265–2100

Grafton Motel
300 Moritz Ave.
Grafton, WV 26354
(304) 265–2100

Philipi Motel
P.O. Box 304
Philipi, WV 26416
(304) 457–1280

Tygart Lake State Park Lodge
Rt. 1, Box 260
Grafton, WV 26354
(800) 225–5982

Campgrounds
Pleasant Creek Campground
Rt. 3, Box 180
Philipi, WV 26416
(304) 457–1280

Tygart Lake State Park
Rt. 1, Box 260
Grafton, WV 26354
(304) 265–3383

Shenandoah River, West Virginia

Lodging
Cliffside Inn
Rt. 340
Harpers Ferry, WV 25425
(304) 535–6302

Comfort Inn
Rt. 340
Harpers Ferry, WV 25425
(304) 535–6391

Hillside Motel
Rt. 340
Knoxville, MD 21758
(301) 834–8144

Hilltop House Hotel
P.O. Box 806
Harpers Ferry, WV 25425
(304) 535–6321

Campgrounds
Brunswick Campground
20 East A Street
Brunswick, MD 21716
(301) 834–8050

Maple Tree Campground
Townsend Road
Gapland, MD 21736
(301) 432–5585

James River, Virginia

Richmond Convention and Visitors
  Bureau
550 E. Marshall St.
Richmond, VA 23219
(800) 365–7272
(804) 782–2777

Lodging
Best Western James River Inn
8008 W. Broad St.
Richmond, VA 23294
(804) 346–0000

Comfort Inn Midtown
3200 W. Broad St.
Richmond, VA 23230
(804) 359–4061

Days Inn Downtown
612 E. Marshall St.
Richmond, VA 23240
(804) 649–2378

Campgrounds
KOA Richmond East
Rt. 1, Box 120
New Kent, VA 23124
(804) 932–4776

Kings Dominion Campground
Rt. 1, Box 57
Doswell, VA 23047
(804) 876–5355

**CHAPTER 16:
SOUTHEAST STATES**

*Chattooga River, Georgia/
  South Carolina*

Lodging
A Small Motel & Lodge
U.S. 76 E.
Clayton, GA 30525
(706) 782–6488

Best Western Dillard
Hwy. 441
Dillard, GA 30537
(706) 746–5321

Days Inn Seneca
Hwy. 123, 11015 Radio Station Rd.
Seneca, SC 29678
(803) 885–0710

Dillard House Inn
Hwy. 441
Dillard, GA 30537
(706) 746–5348

English Manor Inn
Hwy. 76 E., P.O. Box 1605
Clayton, GA 30525
(800) 782–5780
(706) 782–5789

Quality Mountain Valley Inn
Hwy. 441 N.
Dillard, GA 30537
(706) 746–5373

The Stonebrook Inn
P.O. Box 341
Clayton, GA 30525
(706) 782–2214

Campgrounds
Black Rock Mountain State Park
Mountain City, GA 30562
(706) 746–2141

Oconee State Park
624 State Park Rd.
Mountain Rest, SC 29664
(803) 638–5353

Nantahala River, North Carolina

Cherokee Visitors Center
441 Main St.
Cherokee, NC 28719
(704) 497–9195

Lodging
Freeman's Motel
NC 28 North
Almond, NC 28702
(704) 488–2737

Fryemont Inn
Fryemont Rd., P.O. Box 459
Bryson City, NC 28713
(704) 488–2159

Hemlock Inn
U.S. 19 N.
Bryson City, NC 28713
(704) 488–2885

Nantahala Village
9400 Hwy. 19 W.
Almond, NC 28702
(704) 488–2826

Peppertree Fontana Village
Fontana Dam, NC 28733
(800) 438–8080
(704) 498–2211

Campgrounds
Deep Creek Campground
Deep Creek Rd.
Bryson City, NC 28713
(704) 488–3184

Lost Mine Campground
Silvermine Rd., Box 40
Wesser, NC 28713
(704) 488–6445

Turkey Creek Campground
P.O. Box 93
Almond, NC 28702
(704) 488–8966

Tuckaseigee River, North Carolina

Lodging
Chalet Inn
Rt. 2, Box 99
Whittier, NC 28789
(704) 586–0251

Comfort Inn Dillsboro/Sylva
U.S. 23 & 74
Sylva, NC 28779
(704) 586–3315

Squire Watkins Inn B&B
P.O. Box 430
Dillsboro, NC 28725
(704) 586–5244

Campground
Great Smoky Mountain RV Park &
  Campground
Hwy. 441
Whittier, NC 28789
(704) 497–2470

French Broad River, North Carolina

Asheville Chamber of Commerce
151 Haywood St.
Asheville, NC 28801
(800) 257–1300
(704) 258–3858

Lodging
Alpine Court Motel
P.O. Box 246
Hot Springs, NC 28743
(704) 622–3231

Best Western Asheville Central
22 Woodfin St.
Asheville, NC 28801
(704) 253–1851

Days Inn Downtown
120 Patton Ave.
Asheville, NC 28801
(704) 254–9661

Marshall House B&B
5 Hill St.
Marshall, NC 28753
(704) 649–9205

Mars Hill College
Mars Hill, NC 28754
(704) 689–1166

Campgrounds
Hot Springs Resort Campground
One Bridge St.
Hot Springs, NC 28743
(704) 622–7676

Mountain Laurel Campground
Rt. 3, Puncheon Fork Rd.
Mars Hill, NC 28754
(704) 689–3602

Wilson Creek, North Carolina, and Watauga River, North Carolina/ Tennessee

Lodging
Comfort Inn
1515 U.S. 19 E. Bypass
Elizabethton, TN 37643
(615) 542–4466

Days Inn Mountain City
Hwy. 421, Rt. 4
Mountain City, TN 37683
(615) 727–7311

EconoLodge
SR 105, Rt. 6, Box 46
Boone, NC 28607
(704) 264–4133

Holiday Inn Boone
710 Blowing Rock Rd.
Boone, NC 28607
(704) 264–2451

Lakeshore Resort
Rt. 2
Hampton, TN 37658
(615) 725–2201

Campgrounds
Boone KOA Campground
Rt. 2, Box 205
Boone, NC 28607
(704) 264–7250

Pioneer Landing Campground
Rt. 1, Box 2735
Butler, TN 37640
(615) 768–3164

Nolichucky River, North Carolina/Tennessee

Erwin Chamber of Commerce
Erwin, TN 37650
(615) 743–3000

Lodging
Carolina Country Inn
600 W. Main St.
Burnsville, NC 28714
(704) 682–6033

Erwin Motel
1315 Asheville Hwy.
Erwin, TN 37650
(615) 743–6438

Family Inns of America
100 Country Club Dr.
Unicoi, TN 37692
(615) 743–9181

Garden Plaza Hotel
211 Mockingbird Ln.
Johnson City, TN 37601
(615) 929–2000

Nu-Wray Inn
Town Square
Burnsville, NC 28714
(704) 682–2329

Campgrounds
Hot Springs Resort Campground
One Bridge St.
Hot Springs, NC 28743
(704) 622–7676

Indian Creek Campground
Hwy. 19/23
Erwin, TN 37650
(615) 743–6485

Big Pigeon River, Tennessee

Lodging
Best Western Crossroads Motor Lodge
440 Parkway
Gatlinburg, TN 37738
(615) 436–5661

Best Western Newport
I–40 & Cosby Hwy. 32
Newport, TN 37821
(615) 623–8713

Hampton Inn
965 Parkway
Gatlinburg, TN 37738
(615) 436–4878

Rocky Waters Motor Lodge
333 Parkway
Gatlinburg, TN 37738
(615) 436–7861

Campgrounds
Trout Creek Campground
Hwy. 321 N.
Gatlinburg, TN 37738
(615) 436–5905

Twin Creek Campground
Hwy. 321 N.
Gatlinburg, TN 37738
(615) 436–7081

Ocoee River, Tennessee

Cleveland Chamber of Commerce
2145 Keith St. NW
Cleveland, TN 37311
(615) 742–6587

Lodging

Applegate Inn
Hwy. 64 Bypass
Cleveland, TN 37311
(615) 479–9915

Best Western Copper Inn
U.S. Hwy. 64
Ducktown, TN 37326
(615) 496–5541

Best Western Inn Murphy
588 Andrews Rd.
Murphy, NC 28906
(704) 837–3060

Georgetown Inn
I–75 and Hwy. 60
Cleveland, TN 37311
(615) 478–1137

Village Inn
Keith St.
Cleveland, TN 37311
(615) 478–1161

Campgrounds

Chilhowee Recreation Area
Parksville Lake Recreation Area
Rt. 1, Box 346
Benton, TN 37307
(615) 338–5201

Cleveland KOA Campground
P.O. Box 3232
Cleveland, TN 37311
(615) 472–8928

Gee Creek Campground
Hwy. 411
Benton, TN 37307
(615) 388–4133

Cumberland River (Big South Fork), Tennessee

Lodging

Classic Inn
Hwy. 27
Oneida, TN 37841
(615) 569–6376

Tobes Motel
Hwy. 27
Oneida, TN 37841
(615) 569–8581

Campground

Bandy Creek Campground
Big South Fork NRRA
P.O. Box 630
Oneida, TN 37841
(615) 346–6295

Cumberland and Rockcastle Rivers, Kentucky

Lodging

Best Western Corbin Inn
2630 Cumberland Falls Rd.
Corbin, KY 40701
(606) 528–2100

Cumberland Falls State Resort Park
Dupont Lodge, Rt. 6
Corbin, KY 40701
(606) 528–4121

Days Inn Corbin
I–75 & U.S. 25 W
Corbin, KY 40701
(606) 528–8150

Quality Inn Corbin
I–75 and U.S. 25 E.
Corbin, KY 40701
(606) 528–4802

Campgrounds

Cumberland Falls State Resort Park
Rt. 6
Corbin, KY 40701
(606) 528–4121

Laurel Lake Family Campground
2660 Hightop Rd.
Corbin, KY 40701
(606) 528–0042

Levisa River, Virginia/Kentucky

Lodging

Days Inn Pikeville
518 S. Mayo Trail
Pikeville, KY 41501
(606) 432–0314

Landmark Inn
146 S. Mayo Trail
Pikeville, KY 41501
(606) 432–2545

Campground

Breaks Interstate Park
P.O. Box 100
Breaks, VA 24607
(703) 865–4413

CHAPTER 17:
WESTERN CANADA

Birkenhead, Green, and Elaho and Squamish Rivers, British Columbia

Whistler Travel Infocentre
2097 Lake Placid Rd., P.O. Box 181
Whistler, British Columbia
Canada V0N 1B0
(604) 932–5528

Lodging

Listel Whistler Hotel
4121 Village Green, P.O. Box 93
Whistler, British Columbia
Canada V0N 1B0
(604) 932–1133

Nancy Greene Lodge
4154 Village Green
Whistler, British Columbia
Canada V0N 1B0
(800) 667–3363
(604) 932–2211

Whistler Fairways Hotel
4005 Whistler Way, P.O. Box 1012
Whistler, British Columbia
Canada V0N 1B0
(604) 932–2522

Campground

Whistler Campground & RV Park
8000 Mons Rd., P.O. Box 749
Whistler, British Columbia
Canada V0N 1B0
(604) 932–5181

Thompson River, British Columbia

Lodging

Braeden Lodge Motel
223 Main St.
Lytton, British Columbia
Canada V0K 1Z0
(604) 455–2334

Lytton Hotel
P.O. Box 113
Lytton, British Columbia
Canada V0K 1Z0
(604) 455–2211

Lytton Pines Motel
Trans Canada Hwy., P.O. Box 249
Lytton, British Columbia
Canada V0K 1Z0
(604) 455–2322

Totem Motel and Lodge
320 Fraser St.
Lytton, British Columbia
Canada V0K 1Z0
(604) 455–2321

Campground
Jade Springs Park
Trans Canada Hwy., P.O. Box 488
Lytton, British Columbia
Canada V0K 1Z0
(604) 455–2420

Nahatlatch and Fraser Rivers, British Columbia

Lodging
Canyon Alpine Motel
50530 Trans Canada Hwy., P.O. Box 395
Boston Bar, British Columbia
Canada V0K 1C0
(604) 867–9295

Charles Hotel
P.O. Box 190
Boston Bar, British Columbia
Canada V0K 1C0
(604) 867–9221

Fort Yale Motel
13265 Trans Canada Hwy., P.O. Box 44
Yale, British Columbia
Canada V0K 2S0
(604) 863–2216

Campground
Blue Lake Resort
63452 Blue Lake Rd.
Boston Bar, British Columbia
Canada V0K 1C0
(604) 867–9246

Chilliwack River, British Columbia

Lodging
Best Western Rainbow Country Inn
43971 Industrial Way
Sardis, British Columbia
Canada V2R 1A9
(604) 795–3828

Cottonwood Inn Chilliwack
45466 Yale Rd.
Chilliwack, British Columbia
Canada V2R 1A9
(604) 792–4240

Rainbow Motor Inn
45620 Yale Rd. W.
Chilliwack, British Columbia
Canada V2P 2N2
(604) 792–6412

Campground
Cultus Lake Provincial Park
P.O. Box 10
Cultus Lake, British Columbia
Canada V0X 1H0
(604) 858–4515

Clearwater River, British Columbia

Clearwater Travel Infocentre
425 E. Yellowhead Hwy.
Clearwater, British Columbia
Canada V0E 1N0
(604) 674–2646

Lodging
Dutch Lake Motel
333 Roy Rd., P.O. Box 5116
Clearwater, British Columbia
Canada V0E 1N0
(604) 674–3325

Wells Gray Inn
Clearwater Village Rd. & Hwy. 5
Clearwater, British Columbia
Canada V0E 1N0
(604) 674–2214

Campground
Nordstrom's Resort & RV Park
361 Ridge Rd., RR 2, Box 2160
Clearwater, British Columbia
Canada V0E 1N0
(604) 674–3351

Adams River, British Columbia

Chase Travel Infocentre
120 Chase St.
Chase, British Columbia
Canada V0E 1M0
(604) 679–8432

Lodging
Overlander Motel
181 Shuswap Ave., P.O. Box 92
Chase, British Columbia
Canada V0E 1M0
(604) 679–8633

Sorrento Motor Inn
Trans Canada Hwy., P.O. Box 30
Sorrento, British Columbia
Canada V0E 2W0
(6040 675–2454

Campground
Chase Country Inn and RV Park
807 Cedar Ave., P.O. Box 1031
Chase, British Columbia
Canada V0E 1M0
(604) 679–3333

Kicking Horse River, British Columbia

Golden Travel Infocentre
500 10th Avenue N.
Golden, British Columbia
Canada V0A 1H0
(604) 344–7125

Lodging
Golden Rim Motor Inn
1416 Golden View Rd.
Golden, British Columbia
Canada V0A 1H0
(604) 344–2216

Golden Village Motor Inn
Trans Canada Highway, P.O. Box 371
Golden, British Columbia
Canada V0A 1H0
(604) 344–5996

Rondo Motel
904 Park Dr.
Golden, British Columbia
Canada V0A 1H0
(604) 344–5295

Campground
Golden Municipal Campground
1407 South 9th St.
Golden, British Columbia
Canada V0A 1H0
(604) 344–5412

Chilko, Chilcotin, and Fraser Rivers, British Columbia

Williams Lake & District Travel Infocentre
1148 Broadway S.
Williams Lake, British Columbia
Canada V2G 1A2
(604) 392–5025

Lodging
Drummond Lodge Motel
1405 Cariboo Hwy. East
Williams Lake, British Columbia
Canada V2G 2W3
(604) 392–5334

Sandman Inn
664 Oliver St.
Williams Lake, British Columbia
Canada V2G 1M6
(604) 392–6557

Valley View Motel
1523 Cariboo Highway
Williams Lake, British Columbia
Canada V2G 2W3
(604) 392–4655

Babine River, British Columbia

Smithers Travel Infocentre
1425 Main St.
Smithers, British Columbia
Canada V0J 2N0
(604) 847–9854

Lodging
Aspen Motor Inn
4268 Hwy. 16, P.O. Box 756
Smithers, British Columbia
Canada V0J 2N0
(604) 847–4551

Capri Motor Inn
3984 Hwy. 16 W., Box 3418
Smithers, British Columbia
Canada V0J 2N0
(604) 847–4226

Campground
Riverside Park Municipal Campsite
19th Ave., P.O. Box 879
Smithers, British Columbia
Canada V0J 2N0
(604) 847–3251

Red Deer River, Alberta

Lodging
Parkwood Motor Inn
P.O. Box 11
Sundre, Alberta
Canada T0M 1X0
(403) 638–4424

Sundre Motor Inn
P.O. Box 810
Sundre, Alberta
Canada T0M 1X0
(4030 638–4440

Campground
Tall Timbers Campground
P.O. Box 24
Sundre, Alberta
Canada T0M 1X0
(403) 638–3555

*Maligne and Athabasca Rivers,
Alberta*

Jasper Park Chamber of Commerce
Jasper National Park, Box 98
Jasper, Alberta
Canada T0E 1E0
(403) 852–3858

Lodging
Jasper Park Lodge
P.O. Box 40
Jasper, Alberta
Canada T0E 1E0
(403) 852–3301

Maligne Lodge
925 Connaught Dr.
Japser, Alberta
Canada T0E 1E0
(403) 852–3143

Marmot Lodge
94 Connaught Dr.
Jasper, Alberta
Canada T0E 1E0
(403) 852–4471

Campground
Canadian Parks Information Office
Connaught Drive
Jasper, Alberta
Canada T0E 1E0
(403) 852–6161

Bow River, Alberta

Banff–Lake Louise Tourism Bureau
P.O. Box 1298
Banff, Alberta
Canada T0L 0C0
(403) 762–0270

Lodging
Banff Caribou Lodge
521 Banff Ave., P.O. Box 279
Banff, Alberta
Canada T0L 0C0
(800) 563–8764
(403) 762–5887

Banff Park Lodge
222 Lynx St., P.O. Box 1228
Banff, Alberta
Canada T0L 0C0
(800) 661–9266
(403) 762–4433

Best Western Siding 29 Lodge
453 Marten St., P.O. Box 1387
Banff, Alberta
Canada T0L 0C0
(403) 762–5575

Rimrock Inn
Mountain Ave., P.O. Box 1110
Banff, Alberta
Canada T0L 0C0
(403) 762–3356

Campground
Tunnell Mountain Campground
Banff, Alberta
Canada T0L 0C0
(403) 762–1550

Kananaskis River, Alberta

Lodging
Best Western Kananaskis Inn
P.O. Box 10
Kananaskis Village, Alberta
Canada T0L 2H0
(403) 591–7500

Kananaskis Guest Ranch
General Delivery
Seebee, Alberta
Canada T0L 1X0
(403) 673–3737

The Lodge at Kananaskis
Kananaskis Village, Alberta
Canada T0L 2H0
(403) 591–7711

Campgrounds
Bow Valley & Willow Rock Provincial Parks
P.O. Box 280
Exhaw, Alberta
Canada T0L 2C0
(403) 673–3663

Mt. Kidd RV Park & Campground
Kananaskis Village, Alberta
Canada T0L 2H0
(403) 591–7700

Highwood River, Alberta

Calgary Convention & Visitors Bureau
237 8th Ave. S.E.
Calgary, Alberta
Canada T2G 3K8
(403) 263–8513

Lodging
Blue Sky Motel
P.O. Box 225
Longview, Alberta
Canada T0L 1H0
(403) 558–3665

Heritage Inn
P.O. Box 1078
High River, Alberta
Canada T0L 1B0
(403) 652–3834

CHAPTER 18:
EASTERN CANADA

Ottawa River, Ontario

Lodging
Best Western Pembroke Inn
One International Drive
Pembroke, Ontario
Canada K8A 6X9
(613) 735–0131

Days Inn Pembroke
900 Pembroke St. E.
Pembroke, Ontario
Canada K8A 3M2
(613) 735–6868

North Way Motel
Hwy. 17
Cobden, Ontario
Canada L0J 1K0
(613) 646–2678

Renfrew Inn
760 Gibbons Rd.
Renfrew, Ontario
Canada K7V 4A2
(613) 432–8109

Victoria House B&B
P.O. Box 23
Foresters Falls, Ontario
Canada K0J 1B0
(613) 646–7638

Campgrounds
Cedar Haven Campground
RR 1
Cobden, Ontario
Canada L0J 1K0
(613) 646–7989

KOA Renfrew
RR 5
Renfrew, Ontario
Canada K7V 3Z8
(613) 432–6280

Madawaska River, Ontario

Lodging
Algonquin Parkway Inn
Whitney, Ontario
Canada K0J 2M0
(613) 637–2760

Pinewood Inn
Hwy. 62 S.
Barry's Bay, Ontario
Canada K0J 1B0
(613) 756–2646

Campground
Riverland Tent & Trailer Park
P.O. Box 98
Madawaska, Ontario
Canada K0J 2C0
(613) 637–5338

Rouge River, Quebec

Lodging
Auberge Val Carroll
RR 2, Calumet
Harrington, Quebec
Canada J0V 1B0
(819) 242–7041

Best Western L'Heritage
1575 Tupper St.
Hawkesbury, Ontario
Canada K6A 3E1
(613) 632–5941

Carling Lake Resort Hotel
Rt. 327 N.
Pine Hill, Quebec
Canada J0V 1A0
(514) 633–9211

Château Montebello
392 Notre Dame St.
Montebello, Quebec
Canada J0V 1L0
(819) 423–6341

Holiday Motel
261 McGill St.
Hawkesbury, Ontario
Canada K6A 1B9
(613) 632–7087

Campgrounds
Camping Val Carroll
RR 2
Calumet, Quebec
Canada J0V 1B0
(819) 242–7041

Camping Valée de la Rivière Rouge
RR 2
Calumet, Quebec
Canada J0V 1B0
(819) 242–0277

Jacques Cartier River, Quebec

Tourism Quebec
1010 St. Catherine W.
Montreal, Quebec
Canada H3B 1G2
(800) 363–7372

Lodging
Château Laurier
695 Grand Allée E.
Quebec City, Quebec
Canada G1R 2K4
(418) 522–8108

Oncle Sam Motel
7025 W. Hamel Blvd.
Ste-Foy, Quebec
Canada G2G 1B6
(418) 872–1488

Hotel Quebec
315 Laurier Blvd.
Ste-Foy, Quebec
Canada G1W 3Z6
(418) 658–5120

Quebec Inn
5175 W. Hamel Blvd.
Ste-Foy, Quebec
Canada G2G 1B6
(418) 872–9831

Campground
KOA Quebec City
684 Chemin Olivier
Bernières, Quebec
Canada G0S 1C0
(418) 831–1813

Batiscan River, Quebec

Tourism Quebec
1010 St. Catherine W.
Montreal, Quebec
Canada H3B 1G2
(800) 363–7372

Lodging
Auberge des Gouverneurs
975 Hart St.
Trois Rivières, Quebec
Canada G9A 4S3
(819) 379–4550

Hotel Chez Doris
101 Commercial
Rivière-à-Pierre, Quebec
Canada G0A 3A0
(418) 323–2072

Campground
Camp Royal
590 Rt. 138
Champlain, Quebec
Canada G0X 1C0
(819) 374–7782

St. Lawrence River, Quebec

Tourism Quebec
1010 St. Catherine W.
Montreal, Quebec
Canada H3B 1G2
(800) 363–7372

CHAPTER 19:
MEXICO AND COSTA RICA

Rio Usumacinta and Rio Jatate,
  Mexico

Lodging
Quality Hotel Calinda Viva
Av. Ruiz Cortinez y Paseo
Villahermosa, Tabasco, Mexico
011 931–50000

Rio Antigua, Mexico

Lodging
Howard Johnson Hotel
Blvd. Avila Camacho 1263
Veracruz, Veracruz 91799, Mexico
011 52 29 310011

Costa Rica Rivers

Lodging
Aurola Holiday Inn
Avenida Holiday Inn
Avenida 5.5 Str.
San José, Costa Rica, C.A.
011 (506) 233–7233

Balmoral Hotel
Central Avenida, 7 & 9 Str.
San José, Costa Rica, C.A.
011 (506) 222–5022

Cariari Hotel
Ciudad Cariari, H.
San José, Costa Rica, C.A.
011 (506) 239–0022

Corobici Hotel
La Sabana
San José, Costa Rica, C.A.
011 (506) 232–8122

Europa
3 & 5 Ave., Central St.
San José, Costa Rica, C.A.
011 (506) 222–1222

Quality Fiesta Resort & Casino
Box 155-4005 San Antonio de Belen
El Roble, Puntarenas, 1715400, Costa
  Rica, C.A.
011 (506) 663–0808

River Index

Best Half-Day Trips for Beginners, Small Children, and Seniors

Best Intermediate One-Day Trips

California
American (South Fork), 30
  Chili Bar and Gorge, 30
Kings, 39
Klamath (Upper), 45

Pacific Northwest States
Sauk, 58
Skykomish, 61
Wenatchee, 52

Northern Rocky Mountain States
Flathead (Middle Fork), 85
Flathead (Lower), 87
Payette, 84

Colorado
Arkansas
  Browns Canyon, 99
  Royal Gorge, 100
Cache la Poudre, 101

Southwest States
Colorado (Westwater), 124
Rio Grande (Taos Box), 133

Northeast States
Black, 164
Hudson, 161
Kennebec, 158

Mid-Atlantic States
Cheat, 174
Gauley (Lower), 177
Lehigh (Sections I and II), 171
New (Lower), 175
Youghiogeny (Lower), 172

Southeast States
Chattooga (Section III), 187
Nolichucky, 193
Ocoee, 195

Western Canada
Red Deer, 214
Thompson, 208

Eastern Canada
Ottawa, 222
Rouge, 224

Mexico and Costa Rica
Rio Reventazon (Tucurrique), 234

Best Advanced One-Day Trips

Best Multiday Trips

Pacific Northwest
Rogue (Wild), 63

Northern Rocky Mountain States
Lochsa, 82
Salmon (Middle Fork), 76
Salmon (Main), 77
Salmon (Lower), 78
Selway, 83
Snake (Hells Canyon), 81

Colorado
Colorado (Upper), 105
Dolores, 115
Yampa and Green, 117

Southwest States
Colorado (Cataract), 125
Colorado (Grand Canyon), 128
Green (Desolation), 124
Rio Chama, 132
Rio Grande (Big Bend), 134
San Juan, 127

Alaska
Alsek and Tatchenshini, 146

Western Canada
Chilko, Chilcotin, and Fraser, 212

Mexico and Costa Rica
Rio General, 235

About the Author

Lloyd Armstead has been an avid whitewater enthusiast for fifteen years. Today he is widely recognized and respected by rafters and outfitters for his accurate and detailed river research. His books have been reviewed and praised by recreational editors in numerous national and regional magazines and newspapers.

Lloyd has traveled extensively in all fifty states and in fifty-five foreign countries. He is personally familiar with most of the whitewater rivers and professional rafting outfitters listed in this book. In his untiring quest for firsthand experience on North America's recreational whitewater stretches, Lloyd has now rafted and kayaked rivers in twenty-one states, three Canadian provinces, and Costa Rica. He lives with his wife, Connie, in Fairfax County, Virginia, near Washington, D.C.